THE VEILED WOMAN
OF
ACHILL
ISLAND OUTRAGE & A PLAYBOY DRAMA

Patricia Byrne is a Mayo-born writer living in Limerick and a graduate of the MA (Writing) programme of NUI Galway. Her interest in the Valley House story arose out of family history. Her great granduncle, Brother Paul Carney, served as a Franciscan monk on Achill Island in the late nineteenth century and wrote extensive journals, including a narrative of the life of James Lynchehaun.
patricia05@eircom.net

For Mick, Breon and Michael

This is a true story of actual historical events written in the narrative non-fiction style. There are no fictional characters in the book and all direct speech is taken directly, or adapted, from contemporary historical accounts. Scenes are dramatised using setting, personal gestures, and internal thoughts of characters. Source notes for individual chapters are indicated at the end of the book.

THE VEILED WOMAN
OF
ACHILL

ISLAND OUTRAGE & A PLAYBOY DRAMA

PATRICIA BYRNE

The Collins Press

First published in 2012 by
The Collins Press
West Link Park
Doughcloyne
Wilton
Cork
T12 N5EF
Ireland

Reprinted 2014, 2016

British Library Cataloguing in Publication Data

Byrne, Patricia.
  Veiled woman of Achill : island outrage & a playboy drama.
  1. MacDonnell, Agnes, d. 1923. 2. Lynchehaun, James, ca.
  1860-ca. 1937. 3. Lynchehaun, James, ca. 1860-ca. 1937—
  Trials, litigation, etc. 4. Women landowners—Crimes
  against—Ireland—Achill Island—History—19th century.
  5. Carney, Paul. 6. Synge, J. M. (John Millington),
  1871-1909—Characters—Christy Mahon. 7. Achill Island
  (Ireland)—Social conditions—19th century.
  I. Title
  364.1'5'092-dc23

Paperback ISBN-13: 978-1-84889-147-0
PDF ISBN: 978-1-84889-810-3
ePub ISBN: 978-1-84889-953-7
Mobi ISBN: 978-1-84889-954-4

Typesetting by The Collins Press
Typeset in Bembo

Printed in Ireland by Essentra

Contents

Acknowledgements

I am grateful to my cousin Michael McDonnell who, during my visit to his then home in Kiltimagh in the spring of 2006, whetted my appetite for this story as we talked about family history. My thanks to the Franciscan community for facilitating access to the manuscripts of my great granduncle, Brother Paul Carney.

This project would not have seen the light of day if I hadn't participated in the MA (Writing) Programme at NUI Galway (2007–2008), where I was greatly encouraged by Professor Adrian Frazier, Dr John Kenny and Dr Patrick Lonergan, as well as by my fellow writing students.

I am thankful for the resources of the following libraries: Achill branch library (Pauline Quinn); Castlebar County Library (Ivor Hamrock); the Hardiman Library, NUI Galway (Marie Boran and Kieran Hoare); National Folklore Collection, University College Dublin; National Library of Ireland; Trinity College Library; Representative Church Body Library, Dublin. I was able to draw on the resources of the Berg Room, New York Public Library, and the Brooklyn Historical Society Library, while on a visit to the USA in September 2009.

I was privileged to spend time at the Heinrich Böll cottage in the shadows of Achill's Slievemore in January 2009 while researching this book. I am grateful to John McHugh and to the Heinrich Böll Foundation for the residency, and also for the opportunity to present at the Heinrich Böll Weekend in May 2009. John O'Shea, Dooagh, was a mine of information on Achill, as was Pat Gallagher of the Valley House who responded to my numerous queries. I appreciate the valuable information received from relatives of Agnes and Randal MacDonnell and Irene Elliot: Jim and Marilyn Rankin, Ann and Richard MacDonnell and Randal MacDonnell.

Acknowledgements

It was helpful to have aspects of the research for this story published in a number of journals and magazines and I am grateful to the following publications and editors: the *Journal of the Galway Archaeological and Historical Society* (Dr Diarmuid Ó Cearbhaill); *Cathair na Mart – Journal of the Westport Historical Society* (Aiden Clarke); *Verbal Magazine* (Catherine McGrotty); *The Irish Story* (Eoin Purcell). I was also encouraged at being included among the prize winners in the Unbound Press (UK) competition for opening nonfiction chapters in 2010, and for inclusion in their anthology.

For their assistance with images and illustrations for the book, I am grateful to Glenn Dunne and Berni Metcalfe of the National Library of Ireland; Tom Kennedy, on behalf of the Wynne Collection; Isaac Gewirtz and Tom Lisanti of the Berg Collection, New York Public Library; Ivor Hamrock, Mayo County Library; Ann & Richard MacDonnell, UK; Michael McDonnell, Galway; and *The Mayo News* archives.

I appreciate the support of my siblings, Kathleen, Noreen and Paddy. On a sunny St Patrick's Day in 2009 my brother, Paddy Murphy, and I visited a number of places associated with Brother Paul Carney around Ballyhaunis, County Mayo, including his birthplace in Ballindrehid, the site of the former Granlahan Monastery, and the graveyard of the Augustinian Friary, Ballyhaunis, where the monk's parents (my great great grandparents) are buried.

I would like to thank Kathleen Thorne, David Rice and my fellow writers from the Killaloe Hedge School Writer Group for their constant support, and especially Ciarán Ó Gríofa for his detailed and perceptive comments on the draft manuscript. I am also grateful to my fellow book club readers in The Kyleglass Book Worms who have taught me much about reading and writing, and to Margaret Enright for reading the manuscript. Many friends in The Duck Walkers and Gawbatas listened patiently to accounts of my writing progess while rambling the hills and walking trails of Limerick, Clare and Tippeary.

Thanks to The Collins Press for accepting my manuscript for publication and for their work in getting this story into print. Thanks also to Isobel Creed, Vanessa O'Loughlin and Patricia O'Reilly for their professional inputs.

Finally, thanks to Mick, my best reader, for his love and encouragement.

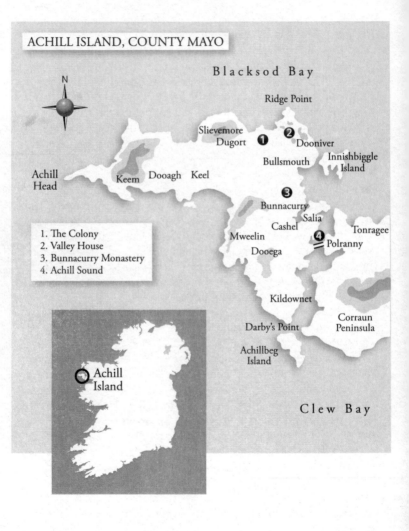

ACHILL ISLAND, COUNTY MAYO

Blacksod Bay

N

Ridge Point

Slievemore
Dugort ❶ ❷ Dooniver

Achill
Head

Bullsmouth

Innishbiggle
Island

Keem   Dooagh   Keel

❸
Bunnacurry

Salia

1. The Colony
2. Valley House
3. Bunnacurry Monastery
4. Achill Sound

Cashel

Tonragee

Mweelin   ❹ Polranny

Dooega

Kildownet

Corraun
Peninsula

Achill
Island

Darby's Point

Achillbeg
Island

Clew Bay

PROLOGUE
Achill
Summer 1888

Agnes MacDonnell is exhausted. She has travelled by rail across England from her London home at Belsize Square, from Holyhead by steamer to Kingstown, and then the final leg of her journey across the breadth of Ireland on the Midland Great Western Railway train to Westport. She crosses the bridge to Achill Island to the rattle of car wheels and the clip clop of horse hooves, her body jerking from side to side with the movement. The glint of new steel on the railings reminds her of the city she has left behind. Had she travelled to the island a year earlier while the swivel bridge was under construction, the car would have had to wait until low tide to pass through the channel at the village of Achill Sound. It is just ten more miles to her new home at the Valley House in Achill's northwest corner. There she will rest, replenish her energies, and tackle the challenges of the 2,000 acre estate she now owns.

Many travellers before her have come to this remote place. They followed the same approach road that swings in an arc around the south shores of Blacksod Bay. Four miles out from Achill, on turning the bend of Tonragee, the visitor faces the spectacle of Slievemore Mountain, mottled with shadows like patches on a piebald horse. The mountain overpowers the island and it is as if it wraps within its entrails the dramas that unfolded beneath its shade. The travellers to Achill in the previous half-century were many and varied: proselytisers imbued with a

I

zeal to convert souls; independent Victorian women who wrote of famine horrors; men who hunted for red-brown grouse on mountain slopes; artists, mesmerised by the island's shifting light, who set up their easels at the Atlantic's edge; seekers of the amethyst's purple glow at the quartz quarry in Keem.

From Achill Sound the horse gallops along the island's spine road as far as Bunnacurry, where the tower of the Franciscan monastery juts into the sky. The car veers north through a treeless landscape where an expanse of bog stretches away as far as Agnes can see. Women in scarlet petticoats walk at the roadside in single file, bent beneath creels of turf and seaweed like beasts of burden. Children in bare feet shout and scamper after the car. Old men suck clay pipes and stare at her from the dark doorways of cottages. Agnes may not have yet observed how few young people there are on the island, many of them having made the annual migrant journey to the harvest-fields of Scotland and England. Everywhere, there is the smell of peat-smoke that oozes and circles languorously into the island skies.

If she is able to peer beyond the cottage doors, Agnes MacDonnell will see that pigs and cattle share the gloomy spaces with the inhabitants. But she is a woman who does not dwell on such things. She is practical, single-minded, her thoughts fixed on the place she is moving towards. She will reclaim the barren fields and breed the best horses in the locality. She will take no nonsense from her tenants and will collect the outstanding rents. Her strength will be in her discipline and diligent work, in her religious faith, and in recourse to the law to protect her rights.

The car has almost reached its destination. The horse canters through the village of Dugort, past the settlement of The Colony where the Achill Mission set up its base a half-century earlier and transformed the mountain slopes into arable fields. The rectangular development of sturdy slated houses nestles against the slopes of Slievemore, which looks down on the rust-charcoal stone of St Thomas' Church where she will worship.

The driver reins in the horse at the Valley crossroads where the car wheels about, passing through a pair of white pillars by the gate lodge and on to the driveway that curves up to the Valley House. Agnes MacDonnell has arrived at her Achill home and alights within earshot of the breaking waves on Blacksod Bay. When she lifts her head she is looking straight at the mountain that appears, from the angle at which she watches, as if a giant hand has gouged out a hollow in its face. Her lands stretch out in front of her, reaching into the bogs and up into the mountain slopes. All around are the cottages of her tenants who will make their weary way up the driveway to hand over sweat-greased coins to their new landlord. When she moves to an upstairs room she can look out beyond her estate to the Mullet Peninsula and the Inishkea Islands of north Mayo.

Few outsiders have heard of the townland of Valley, for it has not drawn attention to itself. However, the arrival of Agnes MacDonnell will set into motion happenings that will culminate in an outburst of ferocious passion. In the darkness of an October night, sounds, other than the usual ones of breaking waves or barking dogs, will erupt: screams of horror, shouts of rage, and the crackle of flames shooting into the sky. These events will reverberate for years to come across Ireland, Britain and America, and many will find release from the reality of their lives in recounting, over and over again, what happened. A folk hero will glow in the public imagination. During long winter nights, storytellers will give their accounts of these events, often blurring the lines between truth and fiction and reality and fantasy, helping to make the actuality of desperate lives bearable and meaningful.

What happens in the townland of Valley, on the island of Achill, will test the endurance and the resolve of Agnes MacDonnell.

Part 1

1

The Island Drowned

June 1894

The train rounded the bend where butter-yellow gorse snaked across the hill. The locomotive whistled clouds of steam and belched out a froth of vapour and grime. It shook and rattled to a halt at the temporary rail platform in Achill Sound. The eyes of the children bulged in dirt-streaked faces as they cowered, terrified that the monster-machine was about to explode before their eyes. The new railway line from Mulranny to Achill was not yet commissioned and the station building was still under construction. The first train to the island carried a desolate cargo on the June afternoon of 1894.

Those who waited had risen before dawn to make their way by foot and by cart from Achill's four corners. They had come from the townlands of Dugort and Dookinella in the north, from Dooagh and Pollach in the west, from Dooega and Shraheens in the south. Many carried cloth bundles of bread and cold potatoes with tilly-cans of milk or stewed tea. By eight o'clock they were thronging into the village, passing in and out of the Telegraph Office and asking in low voices, 'When will the train be here?'

By mid-morning the crowd had swelled to over 400 people who thronged the hillside that flashed with crimson petticoats and white calico mourning bands. Some held aloft black flags tied to ash-sticks. A string of carts lined the roadway and it seemed as if every donkey and pony from the island had been drawn into service. The animals shifted restlessly, harnesses jangling and cart wheels rattling. The smells of fresh animal dung, sweet gorse petals, and seaweed coursed through the air and black-faced sheep bleated from the purple hills. The wind was freshening, a sure sign that the weather would change before the day was out.

An arc of constables, smelling of carbolic soap and boot blackening, linked arms along the length of the train. They strained their muscles, the taste of salt-water on their clenched lips. Sergeant Scully fretted; would his men be able to hold back the surge? Would things get out of control? He raised a long uniformed arm and squealed in a hoarse voice, 'Move back there. For God's sake, move back.'

A cascade of noise rippled through the mass of islanders. Women wailed; children whimpered; dogs barked; young and old shuffled forward in a throng of humanity that reeked of alcohol, urine and stale perspiration. They piled down the hill, crushing and surging towards the train where men were uncovering the wagons and stacking the white deal coffins on the ground among the swirling fumes. The keen of the women started up, rose and fell, built and waned, as the coffins were lifted to the ground.

Mr Gray of the Railway Company barked out the name of each of the deceased as groups of men stepped forward, heads bent, to claim the dead. Feet set apart, the men grasped the pale wood, hoisted a coffin, twisted their bodies and walked with scrunching steps to where the carts were lined up on the roadway. The onlookers opened a pathway, genuflected, crossed themselves, and intoned prayers and blessings. A woman knelt and prostrated her body on the pale wood of a coffin next to a cart. She pounded the wooden box with clenched hands, aching to touch the flesh of her daughter.

'Let me see her. Let me see her,' she screamed.

Relatives circled the woman and raised her to her feet: 'Leave it be, Mary. Let it be.'

Wood scraped against wood as they loaded thirty coffins

on to the waiting carts for the five-mile journey south to Kildownet. The burial ground was within yards of the shore and close to the ruined castle of Grace O'Malley, the ancient Pirate Queen of the West.

Among the mourners was James Lynchehaun who had travelled the ten miles from his home in the north of the island. He knew many of those who had drowned: the three Malley sisters – Mary, Margaret and Annie – came from the townland of Valley where he ran his grocery business; Bridget Joyce and Pat Cafferkey lived in Tonragee, close to his birthplace; Catherine Gallagher grew up in Corraun where he had tended his father's sheep as a boy.

That summer James Lynchehaun was in his mid thirties, five foot ten inches in height, a well-built, dark-haired man with broad shoulders and a square-jawed face. He had startling bright eyes, nostrils that twitched like a lively colt's, and a peculiar habit of wrinkling his forehead in conversation. His was a restless and volatile spirit and those who knew said that drink had a disastrous effect on him. The stories of his youthful exploits were legendary, but he had recently married Catherine Gallagher and was the father of an infant son. Perhaps he had sown his wild oats.

The islanders talked and whispered behind cupped hands, exchanging scraps of information about what had happened: 'Did you hear that Mary McLaughlin held on to her sister's hand in the water as long as she could? In the end she slipped away. Poor Mary, she'll have Bridget's grip on her wrist for the rest of her days. God help her.'

'Mary Lavelle was only thirteen and the eldest of seven boys and girls.'

'Is there no news yet of young Pat Cafferkey? His father is going about everywhere looking for him.'

'What will Owen Malley do now with his three daughters gone and he left childless?'

'There's Mister Kelly. What does he say?'

P. J. Kelly of the Westport Board of Guardians moved among the families of the victims and dispensed financial assistance to the bereaved. It could be a tricky situation for the Guardians who had responsibility for collecting the seed potato rates in Achill. The official knew only too well that there were low-voiced mutterings that the migrants had to go to Scotland to earn enough money to pay the rents. He handed Owen O'Malley a sovereign, shook his hand energetically and murmured, 'So sorry for your troubles.'

The grieving man sniffled and asked plaintively, 'Sir, will we have to give this back for the seed payment? If we have, it is better for us not to take it.'

P. J. Kelly assured him that there was no need to be fearful of any such harassment from the rate collectors. His words were of little comfort.

Nearby, a man muttered loudly, 'Wasn't Mr Balfour, the Chief Secretary, here only two years ago with his sister, and didn't he see for himself the way things are? Didn't he bring in the seed rate after that and now it's worse than ever!' People nodded in agreement. The official moved on.

Father Connolly, Achill parish priest, faced the cortège, tracing the sign of the cross in the air with a plump hand, and led the mourners in prayer. The procession queue got ready as the carts moved to the centre of the road, lined up, then set off across the span of Michael Davitt Bridge, the cart shafts swinging rhythmically at the animals' sides. The gulls wheeled overhead, screeching their funeral dirge. On the far side of the bridge the half-mile procession curled south, hugging the channel of water that separated the island from Corraun Peninsula. The people crowded in close to the cortège, the keening women hanging off the cart shafts while children clung to their skirts. The carts clattered past houses, where yellow laburnum drooped low in the gardens, and ferried the dead to their final resting place.

The burial destination in Kildownet was a short distance from the pier at Darby's Point where those, who now lay motionless on carts, had gathered just two days earlier at the start of their migrant journey. There had been a hubbub of excitement throughout Achill from early morning on the day they set out. Over 400 of the islanders, most of them young girls, had made the dawn journey dressed in their Sunday best and carrying their few possessions in tied cloth bundles. Those who travelled from Keem, Dooagh and Keel in the west met up with others from the townlands of Dookinella, Dugort and Valley at Bunnacurry crossroads on the brow of the hill. The morning air was filled with laughter, shouts, calls of greeting, and cheers as they headed on their way. They would travel by hooker, the traditional island sailing boat, as far as Westport Quay where they would board the Laird steamer SS *Elm* for the onward journey to Glasgow and the harvest fields of Scotland. Cart after cart had arrived at Darby's Point where four hookers waited out in the channel, their sails flapping in the morning breeze. John and Pat Healy had taken their hooker, *Victory,* around from Belfarsad to await their passengers who were being rowed out from the pier by currach. By eight o'clock there were more than 100 passengers on the *Victory* deck and yet more clambered on board. The tide was going out and the crews knew that they needed to get on their way. By nine o'clock the four hookers were under sail as a crowd gathered on Achill Beg to wave them off. John Healy moved among his passengers trying to collect the six penny fare. Some had borrowed the money for the passage from local shopkeepers while others had it sent to them by their host farmers in Scotland. Healy later claimed that the *Victory* was carrying 75 passengers but the police would conclude that there were 126 people on the ship.

Two and a half hours after departing Darby's Point, the *Victory* sailed past Annagh Head and moved towards Westport Quay where the steamer waited about a mile from the quay for the incoming tide to allow her to berth. On board the SS *Elm* were Captain Carswell, pilot Thomas Gibbons, and a number of crew under the supervision of stevedore Michael O'Malley. As the *Victory* closed the distance between it and the steamer, the hooker passengers shouted to one another to come and look at the ship that would take them to Glasgow. They streamed up from the *Victory* hold and piled on to one side of the hooker to get a better view.

Thomas Gibbons was the first to spot the danger from the deck of the SS *Elm*. He watched the cheering passengers stream to one side of the *Victory* and knew that the crew would have to jibe quickly, and turn the stern through the wind, but he feared that there was too much top weight on the vessel. He shouted urgently across to the hooker crew, 'Lower your mainsail! Lower your mainsail!'

John and Pat Healy were, by then, aware of the hazard and yelled at the excited passengers to sit down. John Healy shouted that he was going to bring the boat around in a jibe but did not appear to slacken the sheet or to lower the mainsail. The sudden movements of the boom and sail brought the vessel over violently. The *Victory* capsized and most of the passengers were thrown into the water. The sounds would stay forever with those who witnessed the scene: frantic splashes, screams for help, choking coughs and cries of terror. They were the pitiful sounds of the drowning and the dying.

Some tried to swim to safety but became entangled in the hooker's huge sails; others were pinned in the boat's hold by falling spars and deck gear. Heads bobbed in the water beneath the sails like footballs, and it was impossible to release them due to the pressure of the water as bodies drifted away helplessly on the tide. John Healy caught hold of a plank and kept himself afloat until rescued. The teenager, Edward O'Malley, was approaching the SS *Elm* in a rowing boat from the opposite direction to collect cargo from the steamer. 'At first glance,' he said afterwards, 'we were able to see that, when the mast struck the water, the mainsail and the jib had imprisoned several of the poor islanders. The water was a struggling, screaming mass of human beings. Some were grabbing their companions in order to try and save themselves, but the inevitable result was that they were dragging one another underneath.'

Four boats were launched from the SS *Elm* and more craft put out from the quays. Within the hour boatloads of survivors were arriving on Westport Quay where they walked dazed among the sodden corpses of their neighbours and friends. By late afternoon thirty bodies lay side by side in the temporary morgue, light shawls covered their still, fear-wracked faces.

Frank Molloy of Breanaskil was one of the lucky ones and later spoke of his good fortune in not travelling on the *Victory* on account of not having the fare: 'I did not come by Healy's hooker but walked round by the road. I started from home about ten o'clock. The distance is about twenty-nine Irish miles. I left Achill for the purpose of going to England and I intended leaving Newport by rail but came on to Westport Quay when I heard about the accident. I was told that the Healy boat was capsized.'

Many of the survivors sailed for Glasgow on the SS *Elm* later that evening. Some carried their bundles of drenched possessions, while others had lost everything they had taken from home that morning. Some had not wanted to leave but they knew that the lack of their harvest remittances could lead to eviction for their families if the seed rent wasn't paid in the autumn. They had to go.

The funeral carts reached Kildownet cemetery in a hollow of ground to the sucking sounds of an ebbing tide. The evening shadows moved on Corraun Hill as if an oversized fox sloped there. They unloaded the carts and rows of pale wooden boxes shone bright against the purple heather. Relatives of the dead had agreed to Father Connolly's suggestion that they bury their dead in a communal plot. A group of seventy men stepped forward, armed with pickaxes, shovels and spades, the breeze lifting the hair on their bare heads. Soon there was the ring of spades off rocks, the thud of pick axes against stones, and the crunch of shovels scooping up clay. The men bent and lifted shovel after shovel of brown-black earth. Occasionally, a man paused to lean his implement against his wet body, spitting warm saliva into his palms and rubbing his calloused hands before reaching for a drink and gulping down sharp, butter-clotted milk. Soon the diggers stood shoulder-deep in the earth.

The sun was low in the Atlantic sky when Father Connolly, dressed in white surplice, moved along the coffin rows sprinkling holy water with a heavy hand from a silver aspersorium, and intoning, 'May perpetual light shine upon them; may they rest in peace.' Men slid ropes through weather-beaten hands and lowered the dead into the Kildownet ground. As the first shovels of earth smashed down on wood, a wild lamentation rose into the air. The skies darkened and a heavy shower of slanting rain fell on the fresh earth and the bowed heads. Paraffin lights and candles began to glow from windows across the channel as day drifted into night.

The day after the funeral they towed the ill-fated *Victory* into Westport Quay as torn shawls, baskets, ribbons, and remnants of clothing lay strewn at the edges of Clew Bay. Soon, a full scale fund-raising effort got under way to relieve the plight of the Achill islanders. The County Mayo High Sheriff sent an urgent letter by telegraph to the main newspapers:

Sir, -
As the Press has fully depicted the terrible disaster at Westport on Thursday last, it is unnecessary for me to enter into details. Up to this the dead bodies of 25 girls and seven men have been recovered, and two men are still missing. Each of these is bread-winner to a family, so that there are 34 impoverished as well as desolate homes in Achill today. Each of the girls would have brought home £8 to £10 at the end of the harvest season, and each of the men from £12 to £15, so that the magnitude of the loss for this single year can be at once seen. Subscriptions will be received by the Bank of Ireland and the Ulster Bank, Westport, or by me, and acknowledged through the Press. A committee is being formed to distribute the funds which we hope to receive.

I am, Sir, your obedient servant,

E. Thomas O'Donel,
High Sheriff, County Mayo
Newport House, Newport.

The situation was dangerous and things could easily turn nasty. The tragedy could heighten anger about the seed potato rates and increase hostilities between landlords and tenants on the island. Those with influence rushed to print and sought to take the high moral ground. Cardinal Logue wrote to Father O'Connor to express his concerns about the hardship 'that forces young girls of tender years to quit the shelter of their homes and the security of their simple family lives ... to seek in the harvest fields of England and Scotland employment which for many reasons is unsuited to their sex and age. Surely there must be some remedy for this crying evil, if those who have the power had only the will to seek it out and apply it?'

The Trustees of the Achill Mission estate in north Achill represented the largest landlords on the island. They responded quickly by contributing £20 to the Achill-Westport fund and expressed their relief that, among the list of those who perished, there were none of the tenants of the Achill Mission estate. When the Westport Committee later published a list of fund subscribers, a £5 contribution from Agnes MacDonnell, owner of the Valley House estate, was acknowledged.

There was now intense national and international interest in the plight of Achill. *The Irish Times* urged the public to support the Achill Fund and gave an upbeat prognosis for the island's prospects which may not have been shared by many of the Achill inhabitants: 'There is a future for Achill. Its healthfulness, its natural beauty, its inspiring scenery and, not less than these attractions, its honesty and kindliness of its people must draw strangers to its coasts and headlands when once the railway is opened and a new era for the locality has begun. This very disaster must cause many more in distant places to make Inquiry as to what Achill is.'

The Times of London drew attention to the bitter resentment among the Achill islanders to the seed potato rate and linked it directly to the ever growing numbers of young harvesters leaving the island each summer. The paper reminded readers how, two years earlier, Mr Balfour, Chief Secretary of Ireland, had visited Achill and afterwards secured a grant for the Poor Law Guardians to purchase seed potatoes: 'Upwards of £4,000 worth of seed was given to the people in this way, large quantities of which failed.' It was the view of *The Times* that the seed rate issue was becoming explosive as the Government refused to extend the two-year limit on the repayment of loans advanced to tenant farmers for seed purchase.

In the week following the funeral of the drowned, a newspaper reporter had an unusual experience while travelling between Newport and Achill when he and his driver gave a lift to a girl they met walking back from Westport. She was one of those rescued from the sea when the *Victory* capsized. 'I would not travel on the steamer after what happened,' she told them. 'I could not face it.' She had started out by foot from Achill the previous day to walk to Westport. 'I wanted to find my sister's clothes. She was lost.'

Did she find anything belonging to her sister?

She had found nothing. She was going home, back to the island.

Before the month was out the inquest into the deaths of the *Victory* victims resumed in Westport and reached a verdict: 'We consider that the deceased were drowned abreast of Islandrue in the County of Mayo on 14 June 1894 by the capsizing of the hooker *Victory* and which said hooker was in the charge of John Healy, and we consider the capsizing took place by the passengers on board rushing to the side of the hooker nearest to the steamship *Elm*. We consider that the hooker was not properly ballasted when she left Achill and we consider that the hooker was grossly overcrowded.'

Meanwhile, when the hot-blooded James Lynchehaun looked out from his house in north Achill, where he ran his grocery business on the road between Valley and Dugort, bitterness and anger festered in his soul. He could not escape the menacing stare of Slievemore a short distance away, ever changing in aspect as it reflected the shifting clouds above. It was as if the mountain mirrored his agitated nature. He was on a collision course with his landlord, and former employer, Agnes MacDonnell of the Valley House.

2
The Great and the Good
July 1894

A chill needed its heroes. That summer, when Michael Davitt crossed the bridge named in his honour, it was three weeks to the day since the island had buried its dead. Huddles of children followed the gaunt sallow-faced man. Giggling, they pointed small fingers at his flat, flapping jacket sleeve, a dark reminder of the accident at Stellfoxe Victoria Mill that had severed the right arm from his young body. It seemed that everything about the tall, odd-looking figure was dark and brooding: large, brilliant-brown, piercing eyes; coal-black hair, beard and side-burns; a melancholy demeanour that matched the island mood.

Michael Davitt was back in his native county, west of the place where his evicted family had stood homeless and bereft on a Straide roadside. The towns and villages of Mayo marked steps in the growth of his political campaign against landlordism: Irishtown, where the tenant-farmers had gathered in their thousands to protest against unjust rents; Westport, where he had stood side by side with Charles Stewart Parnell, and from where the cry went out 'the land for the people'; Castlebar, where he started the Land League of Mayo in Daly's Hotel on the Mall.

Davitt attended the funeral of Catherine Masterson, who had been among the lucky ones rescued when the *Victory* capsized in Clew Bay, only to die later from her injuries. He met

Mary Mullane whose daughter was also rescued off Westport Quay and took the steamer to Scotland after her ordeal. Like the others who had travelled after the *Victory* capsize, she knew her family's need of the money she would send home to pay the seed rent but, not long after her arrival in Scotland, trauma overtook her. 'The poor girl lost her reason beyond there. She's in a lunatic asylum,' they told him. Would he make a case for relief monies to be paid to her destitute mother? He had come to them in their lowest moments, they said. He would come to their rescue in their latest hour of need.

Michael Davitt went to the home of Owen and Mary Malley who had lost their three daughters. 'Davitt is here,' a boy shouted, as the horse and cart turned at the crossroads and their hero alighted at the house, his dark hair and suit giving his skin an unhealthy pallor. He stooped and stepped into the cottage, shook hands with Owen and Mary Malley, then bent his head towards them, listening and nodding. 'They were good girls, the finest you could ask for,' Mary Malley told him. 'Annie, it was her first time going. She couldn't wait to be with her two sisters. Margaret and Mary would bring home £10 each. Annie would have tried to do as good as them. She was a great little worker.'

'Who is your landlord? Are you behind with the rent?' he asked.

'It's Agnes MacDonnell above in the Valley House,' someone shouted from the doorway.

'We were relying on the girls' money to pay the rent, Mr Davitt,' Owen Malley said. 'The £5 from the relief fund will go on the seed rent. And the crops is poor again. The spuds are only poreens out there.'

Davitt wrote down what he heard, careful to gather the particulars of every case. He had done this in Achill on another occasion almost a decade earlier when he had filled his notebooks with details of the villages and the cabins, the landlords and the rents. Little had changed. He would collate and analyze all the information and work it into arguments and proposals that he would take to the relief committee that was dealing with the distribution of monies to the bereaved families.

He had already laid the groundwork at a meeting with P. J. Kelly of the Board of Guardians on his way through Westport when they had a long conversation about the allocation of the proceeds of the combined relief funds.

Michael Davitt stayed four days on the island. He visited all the bereaved families and listened to their stories, sympathising in a voice that still held the cadences of Lancashire where he had once toiled in a cotton-mill. When he stooped to enter the miserable cabins, he blinked in the smoke that rose above black pots of gruel hanging over weak fires and absorbed the animal smells at the far end of the rooms. He looked into the islanders' eyes, seeing grief, hunger and fear, and the muscles in his pale face tightened with rage.

The relief committee, presided over by Father Connolly, invited Michael Davitt to attend its meeting in Achill Sound on Tuesday, the day before his departure. The applications for assistance were pouring in and the committee was uneasy, for each of the funds was doing its own thing without reference to the Achill committee. Their secretary would write to all the funds and inform them that, once the immediate needs of the families were attended to, it would be advisable not to distribute any money over the heads of the local committee. Such separate action, in their respectful view, would only lead to waste and overlapping.

Davitt came to the meeting with his thoughts marshalled and organised, supporting his proposals with the forensic skills of a modern actuary. He had already calculated the average age of the heads of the bereaved households. 'I propose that the land annuities be paid for the bereaved families,' he told the committee. 'I also think that the families of the drowned should be excused from the seed rate.' He further suggested that those who survived the drowning and were unable to proceed to Scotland should receive a grant equivalent to what they would have earned in migration. The committee concurred. They would forward Mr Davitt's proposals to each of the Achill funds.

It was seven years since Michael Davitt had come to the island to officially open the new swivel bridge named in his honour. Like the new railway line which would be commissioned in a matter of months, the bridge was held out as a piece of infrastructure that would drive Achill's economic development. During its construction the islanders had watched on as the enormous steelwork arrived by sea from Glasgow and workers collected thousands of tons of stone from Achill's shores and hills for the bridge's foundation. Michael Davitt came that September with his young wife, the American Mary Yore, who was said to have dispelled some of his depressive gloom and sharp spurts of temper. A grey drizzle fell on the crowd as Father O'Connor read the welcome address. 'In you, Mr Davitt, we recognise one of Ireland's noblest sons ... You have laid our grievances before the nations of the earth ... When famine swept over this island, and the callous Government of England looked carelessly on, you came promptly to our aid.' The parish priest had especially warm words of greeting for Mrs Davitt, 'the accomplished and charming bride of one of Ireland's greatest patriots'.

'It would be cruel on my part to detain you under this heavy shower of rain,' Davitt told his Achill Sound audience. 'It is on record the numbers of poor people who lost their lives in wintry weather when trying to cross from the mainland to the Mulranny shore.' He knew well the hardship they endured when they brought their cattle and sheep to the fairs in Newport, Westport and Castlebar and were compelled to wait for two or three days before they could make a passage. 'Let us hope that the bridge now formally opened will open a new era of prosperity for this much afflicted island of Achill,' he continued.

The official party proceeded to the new bridge where Mr Davitt formally declared it open. He then walked along the temporary gangway, the first man to do so, to the cheers of the Achill crowd. Afterwards, the weather cleared as the island regatta got into full swing and the distinguished visitors watched the boat races of yawls, currachs and hookers out on the waters of the Sound. There were horse and donkey competitions, athletic events, and the star turn, climbing the greasy pole, with Michael Davitt officiating as a judge and Mrs Davitt presenting the prizes.

There was another man in Achill who saw in the new bridge an opportunity to project himself as a local hero. Within a few weeks of its official opening, Michael Davitt Bridge was ready for horse and cart traffic and there were plans for another official event at which Father O'Connor would ride across by horse and sidecar, the first person to make the crossing by wheeled transport. However, a strange tale involving James Lynchehaun later grew about what happened that day. The story went that, in the early hours of the morning of the day on which the first horse and cart was to cross the bridge, James Lynchehaun harnessed his mare and cart and made his way to the bridge where the channel waters shimmered in the night light. There, he flicked the reins and goaded the animal into a canter across the new structure, thumping his fist in the air when he reached the far side. It was but one of the many tall tales that would be recounted in subsequent decades about the man who was destined to become a folk hero in Achill and beyond.

James Lynchehaun would afterwards cross Michael Davitt Bridge many times as he made the journey from Tonragee, his birthplace on the mainland, to his home in Valley, north Achill. The year that the bridge was officially opened by Michael Davitt, James Lynchehaun was a young man not long returned from England and having already had several skirmishes with the law. He was a lively, spirited fellow who had done well at school and became a school monitor. He progressed to a teaching post at Belfarsad at the slopes of Corraun Hill, but only lasted two years in the position before giving in to the temptation to 'muster up a large roll' and being dismissed for falsifying the school records. He later secured a teaching post in Roundstone, County Galway, where all went well for a year or so before he reverted to his old ways. His propensity for drink and brawls led to his arrest, but he managed to escape and absconded to England. There, it was said, he had joined the Metropolitan Police Force in Manchester until he got into trouble again as a result of his drinking and was dismissed from the force. James Lynchehaun's reputation as an unpredictable and tempestuous character was well established in Achill.

Within months of James Lynchehaun driving his horse and cart over the new swivel bridge, Agnes MacDonnell would make the same crossing on to Achill Island as she came to take possession of her estate in the townland of Valley. Her fate and that of James Lynchehaun would become inextricably linked in a way that nobody could have imagined. What happened between the pair would also lead to the paths of Lynchehaun and Michael Davitt crossing almost a decade later many miles from Achill.

If, in their grief, the inhabitants of Achill looked to Michael Davitt for hope, they also turned with positive anticipation to another distinguished visitor, Ishbel Gordon – Lady Aberdeen – who arrived on the island just a week after Davitt's departure. She had travelled by train to Mulranny, which was then welcoming its first train passengers. Ishbel Gordon and her party arrived on a day when thick grey rain rolled in from the Atlantic and sat on the mountains, obliterating the peaks. The mist crept down to envelop the island's bogs, rivers and dwellings, and lasted the entire day, turning the gaudy bunting in the village into a sodden mess. A banner, emblazoned with the words *Welcome to the Countess – Success to Irish Industries,* hung limp across Davitt Bridge by evening time when the esteemed lady finally arrived.

She was on a whistle-stop tour of Ireland to promote the Irish Home Industries Association established during an earlier stint with her husband, the Irish Viceroy, at Dublin Castle. She had already visited Limerick, Galway, Clifden and Westport, where she had bowed regally to the cheering crowd outside the Railway Hotel. 'I am glad to be able to tell you that there is an increasing demand for our Irish woollens and linens and embroideries and laces,' she told the crowds, repeating these words like a refrain everywhere she travelled. To applause from the waiting crowd at Achill Sound, Ishbel touched on her own Scottish origins: 'As a Scotch woman I am glad the girls going to Scotland are considered to be well treated, and that the migration there every year to work has not brought them any harm but rather the reverse.'

Ishbel Gordon was still in her thirties, a tall, dark-eyed, well-built woman with brown wavy hair, who had not yet put on the weight that was to transform her into the bulky, matronly figure she would become in later years. A formal photograph of the time shows her in Irish traditional dress, looking into the distance, head slightly tilted with a faint self-conscious smile. She was solemn, raised in an intensely religious family, and driven by a desire to do good. Her reputation as a determined organiser and advocate for Irish arts and crafts was sky high following her promotion of the Irish Village at the Chicago World Fair the previous year.

The weather improved next day when the eminent lady and her entourage headed up the tree-lined avenue to their first engagement at the Franciscan monastery at Bunnacurry. Included in the friary reception party was the rotund figure of Brother Paul Carney who took Lady Aberdeen on a tour of the boys' school where he was principal teacher. Afterwards, the friar wrote in his journal that Ishbel took 'wine and biscuits' and that the children in the local school were handed out sweets and given a school holiday to mark her visit. Ishbel's emotions during her Achill trip were a combination of horror at the living conditions and economic plight of the islanders, and intoxication with the magnificence of the island's natural landscape. Her dominant impression, though, was of a place overwhelmed by hopelessness.

A welcome party gathered to greet Lady Aberdeen at the Slievemore Hotel in the heart of The Colony in Dugort. The gathering did not include the Valley House owner, Agnes MacDonnell, who was then visiting her London home. Agnes had a court case pending at the Achill Assizes against local trespassers on her property but, wisely, given the heightened emotions on the island, she had requested a postponement of the case. Ishbel Gordon and Agnes MacDonnell did not, therefore, face one another in Dugort, yet it is intriguing to imagine such an encounter. Two driven women, the younger moving on an international stage with a highly visible project of promoting native crafts and home industries to boost Ireland's economy, the older woman bent on taming the wild lands of her remote estate.

Before leaving Ireland Ishbel Gordon sat down in Dublin's Shelbourne Hotel and penned a letter to *The Irish Times* calling for urgent action to deal with Achill's plight:

Sir,

The late lamentable disaster to the Achill islanders when on their way to Great Britain to earn the livelihood which they are unable to obtain at home has drawn general attention and widespread sympathy towards the inhabitants of that misery-stricken district. And undoubtedly there is a general desire to seize the present opportunity not only to alleviate the distress of the sorrowing relatives of the deceased, but to effect permanent improvements in the condition of a population which is a disgrace to our country.

Having just returned from a visit to the island, and being on the point of embarking to Canada, I venture to ask you to lay before your readers the results of the inquiries made on the spot, and to invoke their generous aid for the regeneration of Achill.

The densely packed villages in which the people live, in most cases distant from their small holdings and presenting a very labyrinth of abject squalor; the low, dark, unventilated, one-roomed houses inhabited in common by human beings, cattle, pigs and poultry; the extraordinary effect produced by seeing a population composed only of aged people and little children, in consequence of nearly all the adults, men and women alike, being absent for the summer's work; the general look of care and hopelessness, even among the children; the mass of bog land only relieved here and there by a prosperous little bit of reclaimed land; the sea with its wealth of fish, but never a harbour and scarcely a pier; all these things contrasted with the beauty of the scenery – the grand cliffs, the lovely outlook over the islands of the Atlantic, and the blue mountains of Connemara, the many other attractions of hill, river, sea, and strand for the visitor, leave a depressing effect on the mind. What avail of all these natural advantages to the people who live among them?

But there is hope of a different state of things if the present opportunity be firmly grasped.

There appears to be more than a chance, with the cooperation of landlords and tenants, of making the people responsible proprietors of their own holdings, of increasing the size of these holdings within the area of the island which the people would be so unwilling to quit, of removing them from their wretched villages to suitable houses on their land, and of giving them inducements to stay at home and reclaim their land.

Already, that admirable body, the Congested Districts Board, and its devoted officers, by means of model holdings throughout the island and the introduction of improved methods of agriculture, are teaching the people what may be done by themselves. Already does the completion of the new railway to Achill Sound suggest the opening up of the island to tourist traffic, and inspire hope amongst the islanders for the ready disposal of their fish and other marketable commodities; and already has our hon. secretary, the Right Hon. T. A. Dickson, been able to arrange for the sending of new improved looms to the weavers, who are very eager to possess them, and who are to repay their cost by instalments.

I beg to entreat for a generous response to the appeal for subscriptions, which may be sent to the treasurers or secretaries of the Achill Improvement Fund, Mansion House, Dublin.

A strong pull, a long pull, and a pull all together, is needed, if a real and abiding change in the condition of the island as a whole is to be effected. Will your readers help!

Yours, etc.,
Ishbel Aberdeen

As the Countess of Aberdeen was setting sail for Canada, visitors thronged to Achill Island, which was becoming a prime destination for those taking the newly opened railway extension to Mulranny. There, the Railway Hotel offered walks, drives and short excursions to its residents, and the one excursion not be missed was that to Achill. Cyclists could take the coast road to the island, or visitors could choose to travel by sidecar. Tourist handbooks particularly recommended a visit to the Seal Caves near Slievemore: 'These caves are at the northern foot of Slievemore about 1½ to 2 miles from the Strand. They are exceedingly fine, and seals are by no means scarce, though sometimes the traveller may not have the luck to happen upon them in their elusive haunts.'

Newspaper reporters, who had swarmed through Achill in the aftermath of the Clew Bay tragedy and during Lady Aberdeen's visit, had reported some strange events. One correspondent attended mass in Dookinella where he listened with disbelief to a sermon by the curate who had some harsh things to tell his congregation. 'Your poverty,' he had thundered, 'if it exists, is mainly due to your own neglect. You come back from Scotland and England, believing that you have nothing to do but take a holiday. If you devoted yourselves to improving your holdings and dwellings, your poverty would be a good deal mitigated.'

Another reporter, while interviewing the Protestant Rector, asked the cleric if he thought the Achill islanders were a peaceable people. The Rector was adamant in his reply: 'I have been here thirteen years on this island and I have always found them peaceable, quiet and well disposed at all times. During all the years I have been here there has not been a single outrage of any kind.' However, the peace and quiet of Achill Island would soon be shattered.

The bloom of the Achill gorse was fading. The families of the drowned made weary journeys to the premises of the relief committee in Achill Sound for assistance. Between the two points of Dugort to the west and the Valley House to the east, James Lynchehaun watched the traffic move over and back as tourists and dignitaries flooded north Achill. He brooded and bided his time. Agnes MacDonnell was due back at the Valley House from London in August. She had the matter of the court case against trespassers on her estate to attend to. And she and he had unfinished business.

3
Handsome Head of Thick, Reddish Hair
August 1894

I t was a bright Sunday morning in August. Agnes MacDonnell
stood ready in the hallway of the Valley House waiting for
the horse and phaeton to be brought round from the yard. She
had returned from London the previous day and was heading
to St Thomas' Church, three miles away, for Sunday service.
It would be a chance to meet up with her friend Dr Thomas
Croly, and others, to get their views on the state of affairs after
the drowning business. She knew that she had to be careful.
She had already sent a contribution to the relief fund and had,
wisely, requested a postponement of consideration of a case
she had brought against some tenants at the Achill Assizes until
emotions had calmed down.

Agnes MacDonnell was in her late forties, a handsome
woman with a head of thick, reddish hair. Contemporary
portraits of her reveal a soft, delicate contour in her side profile,
her braided hair piled high and shining on her head. However,
her mouth could set into a firm, clenched expression, indicating
a determination and a stubbornness of personality which would
afterwards be described as 'a great firmness of character'.

As she stood at the entrance of the Valley House that
morning, Agnes had good reason to be proud of her achieve-
ments. She waited in the wide hallway where doors led into the
two main reception areas: a fine drawing room with a view

out on to the curved entrance avenue and a windowed alcove opening into the well-kept walled garden; through the drawing room doors, the rarely used dining room that was dominated by a large white marble fireplace. Across the hallway was the small sitting room where she kept the estate accounts and tenant records, and where pieces of paper protruded from pigeonholes in the writing table.

It was six years since she had read the London advertisement in *The Times* of London:

> By order of the executors of the late Earl of Cavan – shooting, fishing and yachting – Freehold Estate of 2000 acres with furnished residence and 150 acres of freehold land. Price for the whole only £1,000. Adjoining the Protestant colony of Dugort in the island of Achill and within one day's journey of London.
>
> AUCTION at the Mart, London
> on Wednesday, April 18th.

She had acted decisively and was soon the title-holder of the Irish estate previously owned by the late Frederick Lambart, eighth Earl of Cavan, in a remote corner of a barren island in the west of Ireland. She was aware that the new swivel bridge in Achill could positively impact the projects and ideas that she nurtured for her new property.

What propelled the decision by Agnes MacDonnell to acquire a property in this bleak spot? Was it the call of distant Irish roots? Was it a desire to build an inheritance for her only child, Leslie, from her first marriage to Frederick Charles Elliot? Was it an alienation from her second husband, barrister Randal MacDonnell, who would visit her island home only occasionally? Was it the story of the Achill Mission proselytisers at The Colony that fired her imagination when she read of wild mountainous lands transformed into arable fields? Was it simply a commercial decision – that Agnes MacDonnell judged that she could make a good return from her tenants' remittances, stock sales, horse breeding, and even running a small hotel?

She may well have read the writings of the women travellers who had made the journey to Achill a half-century earlier and had written with passion about their experiences. It was just a decade after the arrival of the Achill Mission proselytisers on the island that Mrs S. C. Hall, the Irish writer living in England, came to Achill to report on Dugort Colony, about which there were contradictory views. Mrs Hall was clear on one matter, that the Protestant faith bestowed positive benefits on all who embraced the faith, not least in the matter of hygiene and cleanliness. She had written: 'Every traveller in Ireland is fully aware that a greater attention to appearance, and neater, cleaner and more orderly habits, distinguish the Protestant from the Catholic at every grade, below the very highest.' As to the benefits of the Achill Mission settlement, Mrs Hall had been unambiguous in her view that it was worse than useless and an instrument of evil rather than good.

A decade after Mrs Hall's visit, the feminist and sociologist, Harriet Martineau, took a more benign view of The Colony when she travelled to north Achill and observed the reclaimed fields of tillage and the healthy faces of the locals. Her verdict was that the Achill Mission 'has been a great blessing to the island' and that Achill had made good progress in the previous twenty years since the time when 'the people were as truly savage as any South Sea Islanders.'

Agnes MacDonnell shared some traits in common with Mrs Hall, Harriet Martineau and Ishbel Gordon: a strong Protestant faith, a resolute and independent spirit, a belief in the virtues of self-control and industry and a single-mindedness of purpose. Agnes, however, did not embark on any evangelical activities; she did not involve herself in improving the lot of the north Achill community in which she lived; she did not write or communicate externally about the abject conditions on Achill. She concentrated her energies on her house and estate, working with unrelenting obstinacy to maximise the returns from her enterprise.

A letter written by Agnes MacDonnell's London solicitors, Dowett, Knight and Co., provides a detailed picture of the Valley House estate, and an intriguing insight into its owner's personality and character:

> The Valley House ... is the residence of the Tonatanvally estate, which was sold by instructions of the late Earl of Cavan in 1888 to Mrs MacDonnell. We also sold to her some English properties, and these transactions caused many personal interviews (as she transacted her personal business matters personally) and her conduct was such as to very strongly impress us that in a remarkable degree she exhibited a great firmness of character in the traits of absolute justice tempered by a true generosity. Mrs MacDonnell is an English lady, though connected by marriage with one of the most ancient lineages of Ireland (the Taafe family).
>
> It may be interesting if we add that the Tonatanvally estate comprised:

	Acres	Roods	Perches
Lands in hand and residence	530	2	21
Lands let in conacre lots	26	2	15
Lands leased to tenants	243	1	20
Turf-fuel land or bog	1,258	2	38
	2,068 [sic]	1	14

Besides this about 150 acres of the slopes of the Slievemore Mountain were held on lease as a sheep run.

Achill Island comprises 50,000 acres, and has a wild seashore frontage of over 80 miles. The Slievemore Mountain rises to over 2,200 feet.

We are, sir, your obedient servants,

Dowett, Knight and Co.,
3 Lincoln Inn-fields
London 9

Agnes MacDonnell climbed into the phaeton, shook the reins, clicked her teeth and the wheels crunched the gravel of the front avenue that inclined down to the roadway. The hay was saved in the fields and the oats ready for harvesting, but the potato yield would be poor and she would have to rely on the turnip crop to feed her stock through the winter months. On her left side she passed the furze-lined path leading the short distance to Lough Gall. The small lake was a peaceful spot where she liked to walk and watch the ripple of the waters that contrasted with the wild swell of the Atlantic a few hundred yards away to her right.

Passing through the white entrance pillars she faced the Sandybanks, the expanse of grassy sand dunes that stretched away as far as the promontory of Ridge Point. The Sandybanks had caused her more problems than anywhere else on her Achill property. She had tried every means at her disposal to stop the trespassing but still they drove their cattle, day and night, to graze on the salt-drenched grass.

The horse turned instinctively at the Valley crossroads, as the three-mile journey to Dugort was a regular one for animal and mistress. It was when they reached Barnynagappul Strand, where the incoming tide almost touched the road, that Agnes MacDonnell may have become anxious for she would soon skirt the passage that led to the cottage of James Lynchehaun, her former employee and now a tenant with whom she was locked in dispute. Many times, in her head, she had retraced their relationship over the half-dozen years she had known him. It had started out so well as he had charmed her with his free-flowing words, his powerful physical stature, and his knowledge of the wily ways of the islanders. When she first arrived in Achill she had needed an agent to keep an eye on her affairs when she was out of the country, and her earliest appointments had not turned out well. She could see now that Lynchehaun had ingratiated himself with her, writing to her in London with complaints about her employees. She could still recall his sly words:

He (your agent) has visited the Valley three or four times since you left, and on any of these occasions I know him to be on his own business, that is, in connection with his fishing. Also, in order to have the freight of the materials ordered for the repairs of the Big House, he ordered all those things for his own hooker which caused considerable delay in delivery. The cleverness of this agent is not yet known to you. I cannot call it 'cleverness', but I dare say it will convey to you a meaning. I am sure at the time of his appointment you did not know his history, not yet is it known to you, but had you been in the country a few years ago you should certainly learn something interesting from those very reverend gentlemen who now look upon P. Sweeney as an infallible man of business and intellect.

She was relieved that there was no sign of Lynchehaun on the road that morning, for she had enough on her mind without having to deal with his scowls and foul language. She urged the horse into a gallop until she was at the brow of the hill looking down on Pollawaddy Strand and facing Slievemore. There were moments when the towering mountain mass appeared to her as sinister and as threatening as Lynchehaun. She knew that she had nobody but herself to blame for having been taken in by him, and for listening to his smooth words about how he would be diligent in looking after her interests: 'Your stock, your hay and your bent will be better taken care of than if you were here on the spot yourself.' She had contracted him the year after her arrival in Achill for an annual salary of £15, and he had taken a lease from her on 'the Scraw' and on two cottages near where she had just passed.

From the way James Lynchehaun had talked she was left with the impression that he would sort out the Sandybanks problem once and for all. He had told her: 'Your instructions to me are "not to allow any tenants' cattle here except those who have paid up", and your instructions will be carried out to the very letter, unless you order otherwise. But I anticipate some trouble from those who have not paid up, and their trouble in that line, by forcing the cattle on to the Banks, will be only play to me. I am a match for their devilment.'

However, she was no match for his devilment and her relationship with Lynchehaun had soured within months. She dismissed him from her service and sought to repossess her properties. In the previous two years the tension between them had intensified and festered. For now she would banish James Lynchehaun from her thoughts and find some temporary solace in the shadows of St Thomas' Church.

The horse slowed to a trot at the bottom of the hill. She was within sight of The Colony with the Constabulary barrack and Dr Croly's residence close to the road and the largest building, the Slievemore Hotel which was now thronged with summer visitors, running along the line of the mountain. The horse turned into the shade of the laurel-lined avenue leading to the church where she would pray to her God, and confirm her resolve to hold steady in her work no matter what the provocation.

Thomas Croly M.D. greeted his friend, two tufts of bushy hair peeping above his large ears. A committed member of St Thomas' Select Vestry for more than three decades, the doctor possessed practical qualities which Agnes admired. Since her arrival in north Achill six years earlier, she had appreciated his efforts to improve the comfort of the congregation, like his arrangement for fires to be lit in the church on Wednesday, Saturday and Sunday when the weather chilled. He had filled her in on the history of St Thomas' and shown her the register with the names of the hundreds of islanders who had read their recantations when they converted to the Protestant faith in the famine years and were rewarded with food and education for their children.

It was through Dr Croly's efforts that a white, marble plaque to the memory of Edward Nangle, the Achill Mission founder, was erected within the church:

Sacred to the Memory of
The Revd Edward Nangle
The Founder of the Achill Mission
who died Sept 9, 1881
in the 83rd year of his age
He devoted his life from the year 1834
to the welfare of the people of Achill
among whom he lived for many years.
He died looking for that blessed hope
and the glorious appearing
of the great God and Saviour
Jesus Christ
Titus 11.13

The Rector led his congregation in prayer, standing beneath three south-facing stained-glass windows depicting crimson-clad biblical figures. When Agnes gazed out the leaded glass windows she could look back at the stretch of countryside through which she had just travelled and see clusters of black-headed, horned sheep grazing in the fields reclaimed by the Achill Mission. The congregation that morning was swelled by August holidaymakers who had come by long-car to Dugort from Westport and Mulranny railway stations. The cars had passed her many times on the road, four passengers facing outwards on either side with the liveried driver high up in the front, whip in hand. The visitors came to fish and to hunt, to cycle, to climb Slievemore, to bathe on the silver strand, and to paint at the Minaun cliffs.

What might Agnes MacDonnell's thoughts have been as she knelt in prayer that summer morning? Was she anguished at the grief of her neighbours who had lost their offspring in Clew Bay's waters? Was her preoccupation with the trespasser case which would soon come before the Achill Assizes? Did she, perhaps, worry about some of the changes of Arthur Balfour, Chief Secretary in Ireland, in establishing the Congested Districts Board which was purchasing estates under the Land Acts and reallocating lands to the tenants? Or did she dwell on her most intractable problem, that of her difficult and unruly tenant, James Lynchehaun?

She had managed to get her case postponed from the Achill Court Petty Session in July, a sensible course of action given the heightened feelings on the island. But she was determined to pursue her rights. She had sued a group of her tenants for allowing their horses to graze her grass at the sides of the path along which they drew seaweed. On the day that the case was heard in Achill Sound the atmosphere was warm and stifling in the courtroom. The crowd had watched on sullenly as Agnes MacDonnell alighted from her car. They had stared at her with narrowed eyes, muttering among themselves. Could the woman not let the slights against her pass for once? Didn't she know how the poor families were suffering with the bad potato crop and the recent drowning tragedy?

'Is this reserved grass we are dealing with?' the magistrate asked her.

'Yes, sir, and these people are continually annoying me by allowing their horses to graze all over the place.'

One of the defendants, a widow, took the stand and pleaded directly for leniency. 'I lost a day's wages walking the fourteen miles to the court today.'

Agnes MacDonnell's reply indicated that, perhaps, she felt a touch of embarrassment at proceeding with the case. 'I only ask, sir, for a nominal fine in these cases,' she said rather defensively.

She got her pound of flesh, but the anger in the court was palpable. Some of the defendants were fined one penny and costs; others six pence with costs. A crowd watched as she departed, following her every movement in silence.

In another courtroom in Castlebar the following year, Mr Justice Gibson would describe Agnes MacDonnell as 'a lady of somewhat peculiar or independent character'. In the same court, she robustly defended her landlord record, admitting that she had summonses served against many people for trespass but had seldom served eviction notices. 'I had no quarrel with my tenants about the Sandybanks. I had six years ago but that was settled. I have twelve or fourteen conacre tenants, and had served notices on them. I was told some cattle were trespassing in my wood. I disbelieved it, and was told if I got up early I would find them. I did get up at four o'clock, and found cattle trespassing. I knocked at the homes of the owners, and they offered me trespass money, which I refused. This was the only time I went out and I am sorry for it.'

One can only imagine the single-minded toughness that took Agnes MacDonnell abroad her estate on her own in the dead of night, determined to protect and safeguard what was lawfully hers at the risk of her personal safety.

If the issue of the trespassers was out of the way, Agnes MacDonnell's arguments with James Lynchehaun were unresolved as she sought to repossess the properties he held on lease from her. After she had discharged him from her service, he had called on all his verbal skills in a new ploy of writing to the authorities to complain that she was not following proper administrative procedures around the stamping of her tenants' receipt books. 'In the interests of justice I think it is very proper to have this case brought under the notice of the authorities,' he had written.

There was more to come in a similar vein when James Lynchehaun offered to assist the authorities in pursuing the English woman for official irregularities: 'I beg to inform you that Mrs Agnes MacDonnell's postal address is the Valley House, Dugort P.O., Achill; or 19 Belsize Square, London, N.W. This Mrs MacDonnell is a small proprietor here. She lives here presently, and will probably be here for a good part of the year. She is an extensive farmer. Any information or assistance that I can render will always be forthcoming. This woman is so economical that to affix a 1d stamp to transactions such as are now before you would in her opinion be sheer extravagance and waste.'

The dispute between Agnes MacDonnell and James Lynchehaun ebbed and flowed, rose and abated, as each tried to outwit the other, one with wiliness and free-flowing words, the other with ruthless determination and resource to the law. A local man, John Gallagher, would afterwards describe the growing tension between the pair: 'James Lynchehaun and Agnes MacDonnell were not good friends. I saw him a few times when she met him on the road, and I used to be with her and he would not speak to her.'

Agnes MacDonnell wanted to get rid of James Lynchehaun from her property. She had issued him with notices to quit the cottages and he was resisting. She was shrewd enough to realise that she needed to be particularly careful in the climate then prevailing in Achill. Several months earlier, she and James Lynchehaun had their last face to face encounter at the rent office in the Valley House before their hostility exploded into ugly viciousness. The line of tenants that day had snaked from the side of the house through the stone arch of the courtyard and down the driveway. Children had darted, shouting, in and out among the trees and around the edges of the whin bushes near where men plodded up the driveway, caps in hands, and women shuffled forward in their long petticoats. There was a hum of low grumbles as they entered the Valley House office through the side-door from the yard.

A man pleaded with Mrs MacDonnell for leniency with the payments he owed. 'We are like fish in a barrel, my lady, me and the missus and the ten children. What can we do? May the Lord look down on me if I am telling you a lie.' This was the pattern at these encounters: pleas, promises and wrangling for more time to pay the rent. Along the queue of those who waited, heads shook and voices were lowered as they moved closer to the door. A woman blessed herself, her hand moving rapidly from forehead to breast, to shoulder, like somebody possessed, as she mumbled to nobody in particular, 'We're in for it this winter. We're in for it.'

Agnes may have sensed Lynchehaun's presence in the doorway for she was expecting him. When he stood in front of her, she could feel the colour rise up from her neck to her cheeks and the muscles in her throat tighten. When she spoke, her voice was high-pitched. 'I suppose you have come to give back possession of the cottages and the Scraw.' He towered over her like a large animal about to assail its smaller prey. He liked these situations when he appeared like a performer in front of a captive audience. The people behind him in the queue pressed closer and strained their necks to better take in what was happening. They were wary of Lynchehaun but got a vicarious thrill from his brashness.

'Can I stay on, Mrs MacDonnell, for two months until I have another house ready?' He looked behind him at those waiting in line, then leaned towards the woman at the table with a sneering grin. She knew that he wanted to humiliate her in front of her tenants. She'd had enough. She would not be hoodwinked and fooled by this man one day longer. 'You will give possession of the cottages and the land, otherwise I will charge treble rent. You hear me, Lynchehaun?' She spluttered out the words, shaking her fist at him in a rage.

Lynchehaun changed his approach, adopting the attitude of an adult calming a frightened child. He moved around to her side of the table and spoke in a soothing voice. 'Can I help you with the money, Mrs MacDonnell? I can help you sort it.' There were guffaws and chuckles from those in the queue.

Agnes MacDonnell stood and spat out the words, 'Clear off. Do you hear me? Pay your money and get out of here. I'm warning you, James Lynchehaun.'

He threw down the coins and they rattled across the table. 'Take your rent, then,' he said through clenched teeth. 'Let you take your rent, then.' Those who witnessed the scene were left in no doubt but that there was trouble brewing.

The summer days of 1894 shortened and the yellow gorse bloom had all but disappeared. The holidaymakers departed Dugort by long-car and spoke of returning the following summer by rail on the new line to Achill Sound. The daggers were drawn between Agnes MacDonnell and James Lynchehaun as two larger-than-life personalities locked horns under the belligerent gaze of Slievemore.

4

Hostile Meeting
September 1894

A tense group gathered at Achill Sound in mid-September. Father Connolly, parish priest of Achill, was in the chair. He had called together the relief committee to arrange for the purchase of annuities for the families of the drowned out of the money received from generous donors. Invitations had been sent out, he said, to the custodians of the various funds but not all had replied. He thanked them for attending, especially Michael Davitt who had come to Achill at great inconvenience. Others present included P. J. Kelly, Chairman of the Westport Union Board of Guardians, Bindon Scott, a Trustee of the Achill Mission estate in Dugort, Brother Paul Carney and his superior, Brother Bonaventure MacDermott, from the Franciscan monastery at Bunnacurry. Each brought a distinctive perspective to the gathering and the parish priest was aware of the danger that the divisions that had bedevilled Achill throughout the century could erupt at the meeting.

The short, stout, brown-clad monk watched on and held his tongue. Brother Paul Carney's waist had long since lost the slender shape of youth as it merged with his stomach and chest to give his body a rotund barrel shape. His crimson cheeks were an inherited family feature, as was a propensity for talk and words that had now grown into a passion for writing in his leather-bound journals. He had taken a summer break in the Franciscan monastery at Granlahan, outside Ballyhaunis, from where he brought summer fruits from the monastery garden when visiting his childhood home on a rounded hillside. He had knelt in prayer at his parents' grave near the gable end of Ballyhaunis Augustinian Friary, where he remembered, too, the island dead.

Brother Paul shared his monastery home in Bunnacurry with Brother Bonaventure and four fellow friars. The handsome driveway led to a solid stone structure amid sixty acres of reclaimed lands. He had spent a quarter of a century in this place, arriving as a raw novice from his east Mayo homeland. As a child he had attended the local hedge school and afterwards trained as a baker in Ballyhaunis, a two-mile walk from his home, before coming under the influence of the friars in nearby Granlahan. Achill had beckoned and he wrote in his notebook (in the third person, as was his style): 'On the 4th of June 1869 he bade farewell to his relatives and entered the Franciscan Monastery in the barren Island of Achill.' He often thought of his birthplace on the hill at the end of a laneway where shadows jumped about on the stone walls. It had taken him time to get used to the sight of the purple mountains in Achill, the sound of Atlantic waves in the winter nights and the overpowering smells of the ocean.

The Franciscans had been in Achill for two decades by the time Paul arrived, having come on the instructions of the Archbishop of Tuam with a strong directive: to counter the influence of Edward Nangle and the Achill Mission. Of his own early island activities, the monk had written:

> His zeal was chiefly devoted to the conversion of fallen Catholics or Jumpers as they were called who in Famine years had fallen away from the Faith. But with instruction and charity around 95% returned in due course to the true faith. In the years of the famine, the Protestant Mission, Dublin, bought most of the land. Then as the landlords they had the whip hand over the poor starving ignorant tenants, equipped as they were with bags of bibles and purses of gold as bribes.

The friar had come a long way since those times. He had progressed to the position of School Principal in Bunnacurry and had held the offices of Bursar and Master of Novices. He mixed easily with influencers and dignitaries: greeting and accompanying Lady Aberdeen on her recent visit; taking a leadership position at the funeral of the Clew Bay victims; sitting on the local relief committee. Brother Paul Carney was a complex man and, beneath his jovial exterior, he had developed a capacity to negotiate with shrewdness between the island establishment and the destitute islanders in whose eyes he saw the fear of famine that reminded him of the look in neighbours' faces from his childhood.

The friar had his own worries that September day. For the previous three years the Achill national teachers had elected him chairman of their group. However, he had learned that an anonymous person had sent a written complaint about him to the Archbishop of Tuam, requesting that he be relieved of his chairmanship role. There was clearly unease among some at his activities, his political leanings and his associations. Brother Paul Carney had every reason to hold his tongue at the relief committee meeting.

P. J. Kelly was likewise on his guard. The Chairman of the Westport Union Board of Guardians, which held responsibility for the collection of the seed rents in Achill, would have been especially wary of Michael Davitt's sharp tongue. The official informed the committee that he was prepared to hand over £508 10s from the Westport Fund. He may have decided against mentioning that one positive outcome of the *Victory* tragedy was that the Achill landlords appeared to have been shamed into paying their arrears of the poor rates levied on landowners. The Guardians had started court proceedings against Agnes MacDonnell but, after the capsize of the *Victory*, she had quickly settled her debt of £13 with the Union.

P. J. Kelly had been caught unawares in June by the Clew Bay misfortune. Alive to the potential of the catastrophe to inflame even further the resentment of the island tenants against the seed rate, the Guardians had quickly sent a telegram to the Achill rate collector, James Conway: 'Mr Conway is on no account to demand or receive from any family connected with the late drowning accident any moneys on account of poor rate or seed rate until further orders.'That was all very well, but James Conway was already under pressure from the Guardians to improve his rate collection output or face dismissal. There had been consternation when, barely two weeks after the drowning calamity, the rate collector was requisitioning the High Sheriff for a large force of police to accompany him to Achill to make seizures for outstanding rents. It was highly embarrassing for P. J. Kelly when the collector claimed that he was acting on the warrant of the Board of Guardians who, then, had to instruct the collector to call off the move for a month.'I think it would look very bad if the police and bailiffs went amongst them at this time,' P. J. Kelly had told the Board.

But it did not take long for the Guardians to revert to their earlier aggressive policy. By August they were passing a resolution that 'with the exception of the families immediately connected with the Achill drowning disaster, Collector Conway is to proceed collecting the seed potato rate as usual ... as it appears he pretends the collection of the seed rate has been suspended generally in his district'.

No wonder, then, that P. J. Kelly was cautious, particularly in the presence of Michael Davitt. He was forced to tread a fine line between the Local Government Board, on the one hand, which was exerting pressure for improved rate returns, and the heightened tensions between Achill landlord and tenants on the other.

However, when hostility did break out at the meeting, it did not involve the spirited friar, Brother Paul Carney, or the nervous official, P. J. Kelly. The antagonism ripped open between the lofty Michael Davitt and the eloquent Bindon Scott, a neighbour of Agnes MacDonnell in north Achill. Scott had been intent on publicising a view that the wretched state of the Achill people was not the result of hostility between landlord and tenant nor, indeed, the issue of the seed rate payments – an opinion that was unlikely to have found favour with Michael Davitt. In a letter to *The Irish Times*, Scott had made some unusual suggestions for the development of Achill's natural resources, including proposals for the manufacture of charcoal from peat, the cultivation of rhubarb, the introduction of Shetland sheep for wool production, and the manufacture of wine cases from straw.

The disagreement between Michael Davitt and Bindon Scott emerged as the relief committee discussed the pooling of resources from the various relief funds. Bindon Scott reported that there was £450 in the Achill Mission fund, £50 of which had already been spent on urgent temporary relief. The Achill Mission Trustees intended purchasing a compound annuity of £68 from an insurance company to allocate among certain bereaved families. The relief committee, he said, could look after the rest of the families. It was clear that the fractures between landlord and tenant, Catholic and Protestant, the Achill Mission and the islanders, were about to surface once more.

'So you want to keep your funds apart from the general fund?' Michael Davitt challenged Scott. 'Why can't you put your funds with ours?'

'I am not acting alone. I have two other trustees and they prefer doing what I say,' Bindon Scott replied.

Davitt persisted: 'But you can see how the thing will overlap. You will have to take a certain number of the families out of the twenty-four.'

'Yes,' replied Scott. 'We will take six out of the twenty-four and you will take eighteen.'

'But why should you stand apart from the other funds?'

'This is a matter for myself and two friends. It is simply that we would like to give an account of our stewardship ourselves.'

'In other words you think that the only way in which to give an account of your stewardship is to stand apart? I understand that this committee will have to give an account of its stewardship to the public.'

'I was only going to give it to a small section of the public.'

'We mean to give an account to the general public, as the general public are interested. Englishmen, Scotchmen, Welshmen, and Irishmen have subscribed to this fund. There are seven funds; six of them agree to pool all the money but you stand out from the six and you say you will distribute your funds in your own way.'

'I don't say I will distribute it in my own way but in a way similar to yours.'

'In that case why not join with the others?'

Bindon Scott knew that he was being backed into a corner and was keen to move the discussion on. He could not win out against Michael Davitt. 'We need not argue it further,' he said. 'I will think it over and communicate with my co-trustees.'

Davitt tried another tack. 'I am quite willing to propose that Mr Salt be one of our co-trustees. That ought to be a good guarantee to you.'

'I will not commit myself or my co-trustees to that today.'

Davitt proposed that they move on with the meeting. 'We will, then, consider the amount in hand apart from Mr Scott's fund.'

There was a truce of sorts. It was not a time to let the divisions of the past explode into public view. They would try to keep a united front. The committee found that when they allowed for the purchase of the annuities, for grants to bereaved families, and for stamp duty, they were left with a balance of £296.

'What are you going to do with the balance?' Bindon Scott asked.

Michael Davitt suggested they might help the fishermen at Corraun and Kildownet in conjunction with the Congested Districts Board. All present agreed that a railing should be erected around the grave of the drowned and a memorial tablet placed there. Brother Paul Carney was charged with this task.

P. J. Kelly continued with a skilful political strategy of public expressions of concern for the Achill islanders while also vigorously pursuing the collection of rents and rates. Within weeks of the acrimonious relief committee meeting the Westport Board of Guardians publicised a lengthy statement concerning the poor harvest, earnestly appealing to the Government 'to take into the most serious consideration the present deplorable condition of the agricultural population of this impoverished Union.' The potato, the stable food of the people, the statement claimed, 'has almost totally failed and their whole year's work in their fields where they toiled so hard, is gone for nothing.' The potatoes were not worth digging up, they continued, and there was nothing with which to feed people, pigs or cattle. The situation was critical. Some reproductive public works were urgently needed to relieve distress, and the Government must 'appeal to the landlords of the west not to press their unfortunate tenantry for rent in this season', since the money that would be forced from the tenantry in rent was all that stood between them and starvation. The Guardians' resolution received wide publicity as did their decision to send the statement to John Morley, Chief Secretary for Ireland, and to Dr Robert Ambrose and William O'Brien, Members of Parliament.

While they were issuing their statements of concern at the state of the harvest in their area, the Board of Guardians was taking a tough line with its rate collector, James Conway, notifying him that his collection rate was unacceptable to the Guardians who found his 'letter of explanation and list of arrears most unsatisfactory'. The Board passed a motion of dismissal: 'having regard to previous conduct and habitual and repeated neglect of duties and irregularities as recorded in previous minutes of this Board, the Guardians hereby suspend him as rate collector and request the Local Government Board to dismiss him from that office in order that steps be taken to provide an efficient collector or collectors for his district'.

In the interest of greater efficiency the Guardians then decided that James Conway's district would henceforth be divided into two areas: District No 1, comprising of the townlands of Achill, Dooega and Slievemore, would become an area in its own right; District No 2 was to comprise of the areas of Ballycroy North, Ballycroy South and Corraun. For the future, the collectors would pursue the collection of rates in Achill with new vigour and efficiency.

As September drew to a close, Inspector Michael Reilly put the finishing touches to his police report for the Belmullet area. Overall, he was glad to inform his superiors, the district was quiet. There had been a small number of outrages during the month: the killing of an ass and the seizure of some cattle impounded by a bailiff for the debt of £1 3s 3d. There had been two evictions, but both tenants 'were readmitted as caretakers and it is believed soon will be back as tenants'. There had been a general reductions of 10-15% on rents in the area and 'the general relations between landlord and tenants are satisfactory'. Reilly wrote.

Political activity in the area was, thankfully, at a low level as 'there are no political associations or other organisations in this district'. Neither was there any evidence of boycotting or intimidation, even though the protection of two policemen was given to a certain James Moran who had taken over three evicted farms. However, on account of the area being a congested district, 'the people are generally poor and the average wages of the labouring class is eight shillings per week without food, and employment at that rate is scarce'. Reilly was pleased to note that harvester remittances were improved for the year and that 'the migratory labourers from the district who went annually to England and Scotland had sent to their friends at home more money than in any of the five previous years'.

The Inspector's biggest worry was the poor potato harvest. 'The potato crop this year in the district is bad and the yield amounts to scarcely half the crop of last year's produce. I personally attended and saw them dug out of the earth in four different, distant, and opposite directions in the district. I am satisfied that the crop this year is not over half the produce of the year '93. In quality for table use they are bad.' Reilly, however, reported that the yields from oats, barley and hay were good and these harvests were largely saved and stacked away.

Michael Reilly concluded his report on a positive note, writing reassuringly that 'the general condition of the people in this district is improving and I do not see any signs of distress although the potato crop is not as productive as last year. The price of meal, flour, and other necessities of life are low in value.'

Officially, all was peaceful in north Mayo and matters were under control. However, in the northwest corner of the district, on the island of Achill, there were undercurrents and rumblings which would soon throw the area into a pandemonium not seen for a long time.

5

I Am Cold

6 October 1894

When Dr Thomas Croly crossed the road between his home in The Colony and St Thomas' Church, he could look down the hill to the sea and watch the Atlantic waves cascade into frothing white whirlpools before exhausting themselves on the strand. After his busy week he looked forward to the rituals of Sunday service and to the soothing sounds of familiar prayers and hymns. There was also the church business to attend to, collection envelopes to be opened, and plans made for the next Select Vestry meeting. Occasionally, there was an unpleasant aspect to being involved so closely in the church affairs, like the case of the sexton which had left a bad taste. The Select Vestry had to pass a resolution condemning their sexton's action in allowing a Roman Catholic priest to visit the sexton's dying mother-in-law. After much heart-searching, they had agreed to reinstate their sexton, concluding that his actions had been more an error of judgement than a deliberate predetermined act.

When he retired to bed on the night of the first Saturday in October, Dr Croly may have hoped that he would not be roused from his sleep to journey by the light of the moon to attend at a birth or a death at a remote island place. When the night call did come, his unpleasant task was to minister to one of his own, a friend and fellow worshipper. Afterwards, he had to set his feelings aside when he meticulously detailed the physical injuries of his patient in cool, dispassionate terms, unclouded by his horror at the savagery unleashed on one of his own congregation.

Three miles west of Dr Croly's home, Agnes MacDonnell's employees were finishing the last of their evening chores and preparing to depart the Valley House. If an observer had been able to look down from a height on the townland of Valley that fateful evening of 6 October 1894, the sight presented would have been a patchwork of grey, black and yellow: the gleaming walls of the Valley House among the trees; the tips of waves on the strand at the Sandybanks; the faint grey of the four roads at Valley crossroads; the sparkle of lantern and candle light across the landscape. That night the islanders closed their doors against the October chill and stoked the fires. Men lit their clay pipes, while women rocked babies to sleep.

Bridget McNeela was a lucky woman. For six weeks she had worked as housekeeper to Agnes MacDonnell, arriving each morning at six o'clock through the side entrance and along the tree-lined passage. At about seven o'clock that evening Bridget was getting ready to leave for home. The dusk air was filled with twilight sounds around the house and its adjacent stables and sheds: clanking buckets in the yard; Mrs MacDonnell's horses neighing in the stables; footsteps falling on cobbled stones; the rattle of bolts and keys. Bridget had tidied away the crockery in the scullery, lit the paraffin lights, and pulled the curtains in Agnes MacDonnell's downstairs bedroom. 'I was the only female servant in the house,' she would say afterwards. The housekeeper left by the back door and went out through the small wicket gate in the yard. On her left was a carriage shed and next to it a boat house and a loose box for horses. In one of the sheds there was a car, a trap, a canoe, a barrel of tar and some other items. Opposite the kitchen door were some stables for housing sheep.

Outside the yard, Bridget McNeela waited for Agnes MacDonnell's herdsman, Matthew Gallagher, and asked about his son, Johnny, who had worked at tidying the kitchen garden that morning until he felt unwell and had to return home at about nine o'clock. There were three others working at the Valley House that day: the brothers, James and Michael McGinty, and

Tom Calvey, a young mason from Ballycroy on the mainland who was engaged by Mrs MacDonnell in constructing a wall on her property.

Michael McGinty was ready to head home. 'Before leaving,' he later said, 'I fed the horse in the stable. That was the stable on the right hand side of the yard as you go in the gate. There was a mare and a foal in a loose box in the same stable. There was a lantern in the stable that Tom Calvey had brought down from the kitchen door.' Meanwhile, Tom Calvey locked up the doors of the stables and the carriage house and then handed the keys to Mrs MacDonnell at the back door. As all three passed through the wicket gate, their employer bade them good night and locked the gate behind them.

Agnes MacDonnell was now alone in the Valley House. She was tired, having had an early start to get ready for the veterinary surgeon who had come that morning to fire the brood mare. She had gained a reputation for having an eye for a good horse and had, at that time, fifteen horses in all on her estate. Asked afterwards if she'd taken a cup of tea before retiring that night, she had replied, somewhat poignantly, 'I could not get any tea because all the fires were out. There was not a spark of fire about the place anywhere in the house.' When all her staff had left, she set about the ritual of locking up. She was intensely security conscious and not without reason, given the animosity some held towards her. She had broken glass placed on top of the perimeter wall where there was high ground outside. 'I used to go round every night carefully,' she said, 'and see that all was secure as I was living alone in the house. I went in by the kitchen door, which I locked, and the door within that I bolted. I went to bed soon after, as I was very tired having been up since five o'clock that morning.'

She would take it easy the next day, the Sabbath, and travel to Dugort for Sunday service where she would meet up with her friends, pray, and steel herself for the week ahead. Soon, all lights were extinguished and the Valley House was in darkness. All was quiet except for the sound of Atlantic waves crashing against the rocks in the darkness.

Matthew Gallagher and Tom Calvey accompanied Bridget McNeela along the perimeter wall of the kitchen garden and down the side entrance of the Valley House. Michael McGinty and his brother had left ahead of them, walking to the end of the passage and turning into John McLoughlin's shebeen, a place without licence where alcohol could be bought. They ordered their drinks and, not long afterwards, James Lynchehaun arrived. According to Michael McGinty's later evidence, Lynchehaun was carrying a light boot in his hand and he asked John McLoughlin if he would put a stitch in it. Lynchehaun, he said, was wearing a soft hat with a broad leaf, but had no coat. He left the boot to be fixed and went away.

Meanwhile, after parting with Bridget McNeela, Matthew Gallagher and Tom Calvey turned right at the end of the pathway and walked northwards to Peggy Cleary's shebeen on the road to Ridge Point. They were there a short time when James Lynchehaun arrived with three men who were, they learned, all working with him on a road maintenance job. According to Tom Calvey, Lynchehaun called for half a pint of whiskey and, when that was taken, he ordered a half-pint more. Lynchehaun left before the others, telling them that he wanted to collect his boot that was being mended by John McLoughlin. Matthew Gallagher and Tom Calvey left for home shortly afterwards.

James Lynchehaun returned to John McLoughlin's where the McGinty brothers were still drinking, collected his boot and left. James and Michael McGinty departed the shebeen for home at about a quarter past eight. Soon afterwards, like the sudden eruption of a powerful storm, the dark silence of the Valley House was shattered by a hard rap of knuckles on the front door. Amid the normal nocturnal sounds of ocean waves breaking at Ridge Point and dogs barking at Valley crossroads, other sounds of terror would explode into the night skies of north Achill.

Mary Gallagher was not one of Agnes MacDonnell's employees but lived next door to Peggy Cleary's shebeen where she and Peggy sat talking when her mother appeared at the door shouting, 'The big house is on fire.' They set off, running as fast as they could up the side avenue to the Valley House. They could see a crowd of people ahead of them, running towards the blaze as flames lunged into the sky, the sparks hissing and spitting in the darkness. Before passing through the wicket-gate, Mary heard a voice that she recognised as that of James Lynchehaun. When she entered the yard she saw Agnes MacDonnell and Lynchehaun facing the fire, the pair of them etched against the backdrop of the inferno. Mary Gallagher's first thought was that Lynchehaun was trying to save Mrs MacDonnell from the flames. 'As I was going over,' she said, 'I saw James Lynchehaun catching a hold of her round the waist with his two hands; she had nothing on but her nightdress. When he caught Mrs MacDonnell she called him in a loud voice to let her out, and she said this more than once but I cannot say how often. She was trying to pull herself away from him. Lynchehaun had a hold of her and they went very near to the fire, and he brought her right up close to the blaze. Then she was inside the stable door and she fell; her head was turned out towards the door.' Mary said that Agnes MacDonnell was screaming at James Lynchehaun to let her go.

Mary ran towards them. 'I said to James Lynchehaun, "Keep away, you murderer, you." James Lynchehaun looked at me with a cross look. I caught hold of Mrs MacDonnell and lifted her and took her out of the stable – that was the stable which was the one that the flames were going through the roof of. When I was taking Mrs MacDonnell out of the stable she said to me, "Oh woman, take me away from this scoundrel."' Agnes MacDonnell was, Mary said, in a most excitable state. 'She went to the back door of the house and I went over after her. When I was speaking to her at the back door James Lynchehaun was standing at the corner of the house in the yard. He told me to come out of that before I got burnt. I told him I would not. I told him to get out. I saw Mrs MacDonnell going away from the back door and into the house. There was no sign of fire in the house. The fire was only in the stables.'

Mary waited in the yard until Agnes MacDonnell came back out wearing a black cloak over her nightdress. James

Lynchehaun was still there with the others who were trying to put out the fire and Mrs MacDonnell raised her fist to him and shouted: 'Remember that, James Lynchehaun, you'll pay for that.' She kept repeating the words, 'Lynchehaun, you'll pay for that.' Mary then ran back to her own house to get a bucket to help the others douse the flames.

Bridget McNeela was fast asleep in her home when she heard her neighbour, Judy Cooney, shouting from outside that the Valley House was on fire. It was about nine o'clock. In a matter of minutes, Bridget would confront a scene that would haunt her for the rest of her days. At first, the awfulness of what she witnessed would be veiled in the fuzzy night light but, later, her legs would weaken beneath her with shock at what she encountered. She dressed quickly and ran with the others to the big house, taking a short cut to the yard by the whin bushes. The car sheds, car house, and boat house were all on fire in the yard and gangs of people were running about with buckets of water to try and smother the flames. The conflagration was like an enormous bonfire that lit up the faces of the people who held up their hands as a shield from the heat.

Bridget called out Mrs MacDonnell's name and asked if anybody had seen her. Where was she? She kept shouting out to her, asking if she was all right. The people told her not to worry, that her employer had been out in the yard a short time before and was safe. 'I went towards the hall door,' Bridget later testified, 'then I turned down towards the kitchen garden and continued calling and shouting but got no answer.' At that point she heard a sound like a moan coming from the direction of the whin bushes. Bridget followed the sound and came upon her employer, Agnes MacDonnell, lying on the ground and dressed only in her nightdress: 'She had no cloak on her. Her limbs were exposed.' Agnes MacDonnell appeared to her housekeeper to have no feeling whatsoever in her body. 'I took her in my arms and began calling and shouting for help.' The injured woman felt wet all over and Bridget soon discovered that Agnes MacDonnell's body was saturated with blood.

It was about a quarter to ten when James McGinty roused his brother Michael and the pair rushed to the Valley House with other neighbours. Approaching a hay-rick in the field at the front of the house, they heard the women shouting that Mrs MacDonnell was killed. 'I found Bridget McNeela holding up Mrs MacDonnell by the shoulder,' Michael McGinty said, 'and lifting her up off the ground. The other women were around her. I kept going on to the yard and through the wagon door and saw the stables on fire. There was a large crowd in the yard trying to put out the blaze.' One of the first people Michael McGinty encountered was James Lynchehaun: 'I saw him in the yard and he was holding two stones, one in each hand. He had no hat, coat or boots on him and there was blood on his face. It was dripping down on to his waistcoat. His trousers were wet looking. I caught hold of his trousers and asked him what happened and he said he fell coming into the yard.' Michael McGinty asked where his cap and boots were and Lynchehaun replied that he didn't have time to put them on and was on his way to bed when the alarm was raised. 'He then pulled a cap out of his breast and put it on him. I asked him what business he had with the stones but he merely dropped them and made no reply. He was wild looking when I saw him.'

Matthew Gallagher got the call from Judy Cooney at about ten o'clock. He put on a pair of trousers, waistcoat and hat and made for the Valley House, taking the pathway at the gate lodge towards the haystacks. He came upon Agnes MacDonnell between the haystacks and the big house. 'The women and men were holding her up. I spoke to her but she didn't answer. There was nothing on her at the time but a nightdress. They were carrying her away towards Michael Gallagher's house.' Matthew Gallagher then moved into the yard where the men were trying to put out the blaze. By this time the stables were almost burnt to the ground and he went to look for the horses, as he needed to go to Dugort for the doctor, but there was no sign of the animals in the stables. He later learned that the two horses had been stabbed in their flanks. He went to get his own horse and headed at speed for Dugort, accompanied by Pat McNeela.

Tom Calvey rushed to the fire scene with Johnny Gallagher and ran into the yard, intending to let out the sheep, but they found that the animals were already gone. They tried to prevent the fire spreading to the main house by breaking down the roof in one of the stables. Michael McGinty and James Lynchehaun were already there before them and, according to Tom Calvey, James Lynchehaun was bleeding, and wore neither coat nor boots. He told them that he got his injuries while fighting the fire. They went to the house and found the kitchen door open, with a key in the lock on the inside. There was no sign of fire in the Valley House itself and the flames in the stables were, by then, almost extinguished. The wind, Tom Calvey said, was blowing from the southwest.

Joseph Dusting was the sergeant-in-charge at Dugort barrack that night, having returned earlier from London, arriving in Dugort at about half past eight. There were three other officers on duty with him that evening: the senior constable Joseph Morrison, John Sullivan, and Samuel Gwynne, the barrack orderly. Sergeant Dusting had retired to bed at eleven o'clock, only to be awakened half an hour later by Constable Gwynne. 'He told me Matthew Gallagher was below and had reported that the stables of the Valley House were burned and Mrs MacDonnell was injured.' He immediately set out for Valley with Constable Sullivan. They had gone just a short distance when the sergeant decided on a change of plan and directed Constable Sullivan to return to barrack and have Constable Morrison join them. He had a premonition that more resources would be needed. 'This is no ordinary case,' he told his constable.

Bridget felt a faint pulse and knew that Agnes MacDonnell was still alive, but was in urgent need of warmth. She and some others carried the stricken woman down the side avenue as far as Michael Gallagher's cottage, as there was no heat or fire in the Valley House. They stretched her out on a feather bed next to the fire. 'Her face was all black and bruised,' Bridget said, 'you would not say it was the face of a person at all.' She thought that her employer could not possibly survive the night, such was her state.

The police arrived at Michael Gallagher's house at approximately half past midnight and there they saw Agnes MacDonnell stretched out on a bed opposite the kitchen fire 'besmeared with blood'. James Lynchehaun came in shortly afterwards and had, said Sergeant Dusting, 'the appearance of having taken drink.' There were scratches on his face and blood around his mouth and moustache, and on his vest. Lynchehaun moved close to the sergeant and muttered in his ear, 'Arrest Matthew Gallagher, John Gallagher and Tom Calvey, the mason.' The sergeant noticed that Lynchehaun's trousers were wet and dirty from the knees down, that he wore no boots, and that 'he appeared excited, and his eyes seemed to be going everywhere in his head'.

Dr Croly thought his worst fears were realised when, on reaching Gallagher's house, he found his friend in a lifeless condition. However, on hearing his voice, Agnes was heard to whisper, 'I am cold. I am very cold.' When Dr Croly later put pen to paper to detail Agnes' injuries, he cloaked his shock in dispassionate tones: 'Her night dress was saturated with blood. Her pulse was weak and trembling and barely perceptible. Her body was almost cold. Her breathing was weak.' When he first saw the wounded woman he did not think that she could live. 'I gave her some medicine immediately after I went in. I gave her some spirits and she discharged her stomach on two occasions. She discharged a large quantity of black coagulated blood, nearly a couple of quarts.' He applied poultices, stupes and healing lotion in an effort to bring her some relief.

Dr Croly's report would afterwards be dissected word for word by magistrates, barristers, and legal officials. In writing his reports, the doctor had to attempt to put out of his mind all consideration that the mutilated woman was a friend and someone whom he admired for her grit and tenacious spirit. He wrote: 'I found three wounds on the woman's head: the first on the crown reaching over to the left parietal bone was about three inches long. It went to the bone and was what we call a lacerated contused wound. The skull was not fractured there. Some blunt instrument would be likely to cause that wound. A stick or a bar or a long stone would cause it. The second wound was on the left parietal bone, a wound similar to the first but not so long. There was no fracture corresponding with this wound. It was a lacerated and contused wound. The third wound was over the left eye from the angle of the frontal bone half way over to the left temporal. It was a lacerated contused wound also.' There was a deep wound under the left eye which was heavily swollen. There was a semicircular wound passing through the right eye, completely crushing it. It was not only her face that had suffered severe injuries but 'her whole body where there was a large contusion over the two lower ribs of the right side. The lower lobe of the right lung was inflamed and the upper portion of the liver was congested. The bladder itself was inflamed. The right knee was lacerated and the whole of the inner portion of the leg, from knee to ankle, was burned.' Even though Dr Croly would be questioned closely many times as to the detail and causes of Agnes MacDonnell's injuries, there were things that he would not say publicly, no matter how hard he was pressed.

Sometime between two and three o'clock that night, Dr Croly and Sergeant Dusting, who had left a constable in charge at Michael Gallagher's house, went outside to return to Dugort. It was then that they saw flames leaping from the Valley House itself and lighting up the night sky. The doctor realised that Agnes MacDonnell had lost everything: her home, her beauty, and possibly her life.

Sergeant Dusting ran to the Valley House with the Gallaghers. They broke down the front door and found that the room to the right was ablaze, as was the room directly above it. 'We broke in the window to the left of the hall door,' the Sergeant said, 'and found one room on the basement storey where there was no fire and we removed the furniture. We afterwards broke in the window of the upper room on the left. I did not enter that room. John Gallagher did, and he handed out the furniture. I observed two other chair cushions, that is the seats of two chairs, were burning when handed out, and I stamped them out. The wind was blowing from the southwest, from the house towards the stables, at that time.'

As the dawn light seeped across Achill Island in the early hours of Sunday morning, the stricken Agnes MacDonnell did not know of the devastation that had descended on her home. In the hours and days ahead word would spread out from Achill through Ireland, and beyond, of the horror and destruction that had descended on the remote Irish island in the darkness of the October night.

6

An Animal-looking Man
7–10 October 1894

The Irish Times special correspondent quickly learned that things were not always as they appeared on the surface in Achill. On Sunday he travelled from Westport, a distance of some forty miles, to report on the events of the previous night. On his way through the village he called to the telegraph office at Achill Sound to enquire if he could send a wire from the island later in the day, only to be told that the telegraphist was away and wouldn't return until evening. He suspected that there was a closing of ranks and that it would not be an easy task to get to the bottom of what had happened in Valley the previous night, and why.

The odour of smouldering rubble reached his nostrils long before he arrived at Valley early on Sunday afternoon. He made his way towards the gate lodge where knots of people stood around whispering to one another, some with their hands to their mouths. Each time a carriage or cart appeared at the crossroads, a swarm of children chased towards it, pursued by yapping dogs. A photograph of the scene taken on one of the days after the attack shows two constables standing guard at the Valley House entrance while, behind them, a driveway curled towards the main house which could be seen, burnt out and roofless, in the background.

The reporter had his notebook to the ready and was soon getting his first pieces of information from the locals. 'James

Lynchehaun is arrested. He's above in Dugort barrack. He said there should be more arrested than him.'

'Mrs MacDonnell, the poor lady, is deluded above there in Michael Gallagher's house. She thinks it's only the stables is burned. Her nose is smashed and her plaited hair was dragged right off her head.'

'She worked hard superintending her business on the land.'

'The horses were stabbed as well. They've big holes in their flanks.'

'Mrs MacDonnell was going to convert the house into a hotel for pleasure seekers. She was spending a lot of money on the place.'

The early news was not good and, in his first report, the newspaper man wrote that Agnes MacDonnell lay 'in a most precarious condition and there is little hope of her surviving the shocking injuries she sustained'. He enquired from the locals as to what type of woman Agnes MacDonnell was. They were cagey with their answers, but he got a hint of an underlying tension between her and some tenants. She was exacting, they told him, but if tenants got into arrears she allowed them to work on the estate to clear off their debts. 'There was a few did not get on with her. She was in the Assizes a good few times with her tenants.' He formed the impression that Agnes MacDonnell was considered to be eccentric in her habits and, though perceived to be wealthy, she worked hard supervising the business of the estate herself. While her house was spacious and well furnished, she always insisted on being alone at night, not even allowing a female servant to stay with her, something that the locals found strange.

Bit by bit the journalist pieced together the details of what had transpired the previous night. He heard that when the locals found Mrs MacDonnell in a field opposite the main entrance to the house she was in a mutilated condition and was, to all appearances, dead. Some of the stories he heard made his stomach churn, like the one they told him of the police finding a clump of the poor woman's hair, with a hair pin still binding it together. In his report he raised a question, which had preoccupied him since he reached the crime scene: 'The half-dozen thatched cottages of the village line the road on each side quite close to the house, and how the incendiary could have accomplished his purpose so completely without alarming the village is astonishing.'

He carefully set the scene, giving a physical perspective on the Valley House, 'a country mansion of considerable size'. 'It was,' he wrote, 'an oblong building, two storeys high and approached on the front by stone steps up to which there led a well-kept carriage drive. To the back a large yard was surrounded on three sides by stables and sheds, the house itself with the gate entrance to the yard forming the other side of the square and fronting the main road from Achill Sound, a small field only intervening. The half-dozen thatched houses of the village line the road on each side quite close to the house. The house stands on an eminence, commanding a view of the country for miles around.'

The constables were helpful, telling the reporter of what they had found when summoned from Dugort barrack: blood traces from the house to where the unfortunate lady lay, and more blood around the big house itself. Fortunately for their investigations, they soon discovered what they believed to be the attack weapon, 'a stone, several pounds in weight having bloodstains upon it' and they were confident that this was the instrument used to strike the murderous blows that caused such horrible injuries to Mrs MacDonnell. 'She was in her nightdress only,' one of the constables told the reporter, shock etched on his face, 'and in an unconscious condition when they carried her to one of the nearby cottages.' Astonishingly, after her ordeal, it seemed that she partially recovered consciousness during the night and muttered the name of James Lynchehaun. The man had been arrested and was already under custody at Dugort barrack.

The newspaper man continued to probe and to question in an effort to find out what could have provoked such a violent atrocity. 'I made every enquiry as to what could be the motive for such a dastardly outrage on a defenceless female but utterly failed to find any.' He heard that Agnes MacDonnell was on terms of close friendship with the clergy on the island and with the Franciscan monks at Bunnacurry Monastery. Although a Protestant lady herself, it seemed that Agnes MacDonnell had made generous donations to the Catholic Church on the island. The Achill parish priest, Father Connolly, and the curate, Father Fitzgerald, had, he heard, been among the first to visit the unfortunate lady who, even in her distressing condition, recognised and spoke to them. Dr Croly had attended the injured woman again that morning and Mrs MacDonnell was now under the care of Penny FitzGerald, a nurse and daughter of the Dugort Rector.

The reporter obtained an interview with Father Connolly in an effort to further explore the relations between landlord and tenant, Protestant and Catholic, in Achill. The parish priest told him in clear terms that, since coming to the island and so far as he could learn before that, relations between Mrs MacDonnell and her tenants were of the friendliest kind. Only the day after the recent boating disaster, she had forwarded a cheque for £5 to the relief committee, he said.

Much ink would be spent in the coming weeks in a concerted effort to send out the message that there was no religious bigotry at play in the dreadful occurrences in north Achill. 'The poor people into whose house she was removed,' said *The Irish Times* writer, 'are leaving nothing undone, and on all sides the people seem shocked and grief-stricken at such a terrible outrage in their midst.' The writer added that 'the Franciscan monks of Bunnacurry, who were on intimate terms with Mrs MacDonnell, were painfully shocked at the news of the outrage and were early on the scene to visit her.' One can only surmise as to whether Brother Paul Carney was among the early callers.

The reporter picked up on a strange tale concerning James Lynchehaun which would, in time, become part of the folklore attaching to the Achill man; it was the start of a pattern whereby fables and legends about Lynchehaun's feats in outfoxing the authorities took hold of the public imagination, the stories becoming embellished with each telling. The jigsaw pieces of what happened that Sunday morning would only fully fall into place later when Constable Sullivan was charged with permitting the prisoner to change his clothes on the morning of his arrest, and allowing the clothes which the accused wore at the crime scene to disappear from Dugort barrack.

Sergeant Dusting had given the order to arrest James Lynchehaun when the accused awoke from his drunken slumber in the early hours of Sunday morning. Nobody, the sergeant ordered, was to communicate or interfere with the prisoner. The situation was so tense that he had requested police reinforcements from Keel. He instructed Constable Kerrigan to take the prisoner to Dugort: 'You know Lynchehaun well. You know if you give him a quarter of an inch he will take it.' Constables Kerrigan and Sullivan provided the prisoner escort to the barrack and they would afterwards say that they got a strong smell of alcohol from the prisoner while conveying him to Dugort. As they passed the entrance to Lynchehaun's house, about ten yards from the public road, the prisoner asked the officers if he could call to his home for a change of clothes. When Constable Kerrigan refused this request the prisoner spoke in Irish to a boy who stood nearby and asked him to bring a change of clothes and a pair of boots to Dugort barrack.

Constable Kerrigan removed the prisoner's handcuffs when they reached the barrack and left James Lynchehaun in the care of Constable Gwynne, who was relieved of his duties at nine o'clock by Constable Sullivan, who later admitted to seeing a boy at the barrack with clothes for the prisoner. Sullivan also acknowledged that he had left the day-room where Lynchehaun was held to go to the kitchen where Gwynne and Kerrigan were having breakfast. On returning to the day-room Constable Sullivan found that the prisoner had changed out of the clothes he had worn when arrested. He shouted to Kerrigan to pursue the boy, but when they caught up with him there was no sign of the prisoner's clothes. A valuable piece of criminal evidence was missing.

At a constabulary enquiry the following month into the circumstances surrounding the arrest and detention of James Lynchehaun, Constable Sullivan was found not guilty on a charge of negligence in the case of the disappearance of Lynchehaun's clothes, and was admonished with a record for the offences which he did admit. For his role in the incident, Constable Samuel Gwynne was transferred at his own expense to another county.

The journalist returned to Achill Sound from Dugort about six o'clock on Sunday evening, keen to file his story quickly by getting a wired telegraph transmitted through the telegraph office. At first, the telegraphist appeared willing to assist, but then returned with a firm message: 'The postmaster in Westport has ordered me on no account accept any wire.' The correspondent would not give up that easily. He returned to the telegraph office at nine o'clock when the response was even more direct. 'I'm sorry. The message has to pass through the Westport office and the postmaster there has refused to transmit even a sixpenny telegram.' The reporter may have wondered if the lack of cooperation had to do with a diligent observance of the Sabbath or if it was an effort to delay and disrupt the dissemination of a story which many felt cast Achill Island in a poor light with the outside world.

It was Tuesday before *The Irish Times* carried a report from its Achill correspondent:

Terrible Outrage on Achill Island
★★★

A Lady Brutally Assaulted
★★★

Her Life in great Danger
★★★

The Valley Mansion House Burned
★★★

Identification of the Assailant

Photographs accompanying the report showed the roofless

Valley House with its sturdy walls and three chimneys still standing defiant and gaping window holes in its walls. Another image showed a low thatched cottage, with two men posing beside carts on the roadside. This was Michael Gallagher's home where the wounded Agnes MacDonnell lay in the aftermath of her attack.

On the day that *The Irish Times* published its first report of the Achill atrocity, the newspaper had received a letter from Bindon Scott who had lost no time in putting pen to paper to give his authoritative gloss on the recent Achill events:

> Sir,
>
> I have been personally well acquainted with the people of Achill for the last 35 years, and have known them to be a quiet and peaceable people, amongst whom, so far as I have heard, such a crime has never before been committed, and although they, like the peasantry in other parts of Ireland, may easily be excited and their passions roused, yet, even during times of political agitation, they did not resort to acts of violent outrage or crime such as have unfortunately been committed in other places.
>
> I feel fully convinced that none of the residents in Achill feel otherwise than revulsion and horror at the commission of this revolting crime, and that the island should have been so disgraced by it. I therefore hope the public will withhold their judgment respecting these poor people until all the circumstances shall have been fully investigated, when, I have no doubt, it will be found that whatever the cause or motive it was not countenanced nor shared by any of them outside the individual perpetrator or the perpetrators, and that this terrible crime was not of an agrarian character nor connected with the relations of landlord or tenant.
>
> There has been such a general and generous sympathy recently shown for these poor Achill people not only in Ireland but in England also, that I am constrained to confess what I believe to prevent if possible an unjust and

erroneous opinion being formed respecting Achill and its inhabitants.

Yours etc

Bindon Scott
October 9

It was as if James Lynchehaun had two faces. The correspondent watched the accused as he walked, handcuffed, through the crowd into Michael Gallagher's house where the magistrate, Mr T. P. Carr, was due to take a deposition in the presence of Agnes MacDonnell on Sunday evening. On one side of his face the prisoner appeared to have a vicious appearance that would cause a person to move quickly past him; on the other side the features conveyed the aspect of somebody about to wink or break into a smirk. Lynchehaun wore a grey wool cap with a hard peak. His upper body was muscular and he walked through the crowd with no hint of subservience, almost with the air of a bishop moving among his flock, for he did not do obsequious. Chin raised, he looked about him coolly, nodding in the direction of relatives and neighbours in the crowd and letting his eyes rest on the faces of the reporters with what seemed like satisfaction.

A swarm of onlookers pressed towards the doorway after Lynchehaun entered, but a constable raised his hands in a gesture that indicated nobody would be allowed in while the deposition was being taken. While he waited, the reporter passed the time by speaking to and noting down the comments of those who stood around.

'The poor woman inside has lost her eye.'

'Her nose is smashed in. They don't know if she'll make it or not.'

'She said "Let me alone," when they tried to put questions to her.'

'I hear she's in a pitiable sight.'

When Mr Carr emerged after about half an hour, he read

a summary of the charges made against the prisoner: 'That at about 8 o'clock on Saturday evening, James Lynchehaun went to Agnes MacDonnell's house and told her that the place was on fire. She got out of bed and on opening the door, having no clothes on but her nightdress, she went into the yard. Lynchehaun – she deposed – seized her by the waist and endeavoured to throw her back into the flames. She screamed and three or four women – she thought – came into the yard. She made her escape from Lynchehaun to the front of the house and she remembered nothing else until she found herself in the bed where she now lay.'

James Lynchehaun, it appeared, had made no reaction when charged. He was remanded in custody to Dugort barrack for transfer to Castlebar Jail. In court, many months later, Sergeant Scully gave evidence of his conversation with the prisoner as they travelled later that evening between Achill and Castlebar. 'Is this not an extraordinary business,' Lynchehaun had said. 'I was called out of my own house by Judy Cooney when I was going to bed and had my shoes off. When I saw the flames I ran down and saw her [Agnes] in the middle of the fire. I rushed in at her and caught hold of her and shoved her out and she fell in the yard; when she got up I asked for the keys of the stables and she gave them to me and I ran and let the mare and the foal out and I saw no more of her until I saw her in Gallagher's house. The poor woman is destroyed right enough. I don't think she will live. I don't know how it occurred.' James Lynchehaun was not admitting to any wrongdoing.

The correspondent stayed on in Achill, knowing in his bones that there was more mileage in the Achill story. He observed the activity in the vicinity of Dugort during the following days, as if the bustle of the holiday season had returned out of season. Randal MacDonnell arrived from London to the Slievemore Hotel and was said to be most distraught at the turn of events. 'He practised formerly at the London Chancery,' the reporter wrote, 'but retired, having considerable private means. He is closely connected with the Taafe family of Roscommon and has some property in that county. He is a Roman Catholic.'

By Wednesday there were some fresh developments to report when Police Divisional Commissioner Cameron and District Inspectors Hume and Rainsford all travelled to Achill to oversee a further deposition by Agnes MacDonnell, just four days after her attack. Dr Thomas Croly was in attendance, as was Mr J. J. Louden, the Westport barrister and former president of the Mayo Land League founded by Michael Davitt a decade and a half earlier, who came to watch proceedings on behalf of the accused. The correspondent was disappointed that the press was again excluded during the taking of the deposition but he picked up a useful piece of information from a local man: 'They searched James Lynchehaun's house this morning and took away some stuff. But they'll never find the clothes he had on him when it happened.'

Dr Croly was more confident by the day that Mrs MacDonnell would pull through. The police had sifted through the debris of the burnt-out Valley House where they found a considerable amount of gold and silver. The reporter learned that the Valley House was insured for £1,500, and was surprised to hear that notice of a claim for damages and malicious injuries had already been lodged. Afterwards he was told that, during the taking of the second deposition, Agnes MacDonnell lay on a bed in Michael Gallagher's house, with her face almost entirely bandaged. For half an hour or more she described, to the best of her ability given the state of her injuries, the events of the previous Saturday night which would leave her with physical and mental scars for the rest of her days. The most significant piece of additional information to emerge was Agnes MacDonnell's identification of her assailant. She had told the magistrate, 'It was Jim Lynchehaun who did it – the grocer Lynchehaun.'

When asked to describe the man whom she accused, Agnes MacDonnell had replied, 'He is a fine, strong, dark, animal-looking man, square built and stout.'

Agnes MacDonnell's lucid description of her attacker was read out in court several months later. Her words were analysed, parsed, and interpreted for clues to the nature of her relationship with the accused. Was there a suggestion of a physical attraction between the older woman and the younger man? Was there admiration, on her part, for the raw physical strength of the man she accused of her mutilation? Or did she hold James Lynchehaun in contempt as an uncivilised savage with the traits of an animal?

The journalist could only guess at what the traumatised woman meant by those words. What he could not have suspected was the train of events that the Valley House drama would yet unleash. He could scarcely have imagined how quickly he would return to the remote place to report on even more remarkable happenings.

7

He's Off!

20–21 October 1894

The residents of Westport woke on Sunday morning, two weeks after the Achill atrocity, to a loud racket on the streets outside their windows. Leather boots scrunched the cobble stones, horses neighed, carriage wheels trundled, and voices shouted out sharp commands. When the townspeople pulled open their curtains they saw rows of constables march past in dark-green uniforms with metal handcuffs hanging from bright belt buckles. When they slid their door locks and stepped outside into the damp October morning, the smell of fresh dung from dozens of constabulary horses hung in the air. What was happening? Why were the police mobilised? Was it more landlord trouble? Piece by piece, the news of the previous night emerged. The officers had been summoned from their beds, hundreds of them travelling by train to Westport. They had gathered from all over the county, from Castlebar, Ballinrobe, Belmullet and Erris, and were heading west to Polranny, outside Achill. The news was out. James Lynchehaun had escaped from police custody.

The prisoner was being transferred from Dugort to Castlebar Jail on Saturday evening when he bolted near his father's house and made a run for the mountains. Two constables, Ward and Muldoon, were accompanying Lynchehaun in the car and there was a consensus on the streets that both men were in big trouble. 'And Ward's wife is poorly,' one said, 'she'll take this very bad.'

Hordes of constables were now on their way to Polranny. The chase was on and there was general agreement that, given the numbers of officers engaged in the pursuit, it was only a matter of hours before the fugitive was back in custody.

'Did you hear that Albert Purvis, the car-man from Mulranny, was the driver? He had to go all the way back to Achill Sound in the dark to raise the alarm,' a man was heard to say. When news of the escape reached Achill in the middle of the night, a constable had headed for Dugort where District Commissioner Cameron and his senior officers were still in residence dealing with the Valley House investigations. Every available officer from Dugort and Achill proceeded to Polranny to join the hunt for the escapee. At three o'clock in the morning Mr Hume, Acting County Inspector, heard the dismaying information and had the Newport telegraph office in operation within ten minutes.

The news spread like wildfire throughout Westport and some claimed, with authority, that there were as many as 300 police officers already hunting the convict. Knots of people assembled at street corners and outside the church after Mass, all waiting for the news that James Lynchehaun was securely back in police custody once more. There was no way he could evade the mass of constables that packed every corner of Polranny and Achill in hot pursuit. Some were critical of the ineptitude of the constabulary, asking how such an escape could have happened. Wasn't Lynchehaun handcuffed to the officers? How could a criminal, charged with a notorious crime, make his escape with such apparent ease? Who was responsible for the incompetence?

There were whispers that Lynchehaun's own family may have had a hand in the getaway. It was rumoured that after the car carrying the prisoner left Achill Sound and was headed towards Polranny, a relative of Lynchehaun rode a horse close to the car as it approached his father's house. The escape of the accused was already providing an outlet for the wits and the spinners of yarns. One story had it that, when Constable Ward gave chase in pursuit of the escapee and saw Lynchehaun disappear around the gable of a house, the constable fell unceremoniously into a sandpit.

The Mayo News despatched a correspondent from Westport to Polranny where he found the small village clothed in drowsy Sunday quietness, and a few smoking chimneys the only visible signs of life when he looked up at the Corraun hills. When he peered though a pair of field glasses he saw, or imagined he saw, the dark shape of a constable combing the slopes and 'appearing to the naked eye as if he were a crow'. Local people had begun to congregate, pointing at the mist-cloaked heights and asking if Lynchehaun roamed on the bleak hills.

For Divisional Commissioner Cameron the news of Lynchehaun's escape was a humiliation and mortification of the worst kind. He would employ every resource available to him to ensure that James Lynchehaun was returned to custody in the shortest possible time. He would leave no stone unturned in tracking down the renegade and immediately offered a reward of £100 for any information leading to the prisoner's detention. However, the Commissioner knew that he and his officers already faced ridicule and derision, which found expression within days in a hard-hitting piece in *The Mayo News*: 'Why was a prisoner charged with the most atrocious crime despatched in the dark night through the lonely Corraun Mountains in the charge of just two constables upon an outside car? The public are entitled to an explanation.'

A month later, while James Lynchehaun was still at large, the public received some answers to the questions raised by *The Mayo News* when a Court of Inquiry appointed by the Lord Lieutenant of Ireland got under way in Dugort. Its remit was to consider charges against certain members of the constabulary in connection with the arrest, custody, and escape of James Lynchehaun, the prisoner charged with the vicious assault of Agnes MacDonnell at the Valley House. Commissioner Cameron's discomfiture was acute as he sought to defend himself and his officers.

'I have never during my experience, under the conditions prevailing,' the Commissioner told the Inquiry, 'heard of more than two armed men being in charge of a handcuffed prisoner. There was a respectable driver and a good car provided for the conveyance of the prisoner. I consider two armed officers of the RIC amply sufficient to convey a handcuffed prisoner safely whether by day or night anywhere. James Lynchehaun had been remanded in Castlebar Jail. It was necessary to bring him from Castlebar to Valley that day for the purpose of being present during the taking of a deposition by Mr Horne RM, who issued a committal warrant.' Lynchehaun, he explained, on the night of his escape, was to travel by car under police escort to Mulranny and onwards by train to Castlebar the following morning. 'My reasons for considering it more desirable to send the prisoner to Mulranny were that, in the first place, irregularities had occurred in Dugort barrack with reference to this prisoner and there was a lock-up in Mulranny barrack. Secondly, Mulranny was about half-way to Castlebar Jail and consequently a suitable place to send him for the night, it being the terminal point for the train to Castlebar.'

District Inspector Rainsford was the officer with primary responsibility on the night of James Lynchehaun's escape. He deposed to the sworn Inquiry:

> I am District Inspector of the RIC and in charge of Newport district. I was in charge of said district on 20 October last. I had a prisoner on that day (James Lynchehaun) at the Valley before Mr Horne RM. He was charged with murderously assaulting one Mrs Agnes MacDonnell of the Valley House on 6 October. She made a deposition fully identifying James Lynchehaun as her assailant and describing the attack he made upon her on the night of the 6 October. Mr Horne issued a warrant remanding the prisoner to Castlebar Jail, and it was handed to me for execution. I now hold and identify said warrant. In discharge of my duty as District Inspector I, on that day, selected two constables, Patrick Ward and John Muldoon, to convey the prisoner to Mulranny. Constable Ward, being senior, I gave him the warrant.

The gate lodge at the entrance to the burnt-out shell of the Valley House had been turned into a temporary police barrack with about half a dozen officers on duty on the day of Lynchehaun's escape. Sergeant Dusting had, earlier in the day, escorted James Lynchehaun from Castlebar and he watched him leave for the return journey at about half past six in the evening. 'I handcuffed the prisoner and I saw Constables Ward and Muldoon afterwards leaving from the temporary barrack and start for Achill Sound. I saw them get on a car on the avenue leading from the barrack. The two constables were perfectly sober when I saw them leave with the prisoner. They were armed with rifles and swords. The handcuffs I put on the prisoner were Constable Ward's and I handed him the keys.' There was general agreement that the car driver was the best that could be procured to convey the prisoner. He was a thoroughly respectable man.

Constable John Switzer was stationed at Achill Sound when Lynchehaun and his escort arrived at about half past seven and proceeded to the barrack day-room. Soon afterwards, some civilians entered. They were Mary Sweeney, the convict's sister, Frank Sweeney, her husband, and Michael Lynchehaun, the prisoner's brother. They brought food for the detainee and Michael Lynchehaun gave his brother a smoke of a pipe. 'I cannot say if the prisoner was handcuffed or not,' Constable Switzer told the Inquiry, 'but when I entered the day-room I saw handcuffs in Constable Ward's hands and the prisoner was not handcuffed then. He was, however, handcuffed when the party left the barrack. The constable said that it was not unusual for escorts with prisoners to delay for a short time at the police barrack in Achill Sound. He could recall two previous occasions when Lynchehaun's travelling party made a stop there to change escorts when transferring the prisoner between Castlebar and Dugort.

The car had left the barrack at Achill Sound at a quarter past eight. The constables wore heavy coats and capes and had their ammunition pouches strapped outside. Constable Ward and Lynchehaun went to the right side of the car, Constable

Muldoon and the driver to the left. The car headed into the darkness in the direction of Polranny en route to Mulranny.

Perhaps the most reliable account of what happened in Polranny that Saturday evening came from the mouth of the car-man, Albert Purvis, when he gave his evidence to the Inquiry. He started his testimony with the words, 'I live at Mulranny and I am a car owner,' and went on to give his version of events. 'We left the Valley at about six o'clock that Saturday evening. The prisoner Lynchehaun had an overcoat on him that reached about to his knees. We took a break at the Sound, and then started across the bridge towards Mulranny.'

Purvis' father before him ran a car business from Mulranny and for many years they had collected visitors from Westport train station and ferried them to Newport, to Mulranny and to Achill. They received a good amount of what Albert referred to as 'government business' from the Congested Districts Board, the constabulary, and the other official agencies. There was good business too from the railway company and from the ongoing construction work on the railway line extensions. Albert Purvis may have worried that, when the railway station at Achill Sound finally opened the following summer, it could have a negative impact on his car business.

'About a quarter of a mile from The Sound,' Purvis told the investigation, 'we passed by Michael Lynchehaun, the prisoner's brother, who was riding a horse on our side of the road. He shouted something at the prisoner and after we passed him out I quickened the pace of the horses. We trotted on for some distance until we came to a rise in the road about a mile and a half from The Sound and near to a lane leading to the house of Neal Lynchehaun, the prisoner's father.' At this point in the proceedings an official held up a map of the area where James Lynchehaun had escaped, showing the public road from Achill Sound to Mulranny, the laneway along which the fugitive took flight, Neal Lynchehaun's house and a sandpit. The exact distances between each of these points had been measured and noted.

Albert Purvis continued: 'When we came to the hill and the horse stopped trotting, Constable Ward said, "Give me a match one of ye" and then he turned in towards the well of the car and put his left elbow up on it. Constable Muldoon put his hand into his breast pocket as if to get a match, and it was then I felt the car give a spring. When I looked around the prisoner was on the ground, and then he was running up the lane towards his father's house. Constable Ward was shouting "come back" and himself and Constable Muldoon jumped down off the car and ran in pursuit.'

What did he, Purvis, do then?

'I was standing up on the footboard of the car trying to see what was going on. It was a fine starry night. I had a clear view up to about 10 yards from the house when a straw stack cut off my view of the three of them. I heard Constable Ward call out to me from the back of Neal Lynchehaun's house to return to The Sound as quick as I could for more police. At the time Constable Muldoon was running after the prisoner and he was gaining on him and when I lost sight of them he was within, I'd say, five or six yards of Lynchehaun. The prisoner had his hands in front of him apparently still handcuffed.'

What happened next?

'I took off at a gallop to report the news to the constabulary in The Sound and after that in Dugort.'

The Court of Inquiry met for five days in Dugort barrack, between 21 and 26 November. It then adjourned to consider the evidence. It would be a month before it issued its findings.

Meanwhile, James Lynchehaun still evaded the constabulary. Where did he flee to that October night? Where was he hiding out? Some of the answers came, afterward, from the pen of Brother Paul Carney whose quarter of century tenure on Achill Island was then coming to an end. Over at Bunnacurry Monastery the friar was all ears, listening to the local stories and gossip about the fugitive, while being careful to follow the official line of denouncing Lynchehaun in public. When the friar later came to write about Lynchehaun's escapades, he drew on local tales, newspaper reports and official records to produce his own distinctive narrative about the fugitive's adventures. He described what happened immediately after Lynchehaun's jump to freedom:

> So he succeeded in his plans of escape for the time being. Although he was manacled he still had three advantages, in knowing the place in the dark, in being without an overcoat, and in being in the midst of friends, while the police were strangers to the place, loaded with guns and coats, having no friends to direct them. So after a fruitless pursuit they gave it up, returned to the barrack at Achill Sound, told of their mishap, pursuit, and loss of their quarry.

According to the friar, on the night he bolted to freedom, Lynchehaun went to his uncle's house and speaking in Irish asked to be let in. It was about midnight. Recognising the voice his relations opened the door, lit a fire, prepared a good supper, bathed his feet, gave him some clean clothes and broke open the handcuffs that still secured his hands.

James Lynchehaun retraced his steps that night and, according to the monk's account, 'went towards the shore, got a little boat, crossed about a mile of a channel, entered Achill Island, and took up his abode in a friend's house, named James Gallagher, Shraheens, within about half a mile distant from the barrack at Achill Sound. In this house he made or got made a burrow or digging place under a boarded floor in the little room. In this he placed a layer of turf to prevent dampness and over it a pallet, where he could stretch out in time of danger. The entrance to this was covered with an old box into which clothes were carelessly thrown.'

Brother Paul Carney listened to the local gossip and recorded all he heard in his leather-bound notebooks, little realising that this was but the start of a narrative that he would continue to write for several years to come. He took particular delight in describing the panicked and futile pursuit of Lynchehaun in inclement weather throughout the bitter winter of 1894: 'So constables, officers, and magistrates, to the number of about 300 in all, came to the island, searched houses, mountains, valleys and caves, for the space of about three months. Still the fox evaded their grasp, he being snugly in his den, while they traversed the mountains and shores night and day amidst wind and rain, snow and hail.'

There followed a most exhaustive and intensive police search for the escapee in Corraun, in Achill, and – with the aid of a steam cutter – in several of the islands strewn across Clew Bay. Many wild goose chases resulted, such as that described in a frantic headline in *The Freeman's Journal*: 'Is Lynchehaun in Dublin?' The writer of the piece had, it appeared, received some reliable information that he shared enthusiastically with his readers:

> I have heard that a police sergeant who is well acquainted with the appearance of Lynchehaun is at present in Dublin, and is instituting an active search in conjunction with the Castle Detective Department. I have further heard that almost every vessel entering the Liffey for some days past on which the escaped prisoner could possibly be supposed to have boarded, has been searched by members of the G Division from bow to stern, but to no purpose. Similar precautions I hear have been taken at other ports. An idea has also got abroad that Lynchehaun is armed, and that if he is eventually run to earth, a most stubborn and even bloody resistance may be expected.

Weeks went by and, despite the employment of hundreds of police and the substantial reward on offer for information leading to the prisoner's rearrest, James Lynchehaun remained at large. 'The most thrilling stories,' *The Mayo News* reported, 'are told about the hair-breadth escapes which Lynchehaun is said to have had from his pursuers. His relatives are numerous for many miles around, and the police regard this as the greatest difficulty they have had in their chase after him.' Constables who were drafted into the district in pursuit of the prisoner had to be withdrawn in an exhausted condition and large contingents of fresh men sent to replace them.

There were some in Achill who claimed that the fugitive's appearance had changed considerably since his escape, that his usual closely-shaven face was now covered with a coarse beard, and that he had taken on a care-worn and exhausted look. Others said, with confidence, that the convict was in possession of a six-chambered revolver and ammunition. Parents warned their children that a dangerous man was abroad in the winter night. Grave fears were entertained by the police that James Lynchehaun would not be recaptured without a fierce struggle and that members of the public should be on their guard.

8

Frightful Hurricanes
December 1894

Agnes MacDonnell lay in bed at The Rectory in Dugort as the year drifted to a close. Each time she stirred, her forehead furrowed in distress with the movement. The bandages that covered her injured eye and her smashed nose caused the corners of her mouth to tauten, the angry sores and purple bruises giving her face a startling appearance. While the injuries to her face were the most obvious, she felt the results of her wounds over her entire body. There was the tight throbbing at her rib cage; the raw ache of the lacerations on her lower body; the sting of burnt skin from knee to ankle; the smarting wounds in her most intimate areas. The twinge of the individual pains flowed into one another so that she was unable to distinguish one from the other. Her attention did, however, return again and again to the centre of her face as the realisation of her nasal mutilation slowly dawned. After she regained consciousness, the effort of breathing in and out through the shattered nose cartilage was almost unbearable as she held in lungfuls of air to get some relief from the effort of exhaling through her broken nostrils.

They had brought her across from the townland of Valley to stay at The Rectory, which was on an adjoining site to St Thomas' and connected to the church by a pathway through a side gate. Time would heal some, but not all, of her wounds.

She asked herself if she could remain on the island after what had happened. Could she rebuild her life while her attacker was still at large? At night she looked out into the darkness and speculated about the whereabouts of James Lynchehaun. Did he prowl around the debris of her wrecked home three miles away in Valley? Did he pass along the road just a few hundred yards away at the end of the avenue and laugh aloud at her plight? In her bones she knew that he would try to confront and threaten those who could testify about what had happened that night at the Valley House. She would have no peace while the contemptible scoundrel was at large.

At least Agnes MacDonnell had the satisfaction of knowing that her compensation claim had been settled at the Special Presenting Session in Newport Court. She had lost no time in seeking reparation for the malicious damage to her home and the destruction of the stables. The contents of her property were listed for the hearing. The Valley House contained furniture, wearing apparel, £83 in money, a gold watch and other articles of jewellery; the stables housed a car, a canoe and a pleasure boat. Agnes was not in attendance in court for it was Dr Croly's opinion that it would have imperilled his patient's life to travel to Newport to give evidence. Her husband, Randal MacDonnell, was present, having some time earlier posted a copy of the malicious claim notice at each police barrack in Achill.

An engineer, John Smyth CE, had inspected the damaged property and made a ground plan of the house and stables. While the roof of the Valley House was destroyed, he advised the court that the walls were still standing but that the plasterwork was entirely ruined. He then presented to the court a methodology for calculating the cost of rebuilding the house and stables: he first took the cubic area of the buildings, allowed a replacement cost of seven pence per cubic foot as a fair price, then deducted an amount for the cubic area of masonry still standing, to arrive at a cost for the restoration of the buildings.

The District Inspector of the constabulary had told the court that he had not the slightest doubt but that the Valley House property had been damaged maliciously. He had inspected the debris on the morning of 7 October and had found a quantity of gold which, weighed against sovereigns, would represent £50 10s in value. There were five or six sovereigns undamaged and he was told by an eminent dentist that the gold assayed would not be worth £40. He also found a quantity of silver plate, but the silver had been melted off in the heat. 'Any person who has furnished a house,' he said 'would know from experience that the plate would cost £50.' He also discovered a pair of opera glasses, or field glasses, at the scene, the value of which he could not estimate.

Henry Vereker, former agent of Agnes MacDonnell, testified that he knew the Valley House well and had been there frequently. The house, he said, had six rooms and a dairy, was extremely well furnished and, in his view, it would take £260 or £270 to furnish the house to its previous state. He estimated the value of the two destroyed boats at about £8. Henry Vereker was asked if there was ill feeling towards Agnes MacDonnell among her tenants, or anything exceptional in their relations at the time. Were there any harsh acts on her part which could have caused animosity? In his experience, Vereker replied, there was considerable bitterness between Agnes MacDonnell and her tenants, especially over the issue of conacre, or the letting of small parcels of land. When he had acted as Agnes MacDonnell's agent, she wanted him to give notice to the tenants who had held conacre since Lord Cavan's time. Mrs MacDonnell had instructed him that the tenants would have to surrender their letting rights and told him that she intended enforcing this order. 'I don't know anything,' Henry Vereker said, 'that would cause more ill feeling than that. She constantly told the tenants in my presence that she would enforce it.' He explained that this was one of the reasons why he had given up being her agent.

The court awarded Agnes MacDonnell malicious damages compensation of £1,000, which was the full amount claimed, and recommended that the amount should be charged to the county-at-large, as it would be unfair to levy off Achill Island alone. Once the compensation monies were secured, Agnes MacDonnell made plans to return to her London home for

Christmas. She needed to recover her strength and deal with her brutally disfigured face. She planned to recuperate and receive specialist medical help. She would get away, for a time, from the island with its prowling shadows in the night.

Across the road from where Agnes MacDonnell recuperated in The Rectory, the crowds of constabulary had departed following the conclusion of the Inquiry into James Lynchehaun's escape. In Newport, as District Inspector Rainsford awaited the outcome of the Inquiry, he received an unpleasant surprise in the form of a letter, dated 1 December 1894 and post-marked Kirkham, Lancashire, from none other than the fugitive James Lynchehaun:

> Sir,
> I beg to inform you that I have managed to get this far. My object in writing to you is to let you know that I will attend my trial in March next or at any time that you name. You can do this by putting a notice in any of the Dublin papers. I also wish to point out to you that if you wish Mrs MacDonnell to live you will get some other medical man besides Croly. He will put her to death surely for two reasons, (1) to banish me for life, (2) to have an opportunity to buy the Valley estate himself. On this subject I will write to her husband. The wonder is why the poor lady has survived Croly's devilment so long. If you make inquiries you will find that Croly was death on me.
> It may be interesting for you to know how I managed to get here. Well, it was this. I got to Ballycroy that night, crossed into Doohoma, thence to Blacksod into Inishkea, and boarded the first steamer passing. You need not put yourself to any trouble looking for me here. I am something like Mr Balfour in writing and dating his letters. My reason for escaping was I did not like to be such a long time awaiting trial in prison and you need not blame the constables that were with me. Until that moment Ward never lifted a hand out of my overcoat pocket and even if he had the hand there

that minute I had intended to make the plunge. If there were 100 police there at the time I'd go as the night was extremely dark and I knew every nook and turn in the place.

Lest you should have any doubts about this letter being genuine as coming from me, let me remind you that one day in September you were coming out by Mr Hickey's car and that I asked you how you were after your illness. I am not sure now as to the exact words but it was something like what I state, or 'I hope you are all right, sir.' I was road-making that day. I also wish to add that when my trial time comes that I will deliver myself up to Constables Ward and Muldoon but to no others. They did their best to capture me and Muldoon is nothing but a good runner.

I am, Sir,

Yours respectfully
Jas Lynchehaun

The convict was doing his utmost to put the constabulary off his scent. The letter revealed a fierce hostility on Lynchehaun's part towards Dr Croly – an animosity which would later come into public view – as well as some sympathy towards the constables under investigation for dereliction of duty. Lynchehaun's colourful account of his supposed escape route through Doohoma, Blacksod and the Inishkea islands and out of the country reflected some of the outlandish stories then circulating about his exploits.

If Mr Rainsford was experiencing discomfort and embarrassment, so was his superior, Commissioner Cameron, who put pen to paper to write up the report for his Western District in County Mayo for the month of November. He had to construct his account with great care for it was a difficult time for his force with Lynchehaun still evading capture, and his officers under investigation in a formal Inquiry. He needed to reassure his superiors in Dublin Castle that the district was not out of control, and started his report with the confident statement, 'The general state of the county is satisfactory'. His account made no mention of James Lynchehaun.

It was just a month since the Commissioner had written of the events that had thrown his district into turmoil, when he had reported that 'a most barbarous attempt was made to murder Mrs Agnes MacDonnell; that James Lynchehaun was arrested for the crime of which he was the perpetrator, without doubt, the evidence against him being conclusive.' He then had to add the embarrassing information that 'Lynchehaun unfortunately escaped from the custody of his guard while being conveyed to Mulranny en route for Castlebar Jail and has not yet been rearrested. He is believed to be hiding out in Achill and Ballycroy mountains and every possible effort is being made to capture him.' The Commissioner had decided to steer clear of the Lynchehaun business in his most recent report and concentrate instead on the state of landlord-tenant relations in the area. During the month, he reported, twenty-three tenants and eleven sub-tenants were evicted but none of these 'were cases of hardship or likely to disturb the existing relations between tenants and landlords which on the whole are satisfactory'. While three of the evicted farms had been retaken, two by old tenants and one by a new tenant, the Commissioner did not believe that there was any danger of reprisals.

Commissioner Cameron's official accounts almost always included a reference to the potato crop which, he said, had been very variable that year. 'In wet or cold conditions where the land was planted late the return is very bad, in some cases scarcely a fourth. In well drained lands there is a fair average crop. Taken all round there is a short crop, something less than a half crop compared to last year and inferior quality owing to the want of heat in the summer.' The report moved once more into a reassuring mode. 'I do not anticipate distress as food stuffs are abnormally cheap and the people dispense less and less every year on potatoes as the staple article of food.' James Lynchehaun may have turned his force into a laughing stock, and a mutilated woman may have lain stricken on her bed in Dugort, but the Commissioner concluded his report on an upbeat note. 'I see no signs of poverty,' he wrote.

P. J. Kelly and the Westport Board of Guardians were, it seemed, more alert than Commissioner Cameron to the inherent dangers in the state of the potato crop which, in their view, was the poorest in recent times. So serious did they take the situation that the Board had written to the Chief Secretary, John Morley, to express their alarm at the plight of the people in the Union:

> Their staple food and principal source of income, the potato, has almost totally failed and their whole year's work in the fields, where they toiled so hard, is gone for nothing. In most of the districts of the union, the potatoes are not worth digging out and the people's whole industry – feeding of pigs, cattle etc – is therefore paralyzed. Having regard to these facts, we would ask the Government to open up some reproductive public works for the relief of the people, and also to appeal to the landlords of the West not to press their unfortunate tenantry for rent in this season as they have always done in similar circumstances in other bad years, when they knew well those poor people will be without food for themselves and their families, in many instances before Christmas next, and the money now forced from them as rent would be necessary to preserve them for actual starvation.

There was a response of sorts to the Board's appeal. In the closing days of December the Guardians were notified that they would receive a loan without interest to purchase more seed potatoes for those unable to procure a supply. The Board printed up handbills and posted these throughout the district, including on Achill Island, requesting the people to apply to their local guardians for the amount of seed they would need. The tenants would, of course, be required to pay for the seed potatoes distributed.

In the last week of December the Dugort Court of Inquiry issued its ruling. District Inspector Rainsford was found guilty on the charge that, on 20 October 1894, he neglected his duty in not making adequate arrangements for the safe custody and conveyance of the prisoner James Lynchehaun from Valley to Mulranny. The Inspector was transferred to another county at his own expense. Constable Ward was found guilty of serous misdemeanour and dereliction of duty and was dismissed from the force. Constable Muldoon was found guilty of a less serious breach of discipline and was transferred to new duties.

Agnes MacDonnell left Achill for London before Christmas with *The Mayo News* noting her departure: 'On Thursday morning Mrs Agnes MacDonnell, the victim of the Achill outrage, was conveyed from Dugort, Achill, to Mulranny and thence by rail en route to London. To anyone who saw the poor lady immediately after the outrage, her recovery is simply marvellous and reflects great credit on her medical attendant, Dr Croly of Achill.' The journey took her from Dugort by Valley crossroads where, nearby, the soot-splayed walls of her home stood bleak and desolate on the north Achill skyline. Mrs MacDonnell did not yet have the advantage of travelling by train from Achill since the official opening of the new railway extension to the island was still some months off. However, she was about to experience a rare piece of good luck, for she would cross the Irish Sea just hours before the eruption of some of the fiercest storms in living memory. Within hours of her arrival at her home in Belsize Square, London, a powerful southwest gale brought destruction and havoc across Britain and Ireland. *The Freeman's Journal* reported that 'the wind blew in gusts with terrible force and, in some instances pedestrians were nearly blown down by its violence'. On the first night of the high winds the gale increased considerably after midnight and continued to grow in ferocity, as detailed in the newspaper headlines over the Christmas period:

THE GREATEST STORM FOR MANY YEARS
A Frightful Hurricane Rages over the Three Kingdoms
Awful Scenes of Desolation in the Country

The steamer *Banshee* had left Holyhead on the Friday night, carrying two dozen Mayo harvesters returning home for

Christmas. The vessel was due to reach Dublin's North Wall at six o'clock on Saturday morning but did not arrive until a quarter to one. As soon as the ship had made its way beyond Liverpool harbour, heavy seas began striking the vessel's bows and powerful waves dashed over its sides, tossing the vessel about with a ferociousness never before experienced by the crew. Water poured through the port holes, soaking the passengers until they were drenched to the skin. The sea water spilled down from the deck on to the harvesters, the force of the deluge tossing their bundles of belongings about like dice in a box. Soon, the steerage passengers were a sodden, dripping sight, their bodies convulsing with seasickness.

The plight of the harvesters was pitiable. On their arrival in Dublin they had to face the long rail journey to the west and, for the Achill islanders among them, there was the added trauma of returning home for the first time since so many of their neighbours and relatives had been lost in Clew Bay. In the bleak winter days ahead they would listen, wide-eyed, to the Achill stories about the daring feats of James Lynchehaun who still evaded his captors. The tales about the fugitive were growing more bizarre by the day.

The furious squalls continued to rage throughout Christmas week and, on 29 December, a severe windstorm lashed the seas off northwest Mayo, west of the Mullet Peninsula. To the north of the Inishkea islands, two lighthouses on Eagle Island took the full brunt of the squall as the high seas cascaded on to the towers. The east station lighthouse was damaged beyond repair, its lantern glass smashed to pieces and the light extinguished. The high seas breached the 3-foot-thick storm wall and Lizzie Ryan, who was staying at the station at the time, later wrote: 'The like of this storm has not come for hundreds of years.'

It may have been some comfort to Agnes MacDonnell that she passed the storm-filled closing days of 1894 in the safety of her London home, and not on the savage northern edges of Achill. She could no longer look in a mirror and take pride in her handsome face framed by braided auburn hair. Even if she avoided mirrors, she could not escape the shock and disbelief on the faces of her husband and son. She knew that her looks were impaired forever and that her facial beauty had been transformed into a repulsive mask. New skin would grow and conceal the worst of the scars that covered her torso. She visited the oculist to hear the worst about her damaged eye. A physician examined her crushed nose and arranged a nasal prosthesis. For the remainder of her life, Agnes MacDonnell would not appear in public without a veil to conceal her disfigured face.

Back in Achill the Atlantic was in turmoil. A mass of waves – grey, viridian, and turquoise – coiled and curled to the sky in a fury of foam on the far side of Slievemore. It was as if the bloated Atlantic with its giant foam bursts was trying to outdo the reach of the mountain. For days on end there was no break in the swell and lashing of the ocean, or in the screeching flight of the sea-birds in north Achill. As the year drew to an end many looked out from the island towards the distant places of Ballycroy, Doohoma, Blacksod and the Inishkea islands and wondered if James Lynchehaun could possibly have survived being abroad in the ferment of such storms.

Where was James Lynchehaun? Was he still alive?

Portrait of Agnes MacDonnell, *c.* 1880 (*courtesy of Ann and Richard MacDonnell, London*).

James Lynchehaun (above) as he appeared after his capture in January 1895 (*courtesy of* The Mayo News); (below) a sketch of Mr Cooney of New York, alias James Lynchehaun of Cleveland, Ohio, tourist in Achill, 1907 (*courtesy of* The Mayo News).

James Lynchehaun in the United States, *c.* 1910 (*courtesy of Wynne Collection*).

Brother Paul Carney, *c.* 1895 (*courtesy of Michael McDonnell, Galway*).

Bunnacurry Monastery, Achill *c.* 1880 (*courtesy of National Library of Ireland*).

Achill islanders cross the bridge at Achill Sound before the arrival of the train carrying the remains of the drowned from the *Victory* capsize, June 1894 (*courtesy of Wynne Collection*).

Railway line and station under construction at Achill Sound, 1894 (*courtesy of Wynne Collection*).

Coffins of the drowned from the *Victory* capsize, lined up at Westport
Quay, June 1894 (*courtesy of Wynne Collection*).

Michael Davitt Bridge, Achill Sound, *c.* 1890 (*courtesy of National Library of Ireland*).

The Colony, Achill Mission settlement, at Dugort on Achill island, with St Thomas' Church in the foreground and Slievemore rising majestically in the background, *c.* 1880 (*courtesy of National Library of Ireland*).

The Valley House, with Slievemore in the background, *c*. 1880. The estate was bought by Frederick Lambert, 8th Earl of Cavan, in the early 1870s, and used by him as a hunting lodge and holiday residence until his death in 1887 (*courtesy of National Library of Ireland*).

The roofless shell of the Valley House, October 1894 (*courtesy of Wynne Collection*).

Constables at the gate lodge with a roofless Valley House in the background, October 1894 (*courtesy of National Library of Ireland*).

Burnt-out stables at the Valley House, October 1894 (*courtesy of Wynne Collection*).

The Rectory where Agnes MacDonnell recuperated after the Valley House attack, with St Thomas' Church, Dugort, to the left, *c.* 1890 (*courtesy of National Library of Ireland*).

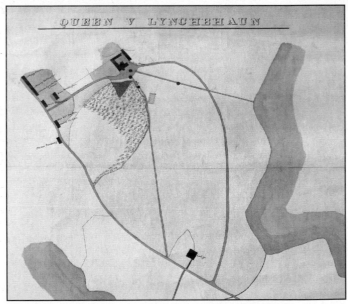

'Queen v Lynchehaun' map of the Valley House crime scene prepared by G. K. Dixon, March 1895, and exhibited at the trial of James Lynchehaun in Castlebar (*courtesy of Mayo County Library*).

The Courthouse and Mall, Castlebar, *c.* 1880. This was the setting
for 'Queen v Lynchehaun' in July 1895, when James Lynchehaun
went on trial for attacking Agnes MacDonnell at the Valley House in
October 1894 (*courtesy of National Library of Ireland*).

Jack Yeats' drawing 'Synge' from his sketchbook *Ireland with Synge 1905* (*courtesy of Berg, New York Public Library;* © *Estate of Jack B. Yeats*).

9

Was This Woman Outraged?
January 1895

The shrill horn sliced the icy January air at Westport railway station, the burst of activity on the platform signalling the arrival of the early morning train from Mulranny. Those waiting turned their heads in unison in the direction of the locomotive noise like soldiers going through a drill, their warm breath looping above their heads. Some curled their toes in their shoes, shifting their feet in an effort to keep warm. The crows that hopped among the railway sleepers flapped their wings and took flight as the roar of the train grew louder. Many in the crowd whispered to one another excitedly:

'Who do you think did the dirty on him?'

'Who will get their hands on the £100 informant money?'

'They say he's changed a lot in appearance.'

'James Gallagher is in big trouble. They arrested him too.'

'There was a poor young girl in the house. She's on the train as well.'

They shuffled in close, bunching together to get a good vantage point. The train screeched into the station with a rattle of wheels and a hiss of brakes. The platform shook and the guard jumped off before the train came to a juddering halt, the carriages wobbling from side to side. The doors swung open and two constables alighted to clear a passage through the crowd. 'Out of the way. Make room there.'

James Lynchehaun stepped onto the platform, handcuffed to two police officers. Heavier than the last time he had been seen in public three months earlier, he now also sported side-whiskers. He held his head high and scanned the crowd with the aura of an arriving dignitary and with the appearance of a man not at all unhappy with the attention he attracted. A pencil-sketch made as the prisoner entered the court that day shows a well-dressed man with a full curling moustache, wearing a soft peaked cap, and looking straight ahead.

By contrast, James Gallagher, the next prisoner to be led out, appeared nervous and edgy, walking with downcast eyes. Mary Masterson walked after them, looking delicate and petrified as she was led, shivering, through the crowd. Westport held bad memories for her as it was scarcely six months since her rescue from the waters of Clew Bay after the *Victory* capsized. The crowd closed in behind the procession of prisoners as it moved towards the convoy of cars where the waiting horses stamped their hooves and tossed their manes. When the prisoners were on board and handcuffed securely to their escorts, whips snapped and the line of carriages moved off smartly on the short trip to Westport courthouse.

It was about eight o'clock that morning when the news broke that James Lynchehaun had been tracked down and recaptured during the night at Shraheens, Achill. He'd been taken under police escort, first to Achill Sound, and then on to Mulranny to catch the early train to Westport. He'd evaded the police for three months throughout the bitter winter. One newspaper reported that Lynchehaun's arrest was no surprise to the people in that part of the country as it was generally known that the renegade had not left the neighbourhood of Achill. Indeed, the report went, 'some of the hair-breadth escapes from the police in search of him were discussed and described with, possibly, a large degree of exaggeration'. The general opinion was that the £100 reward offered by the Government had accomplished what the vigilance of hundreds of police had failed to achieve.

Shortly after noon the three prisoners appeared in the presence of Mr Robert Powell JP in Westport Court. James Gallagher and Mary Masterson were charged with harbouring, concealing and comforting a prisoner charged with felony. District Inspector Rainsford, pleased with his force's night's work, even if he was still smarting from the disciplinary hearings into the earlier police dealings with Lynchehaun, was determined that there would be no bungling this time. He identified the prisoner for the court and described the circumstances of his arrest: 'I found the prisoner, James Lynchehaun, concealed in a hole under the floor in a bedroom in the house of James Gallagher at Shraheens, two miles from Achill Sound. There were several people in the bedroom when we arrested him. James Gallagher, the owner of the house, was in the room when we found [the] accused. I see and identify the man now present.' The Inspector described how, the previous night, he and a party of constables had proceeded to Shraheens. At some distance from James Gallagher's house they divested themselves of their boots. Even though it was an extremely cold night, they approached Gallagher's house in their stockinged feet, arriving at about two o'clock in the morning and surrounding the house on all sides.

Sergeant Scully was one of those in the police party. 'I myself knocked at the front door,' he said. 'We were not admitted for some time. Myself and another sergeant tried to force in the door. We shouted to be let in.' When they gained entry they searched the kitchen and then advanced to the bedroom. There they found a large chest which they dragged from the wall and discovered two planks, about 2 feet long, with bags thrown loosely over them. They removed the planks and found what appeared to be an empty hole with some hay and water at the bottom. On closer examination they established that the hole extended under the floor and was about 7 feet in length, 2½ feet wide and 3 feet deep. It appeared to them that the space had been recently used. There didn't seem to be any way of communicating from the hole with the outer world, and no way of letting air in.

Sergeant Steele, another member of the search party, told the magistrate that he called on Lynchehaun to come out of his hiding place at once and threatened to use his firearm if the prisoner resisted. During the period of the search, he said, James Gallagher 'was very nervous and trembling all over.' Lynchehaun came out of the hole where it appeared as if he was buried alive. He wore only a shirt and made no resistance when arrested. Mary Masterson was present in the room with two young children. 'I asked her,' Inspector Rainsford said, 'what brought her to the house as she did not live there. She gave no explanation. She said she did not know. She lives about half a mile from the house.' James Gallagher's wife cried and pleaded with the police not to take her husband away, claiming that it was her fault that Lynchehaun was found in their house.

There was more incriminating evidence against James Gallagher from Sergeant Michael Glynn who testified about a meeting he had with Gallagher on 1 January on his way to mass in Kildownet, before Lynchehaun's rearrest. The sergeant and Gallagher had walked along together, talking about James Lynchehaun and how the constabulary were killed looking for him night and day. 'James Gallagher said that he believed we would never catch him as he had left the country,' the sergeant testified. 'He also said that if Lynchehaun was the man who committed the crime, no man should allow him into his house as the crime had injured Achill badly.'

There was an unsavoury incident in the court when Farrell Gallagher, the nine-year old son of the prisoner James Gallagher, was produced by Sergeant Scully as a witness against his father. The boy was placed on a table and asked if he understood the oath he was about to take. When the boy replied that he did not, the court refused to take his evidence. All three prisoners were remanded in custody to await further depositions on the charges against them. The police escorted them to Castlebar Jail on the 2.30 p.m. train. During the months of January and February the three prisoners were brought over and back several times from Castlebar Jail to Westport Court. In the course of witness depositions the picture of the Valley House crime scene emerged with greater vividness, like a painting taking on depth and intensity with each stroke of the brush. The atrocity was described in the court with such graphic detail that it continued to send a shudder of shock across Ireland and further afield. It fell to Inspector Rainsford, in his formal statement, to meticulously present a picture of the crime scene which he had encountered at the Valley House. 'I am a District Inspector of the RIC,' the Inspector told the Westport magistrate, 'and I am in charge of this case. I arrived at the Valley House at about 3.30 p.m. on 7 October last. I observed that it and the stables had been burned down except for the outer walls of the house and some of the sheds in the yard. I made a careful examination of the Valley House and the grounds around it.' He and his officers had scrutinised the area between the house and the haystacks. They found what appeared to be a very large quantity of blood on the grass in two or three different places, at about forty yards distant from the house, and it appeared that a trail of blood was going in the direction of the ditch which had whin bushes on top. He observed blood at the spot of the ditch where Bridget McNeela came upon the injured Mrs MacDonnell; it was about 15 or 20 yards from where he had first noticed the blood. In addition, he found a large stained stone at the spot where he detected the largest quantity of blood. 'I directed Constable Carr to take possession of this stone and he has kept it since.'

Inspector Rainsford appeared to stumble on his words when he came to describe a piece of evidence which Constable Carr had found at the scene of the felony. Some in the room took a quick intake of breath when the Inspector held up a clump of hair, apparently twisted into a plait. It appeared, said the officer, to be human hair.

The Inspector described the trail of blood which he found in the Valley House yard: there were blood marks in the stable from where he was told the horses had been let loose; there were droplets of blood in the stable next to the carriage shed that was burned. 'I also saw blood smudges on the wall outside the scullery door. I observed the scullery window was broken completely, large enough to allow a person through. I noticed a black streak from the bottom of the window down to the ground as if some person had come out that way.' The Inspector explained how

Matthew Gallagher had shown him the two injured horses that afternoon and it had been a most distressing sight: 'They were stabbed – the young mare on the right side and the old mare on the left, partly in the stomach. They appeared to be fresh cuts and there was some blood coming from the wounds.'

On the Monday after the Valley House incident, the Inspector said that he had obtained items of Agnes MacDonnell's clothing from Bridget McNeela which included a flannel nightdress, an inside bodice, a shawl and a jersey. 'I now produce these items,' he said, holding up each piece of clothing in turn. He observed that there was a large quantity of blood on the nightdress, bodice and shawl, and a slight trace of blood on the jersey.

The prisoner stood motionless in the court during the Inspector's evidence. His only perceptible movement was of his eyes opening and closing in furious blinks. Inspector Rainsford moved to where Lynchehaun stood and placed some money on the bench in front of the prisoner; it was a sum of £5 2s 6d found in Lynchehaun's possession on arrest. However, the Inspector declined to return some books also found on the accused; these comprised a copy of the New Testament, a manuscript copy of the first chapter of St John's Gospel in Latin, a *Moore's Almanac* for 1895, and a map of England.

Inspector Rainsford told the magistrate that the police were seriously worried at the possibility that witnesses in the case would be interfered with. Already, Michael McGinty had given evidence of Lynchehaun's wife's attempted intimidation some weeks after the crime. 'She came to the house,' McGinty had said, 'and asked could she see me and my brother. She said that we had too much to say in the case against her husband. If we would hang him, she said, we would not hang her and she would be in the Valley long after us.'

By the time Dr Thomas Croly travelled from Dugort to Westport to give his evidence to the court, he knew the style of questioning to expect and he had thought long and carefully about his replies. There were many theories being advanced about the nature of the injuries Agnes MacDonnell had suffered after she had been knocked unconscious with a blow to the head. The doctor knew of these theories and he was resolute in his mind that he would not compound Mrs MacDonnell's public degradation or do anything to further besmirch the character of his friend. He had practised his evidence and was clear on his approach. There were matters he was not prepared to speak of.

'When I saw Agnes MacDonnell first,' Dr Croly told the magistrate, 'I thought she could not live. I attended her from the night of 6 October until December and during that time her life was in imminent danger.' He found three wounds to the head which, in his view, could have been caused by the kick of a boot. Asked if he thought the injuries he saw could have been caused by horses, Dr Croly replied without hesitation, 'I do not.' The doctor said that Agnes MacDonnell had lost the sight in her right eye, which had been crushed in the attack. 'The wound under the left eye would, in my opinion, be caused by some blunt instrument. The wound on the right eye looked as if it was caused by the kick of a toe of a boot.' He described how the whole of the cartilage of the nose was gone and the nasal bone exposed. 'I was of the opinion,' he said calmly, 'that it was bitten off.'

Mr Louden, on behalf of the accused, questioned Dr Croly about his perceived hostility towards the prisoner. 'Now Doctor, do you remember saying to Mrs MacDonnell that you could put a rope round Lynchehaun's neck?'

'I never did.'

'Did you not say that he was guilty?'

'Never.'

'I believe Lynchehaun reported you several times to the Dispensary Committee?'

'Not to my knowledge.'

'Did he ever report you to the Local Government Board?'

'I could not say he did.'

'Did not the Local Government Board send you down a copy of his letter?'

'No. It was supposed to be a copy of a letter signed by a man named Grealis that was sent down.'

It was when Dr Croly was interrogated about Agnes MacDonnell's most intimate injuries that his body stiffened and his face took on a guarded expression. 'The vagina was torn,' the doctor said in an emotionless voice. 'The right side of it was lacerated and torn. I applied poultices, stupes, and healing lotion to that part.' Dr Croly paused, looked at the ground, then continued. 'On the third day I found pieces of whin bushes embedded deeply down in the tissues of the vagina and I removed them.'

'Go on,' said the magistrate.

'Up to that she complained of intense soreness,' the doctor said. 'This relived her very much.'

All in the room listened keenly. Nobody made a sound as Dr Croly was asked for his view as to how pieces of whin came to be lodged in his patient's vagina.

'In my opinion the kicks which lacerated the vagina forced in the whins.'

Dr Croly may have thought that there would be no more questions on this aspect of his painful evidence but Mr Louden had not finished. 'As to the rupture of the urethra, Dr Croly, will you take it upon yourself to swear that it would be caused by a kick?' Louden asked.

Yes,' the doctor replied, 'I believe it was. I believe she got the kick in those parts. The lining membrane of the vagina was torn.'

'How far internally was the vagina lacerated?' Louden persisted.

'Only inside the internal labia. There were three or four distinct tears in the lining membrane of the vagina. In my opinion the internal injury to the vagina was caused by the nails of the boots forced up into it. The inner labia were not ruptured. The external labia were not ruptured.'

'Would a small boot, such as a woman's boot, or a large boot such as a man's be the more likely to pass through the labia without rupturing them so as to cause the laceration of the vagina?'

Dr Croly may not have been surprised by this line of

interrogation if he had heard of the rumours then circulating that Agnes MacDonnell had been attacked in front of the Valley House, not by James Lynchehaun but by a group of local women. The doctor paused for a moment, pursed his lips, then answered in a steely voice: 'I would say that any boot would cause it owing to the laceration of the perineum; a small boot would pass easier than a large one.'

Mr Louden then asked a question that took everybody in the courtroom by surprise: 'The biting of the nose and lip is a very common offence by a woman against a woman on account of jealousy. It is, I believe, a common offence in London?'

The doctor knew that this was a tactic to divert attention away from the prisoner. He replied that he was not aware personally of what the defence had suggested. He had never come across such a thing.

Finally, before concluding his evidence, Dr Croly was pressed further on an issue that was in everybody's mind in the court. 'Can you, as the result of your examination, say whether this woman was outraged or not?' asked Mr Louden.

Dr Croly had his reply ready. He would not deviate from it. He answered in a clear voice, 'I will not say, sir.'

Some time after the taking of the preliminary testimonies in Westport, Dr Croly notified the Crown Solicitor that Agnes MacDonnell would not be in a condition to attend as a witness at the spring Assizes. The Crown then applied for, and received, a postponement of the full hearing in the case to the summer Assizes in Castlebar Court where, for the first time since the events of the previous October, Agnes MacDonnell and James Lynchehaun would come face to face.

10

Queen v Lynchehaun
15 July 1895 – The Morning

There was a hard cold feel to the seats in Castlebar Court where the light from the high windows did not reach. The room smelled of French polish, damp serge and tobacco. There was the scrape of boots on timber floors as people crowded in from where they had waited outside in the court portico in the shade of six high granite colonnades. Summer was in the air on the town's mall in front of the courtroom, where crows cawed noisily and spattered white droppings on oak branches and on freshly-cut grass. It was easy to pick out the Achill inhabitants, their skin tinged tan and crimson from the island sun and winds, their faces furrowed with fine cracks. People piled into the room, settled into their seats and waited with the expectancy of an audience eager for the curtain to rise on a drama performance.

When they lifted their heads the courtroom occupants faced the large exhibit of a map of the Valley House crime scene carrying the bold caption:

Queen v Lynchehaun
G. K. Dixon, Surveyor
16 March 1895

The map showed the waters of Blacksod Bay to the north in a bright sky-blue colour; the Valley House and nearby cottages in black rectangular blocks; the roadways leading from the big house to Valley crossroads and west to Dugort in orange-brown lines. It was unlikely, from where they sat, that those in attendance could see the three cerise blobs on the map, close to the front of the Valley House, indicating the location where Agnes MacDonnell's blood-spattered body had been found. In the lower right-hand corner of the parchment the house of 'James Lynchehaun – Grocer' was indicated, set back from the roadway connecting the townlands of Valley and Dugort. Nearby, on a table, was a wooden model of the Valley House and stables prepared by Mr Lindsey, Castlebar. Map and model would be used in the coming hours and days to indicate homes of witnesses, the areas where fires blazed on the night of 6 October, and the path taken to carry Agnes MacDonnell's broken body to Michael Gallagher's home. The exhibit mapped a night of horror and savagery.

That morning a large number of Achill islanders had travelled from Achill to Castlebar by train. The railway line to Achill had finally opened two months earlier on 13 May in time for the summer tourist season, and *The Irish Times* extolled the delights that awaited the rail traveller to the West and to the island which they hailed as the 'The British Madeira':

> This further opening up of Achill to tourists allowed writers to wax lyrical on the beauties of nature which awaited rail travellers. In previous years many English and American travellers have visited these islands during the summer and autumn seasons, and not a few of them have placed on record their opinion that the sight of the sun sinking in majesty on the horizon of the Atlantic, as seen from these parts, is one such as could not be witnessed save on the West Coast of Ireland, and nowhere even there so grandly as from the islands in Clew and Blacksod Bays. The scenery on the whole seaboard from Mayo to Clare is simply majestic and grand, and the opening of the extension line to Achill Sound, within a couple of hundred yards of Achill Island, will undoubtedly give a

most desirable impetus to tourist development in the hitherto neglected but beautiful West.

Already, the weekend excursion trains of the Midland Great Western Railway were thronged with daytrippers to Achill where every available vehicle was pressed into service to take the visitors around the island. John Sheridan had put on a horse and coach service from Achill Sound to the Slievemore Hotel in Dugort. The Railway Company had produced a fine handbook on Achill's attractions: Dooega Head; the magnificent Keel Strand, 'a two-mile stretch of sand, such as would make the fortune of a watering-place in England'; the striking Cathedral Rocks; the former lodge of the infamous Captain Boycott; the superb spectacle of Croaghaun Mountain. The handbook also contained a strange piece of information titled 'An Achill Cabin':

> Dooagh is a group of funny little cabins that, huddled together below the road, constitutes the hamlet. The interior of a typical Achill cabin must be seen. Some of them are scrupulously tidy as they are quaint, and we have drunk as good tea and eaten as good butter and 'soda-cake' (bread) in them as the most fastidious guest could desire. The sleeping arrangements are often extraordinary, and it speaks volumes for the air of Dooagh that it imparts enough vigour by day to render the people proof against asphyxiation by night.

If tourists and newspaper readers were being treated to the physical delights and wonders of Achill, an altogether different image of the island was about to be projected as the trial of James Lynchehaun got under way in Castlebar. With the early sun at the islanders' backs, the walk from the railway station to the court was less than ten minutes. They passed the time until the court opened by taking a stroll around Castlebar's Mall, past Daly's Hotel where Michael Davitt had started the Irish National Land League a decade and a half earlier, then left by the low Christian Fellowship Church founded by John

Wesley, past the Church of Ireland and the police barrack, before returning to the court building.

Present in the courtroom for James Lynchehaun's trial was Brother Paul Carney who had travelled the couple of miles from Errew Monastery on the outskirts of Castlebar. He had been transferred to Errew just three months earlier, at the end of March, distraught at having to leave the island where he had served for a quarter of a century. The grumblings against him had intensified, and he wrote in his journals that 'some ill-disposed person' had written to the Archbishop of Tuam, urging his removal from the island. It is likely that the Valley House attack hastened his departure given his known association with James Lynchehaun. At least his posting to Errew had the advantage of proximity to Castlebar, allowing him to attend the trial each day.

All waited expectantly in the courtroom. The only sounds were an occasional cough or clearing of a throat, some whispers from the officials at the front of the room, and muffled sounds from the Mall outside. Every now and then, somebody nudged the person next to them, indicating with a head movement where James Lynchehaun's wife sat quietly in a side box of the court with her child. The stillness was broken when everybody rose to their feet as Mr Justice Gibson made his way to the bench.

The legal teams were lined up: The MacDermott (Hugh Hyacinth O'Rorke MacDermott), Attorney General for Ireland, would take the lead for the Crown, his presence indicating the importance which the authorities laid on a conviction. Dr Falconer took the lead for the Defence, assisted by J. J. Louden. The court clock showed the time as eleven o'clock. Turning to The MacDermott, Justice Gibson formally put the question, 'Are you ready to proceed with the trial of the accused man, James Lynchehaun?'

'Yes, my Lord.'

'Let the prisoner come forward.'

All eyes turned in the direction of the accused as he stepped into the dock. Lynchehaun had put on weight and had grown a full beard since his rearrest in January. He was neatly dressed and appeared in good health. He moved without flinching and one newspaper reported that 'his calm, soft-featured countenance created an impression decidedly in his favour.' Another account described the prisoner as 'powerfully built, a rather handsome man' who carried 'a hint of a half-smile on his face'.

The charges against James Lynchehaun were formally read to the court:

> That on 6 October, 1894, he feloniously and unlawfully wounded Mrs Agnes MacDonnell with intent to kill and murder;
> That he caused her bodily harm with the same intention;
> That he feloniously and unlawfully did wound her with intent to disfigure and maim;
> That he feloniously and unlawfully did wound her with intent to do grievous bodily harm;
> That he did wound with intent to commit actual bodily harm.

'What is your plea to these charges?' Justice Gibson asked.

'Not guilty,' James Lynchehaun replied in a clear voice as a murmur spread through the room.

The swearing-in of the jury followed and took a considerable time as the defence exercised their full right to challenge. When they were sworn, His Lordship turned to address the jurors: 'After the prisoner is given in charge you can have no connection with the outer world. You might like to write home to your friends. You had better assume you will be out two nights and I think it would be well for you to write home to your wives.' This suggestion caused some laughter. 'This case is likely to take three days,' the Justice continued, 'and you will not be discharged until Wednesday morning. You will be provided with ink and paper and with the time to write your letters. I will see to it that your notes are posted, or sent by hand, as you wish.'

It was agreed between the Crown and the Defence that witnesses should not be present in court during the hearing of the evidence. His Lordship then directed that all witnesses should retire until called upon. The proceedings proper were about to commence. The MacDermott gathered his papers, rose to full height, took a deep breath, and proceeded to set out the case for the prosecution. He would be on his feet for an hour and a half in the warm, clammy courtroom, and started by directing his comments to the jury: 'You will hear evidence as various and as conclusive as ever was addressed to the intelligence and conscience of a jury, that will place the guilt of the prisoner at the bar beyond any doubt whatsoever. It is my solemn duty to set out the facts of the case against the prisoner James Lynchehaun, facts which the Crown will conclusively prove in the evidence it will bring before this court.'

The MacDermott continued to speak in the hushed room where the shouts of children, and the clatter of carriage wheels, filtered faintly through the court windows. 'James Lynchehaun is not being tried on the capital offence of murder, which might have been the case. Providence, in mercy to the woman who was attacked − a mercy which has fallen indirectly on the prisoner himself − has saved him from completing the crime which undoubtedly the evidence shows he intended to commit that night.' He explained that before drawing the court's attention to the evidence applying to the case, he wished to describe the relative positions of Agnes MacDonnell, the attacked woman, and the prisoner James Lynchehaun, for it was undoubtedly a relationship of some hostility. Newspaper reporters in the court scribbled their notes, some drawing sketches of the prisoner and the jurors.

Agnes MacDonnell, said The MacDermott, was the wife of an Irish barrister resident in London. She had acquired the Valley House estate and moved regularly between her two homes. 'She occasionally came and occasionally went,' he said.

Some time before 6 October her housekeeper died and Mrs MacDonnell consequently came to take charge of the house. When she got this property her first agent was a Mr Salt; secondly she had an agent named Sweeney; thirdly, she had an agent for three   months − not as an agent but rather as an under-agent and steward – and that man was Lynchehaun, the prisoner at the bar. He described himself as James Lynchehaun, grocer, because in one of two houses he held from this lady, he carried on with some success a grocery business. In addition to the two houses he had a small farm which he purchased from a man named Burke and that was known as 'The Scraw'.

The pair had disagreed, The MacDermott told the court, and Agnes MacDonnell served James Lynchehaun with a notice to quit the cottage where he carried on his grocery business, and she also sought to determine the legality of his tenancy of the 'The Scraw'. 'Two notices to quit were served,' he said, 'but she did not succeed because of some errors in service, but a third notice was properly serviced on 19 September 1894, six or seven days before the night on which this attack was made on Mrs MacDonnell.'

The MacDermott then faced the jury and put the question: was there anyone in the world who had a grievance to avenge or a loss to avert more than this man, James Lynchehaun, her dismissed servant from whom she was taking his house and land? What clearer evidence was there of the distance he would go to injure her than the letters – in the prisoner's handwriting – sent to the Collector of Inland revenue in Galway with complaints about unstamped receipts by Agnes MacDonnell?

At this point The MacDermott's address was interrupted by the Foreman of the Grand Jury who approached the bench and handed Justice Gibson the several bills referred to. The prisoner Lynchehaun had listened attentively to The MacDermott, occasionally shuffling his feet or shrugging his shoulders. At one point during the speech he had raised his eyebrows and cast an incredulous smile in the direction of the jury.

The MacDermott warmed to his task. He came to the events of 6 October and he undertook, he said, to convince them, the members of the jury, that James Lynchehaun alone could be the author of the wounds and injuries inflicted on Agnes MacDonnell. He approached the table where the wooden model of Valley House lay and pointed out several buildings in the yard: the entrance gates, the places where the horses were stabled and, in a corner of the yard, the place where a large barrel of petroleum had been stored. 'About a quarter after eight,' The MacDermott continued, 'Mrs MacDonnell, being then in bed, was roused by a knock at the door and looking out the window saw the shed in flames. Please remember that the gate was locked and any person who came in by the back door must have come by some illegitimate means. To her terror, Agnes MacDonnell saw not only the flames outside but, what she would have feared more than the flames, she saw James Lynchehaun.

'The prisoner asked Mrs MacDonnell for the keys of the shed to let out the horses. He therefore drew her out of the place of comparative security; he drew her out into the yard and, having let the horses out, he attempted to push her into the fire. That story is corroborated by the fact that, from her knees to her ankles, she was scorched all over.' This part of the evidence was confirmed, The MacDermott argued, by the testimony of Mary Gallagher, a key prosecution witness since she was the only person, apart from the official witnesses and Mrs MacDonnell's employees, who had testified against the accused. 'A young girl named Mary Gallagher,' he told the court, 'swung the wagon door open, went into the yard and there saw the man, Lynchehaun, with his arms around the woman and she saw him trying to force her towards the flames with considerable force. She thought at first he might be trying to save her, but the more she looked, the more she saw the real intention of Lynchehaun. After Agnes MacDonnell escaped to her house, she went in the kitchen door and barred it inside and Mary Gallagher induced her to open it. She later came out carrying a little fox terrier and her cloak. The terrified woman left her yard and house and disappeared from sight.'

This, the barrister said, was only the start of the woman's torment at the hands of the accused as he had yet to deal with the gross injuries that were inflicted upon her in another place. The terrified woman went around to the front of the house and made in the direction of the haystack. 'She did not remain there long when she made up her mind to return to the house. When she rose to return James Lynchehaun came up and hit her a violent blow upon the head which dashed the light out of her eyes, deprived her of consciousness and stretched her out on the grass.'

All in the courtroom waited. What would The MacDermott say next? All over Achill they had talked about what Lynchehaun had, or had not, done to Agnes MacDonnell that October night. The views and speculations were many and varied. They held their breath as The MacDermott stretched to full height before continuing: 'This man was not satisfied, however, with the blow he struck that reduced the unfortunate woman to unconsciousness. He afterwards maltreated her in the most shocking manner. The lower part of her person and her private parts were broken.' The MacDermott's voice rose as he faced the jury: 'Perhaps, in all the history of human escapes, there is nothing more wonderful − almost a resurrection of life − than the escape of Agnes MacDonnell that night. And this is the man for whom, they were told, there was some sympathy on the island of Achill!'

At this point the prisoner lifted his head and shouted, 'Lies, lies,' before Justice Gibson cracked his anvil and rasped, 'Silence in the court. The prisoner shall not speak.' The Justice reminded the constables present that order must be maintained. He would not allow the proceedings of the court to be disrupted again.

The MacDermott changed tack, turning to what he deemed an attempt by the accused to intimidate Mary Gallagher, a crucial witness for the prosecution. 'There will be evidence,' he said, 'that immediately after this vicious crime, the prisoner tried to silence the evidence which he knew would be brought against him. He was found at the house of Mary Gallagher who had come upon him in the yard trying to pitch Mrs MacDonnell into the flames. He came to her house and told her, "You are the only person who can free me." When she answered that others had seen him as well as her, he replied, "No one will tell on me but you; you are the only one can free me." She said to him, "I am the one that can guilty you."' This, argued The MacDermott, was a clear attempt by the accused to silence the evidence, and he would ask the jury to consider whether this indicated guilt or innocence. It was up to them to decide.

The MacDermott next turned his attention to the fire at the Valley House which, on the basis of the evidence, was set ablaze at about half past one in the morning and started in Mrs

MacDonnell's own bedroom on the ground floor. The person who set fire to the main house, he argued, had entered by the pantry window. There was proof that it was the prisoner at the bar who had done this. First, they had him tracked by a trail of blood; secondly, in the debris of the lady's room were found the keys which, on the night in question, had been given to Lynchehaun to open the stables. 'Who carried the keys there?' The MacDermott asked. 'Lynchehaun. Who dropped the keys there? Lynchehaun. Who went in the pantry window? It was the same blood-stained ruffian, bent on general destruction and conflagration. There is no other explanation.'

The case for the Crown was almost complete. The MacDermott adopted a new tone – that of the incredulous counsel who wondered what plea could possibly be proffered against such overwhelming evidence. He failed utterly to see what form of defence could be suggested. Would witnesses be called to prove that the injuries to Mrs MacDonnell were inflicted by the horses, the Gallaghers, or the McGintys; or that the prisoner was not there at all when the woman was pushed into the flames; or that he came for the first time when he was found bloody and bleeding in the yard? He was at a loss to conceive of any direction from which a defence could come that the prisoner had not destroyed by his own admission.

The MacDermott concluded his address with a powerful appeal: 'No jury has ever had an easier or less difficult task to discharge then you have in this case. You are trying a man who attacked a defenceless woman who had the confidence of the Irish peasantry that she lived unprotected amongst them, and you have a man who inflicted unspeakable injuries on a woman who was once his employer. If there ever was a case that touched the conscience of a jury, sworn to do justice, surely it is the case before you, members of the jury.'

He sat down, pleased with his work. The court adjourned for lunch and the crowd spilled out into the summer sunshine on Castlebar Mall. They would be back. Nobody wanted to miss the testimony of Agnes MacDonnell when she faced her assailant.

11

That is the Man!
15–17 July 1895

Agnes MacDonnell gripped the side of her skirt as she ascended the steps. A constable held her other hand until she had steadied herself in the witness box. She stood with an erect carriage, head high. The cream-grey July light fell on the chocolate-coloured wood panelling in the courtroom. Otherwise, the room was saturated with grey and black clothes, apart from an occasional dash of colour from a woman's skirt or kerchief. Every eye turned in Agnes MacDonnell's direction, each person straining to peer through the netted veil that concealed her face. But it was impossible to catch any glimpse of her red-brown hair, or of the pale skin that she had always rouged in public. The room was quiet. The shuffling of feet, the coughing, and the whispers had all ceased once she entered the high-ceilinged room. She hadn't been seen in public since before the Valley House attack and Agnes MacDonnell's demeanour and evidence in court would crystallise opinions and views about her. Feelings oscillated across a range of emotions: pity and sympathy at her horrific injuries; shock and resentment at her treatment of her tenants; awe at her determination and resolve; some surprise at the extent of her grasping and acquisitive nature.

Agnes MacDonnell smoothed her skirt and waited. She did not look at the man seated diagonally across from her, but she surely sensed him and her body must have tensed and exuded the scent of fear in his presence. James Lynchehaun tilted his head and eyed the woman keenly. Not a muscle in his face moved, except for his eyes which blinked and darted about continuously. He took in the full scene, no doubt picking out friends and neighbours and old enemies in the court. His skin was pale from six months' incarceration away from the Atlantic winds and island sun of Achill, and he watched the proceedings with what appeared to be the suggestion of a leer on his face.

The MacDermott rose heavily from his seat. On behalf of the Crown he would lead the main witness, step by painful step, through the events of the night of 6 October 1894. When Agnes MacDonnell began to answer the questions put to her, she did so at first in a low, weak voice with traces of an English accent. 'My work people stayed with me until everything was locked up that night,' she started. 'I had put broken bottles on the yard wall to stop trespassers.' Gradually her speech grew stronger and more distinct. 'The small door to the yard was barred with iron. I locked the kitchen door and then I locked and barred a door just inside.' She was clear in her mind that she had never had trouble of any sort with her work people. They had always made sure that her horses were looked after and that everything was secure before they left for home. Her passion for horses came through strongly – the animals were, it appeared, her closest companions. 'I had fifteen horses altogether that night. My mare, Lady Jane, was fastened in a field at the back of the house.'

The MacDermott was patient. Carefully, he constructed the setting for the nocturnal felony, allowing a picture to form in the jury's mind of a vulnerable and defenceless woman going about her evening business. 'You heard a knock,' he asked, 'you were surprised at this, were you not?'

'I was occupying a little bedroom on the ground floor. When I heard the knocking I put a large coat on that covered me all over.' There was a faint noise, that could have been a snigger from somewhere in the court. 'I saw Lynchehaun standing outside the front door. It was then that I saw that the stables were on fire from end to end.'

'What kind of night was it?'

'It was a calm night. There was a little wind but not very much.'

'What did he say to you when you opened the door?'

'He said, "Give me the keys. I want to save those horses." I went into the passage and took down the keys. The keys to the gate were tied together and the stable key was separate. I gave him the two sets of keys.'

A few people in the room turned sideways with hands raised to their mouths, no doubt giving their verdict on the woman's evidence. A keen observer might have singled out Agnes MacDonnell's tenants in the room from their weather-beaten faces, and the tight unsympathetic set of their mouths as they watched the veiled witness.

'I stepped a little outside then,' she said, 'and he went and opened the wagon door that was on wheels. I watched him go into the stables. He was there for a good while. Then the horses rushed out through the wagon door, out of the yard on to the grass outside.'

'Go on,' The MacDermott encouraged.

'Then I turned to go back into the house. But he caught hold of me. He dragged me into the burning stables – I think it was the middle one. He tried to force me into the corner where the flames were fiercest. My legs were badly burned from the fire. I was burned from my knees down to my ankles.'

'What happened then?' The MacDermott asked.

Agnes MacDonnell lifted her arms and positioned a hand on either side of her neck, outside the dark veil. Her voice was shrill when she spoke. 'He tried to strangle me,' she said, holding her splayed fingers to her neck. 'I could feel the marks of his fingers on my throat for many months after.'

People shuffled in their chairs. The tension in the stuffy room was beginning to reek with the tang of clammy flesh. The MacDermott waited until he had the full attention of the court and the jury for his next question. He spoke in a solemn voice. 'Now, Mrs MacDonnell, I want to ask you if you have any doubt in your mind as to the identity of the man who attacked you?'

Agnes MacDonnell did not reply immediately. She appeared unable to speak.

The MacDermott tried again. 'Is that the man?' he asked, pointing with his index finger in the direction of the prisoner.

For the first time since she had entered the court, Agnes MacDonnell turned in the direction of the prisoner. She stretched out her arm, faced him through her veil and answered in a fierce voice that echoed through the courtroom: 'That is the man!'

It was some minutes before Justice Gibson restored order to allow Agnes MacDonnell to continue. 'I got away and I think the girl came to my assistance. When I got away from this man, I saw the women there. I remember telling them to go to the lake to get water to put out the fire. I believe after I got away from Lynchehaun I must have gone back to the house because my dog — a fox-terrier — was in the bedroom and could not possibly have got out unless I let him out.' She then went to the haystacks, she said, to look around to see if any of her servants were coming to her assistance. 'I stood there to recover my breath. I made up my mind to return to the house and dress myself and fetch the servants. I saw a man and when he came up to me I saw it was Lynchehaun. He had something in his hand but I could not possibly say what it was. It was a dark night and there was no moon.'

His Lordship intervened to ask, 'When you saw him coming, did you say anything?'

'No. I did not say a word. He gave me a tremendous blow on the head and I felt as if I was shot into a thousand pieces — just on the back of the head. I don't remember anything that happened after that.'

Did she have any doubt, asked The MacDermott, as to who had hit her on this occasion?

'Certainly not. There was no man but Lynchehaun around the place. I am positive it was Lynchehaun. Although it was dark you could see distinctly anything near. He did not appear, as he came towards me, as if he wanted to see me. I recognised him before he came to me and just as he had passed me — he was not a foot past me when he struck me. For days afterwards I think I was only conscious for a short period but I made no mistake about my assailant.'

His Lordship again interrupted to ask the witness if she had good eyesight before the occurrence that night. It was as if he had decided to puncture the proceedings at intervals with studied attempts to recall the court to the severity of the woman's injuries.

Agnes MacDonnell reached up, as though ensuring that her veil was in place. She spoke slowly, as if she had already rehearsed her reply. 'I had my Lord,' she said. 'One eye was burst in my head that night. An eminent oculist who attended me has said that I will never recover full sight in the other.'

For Agnes MacDonnell the easiest part of her testimony was over and she would now face a much tougher, and more hostile, interrogation by Dr Falconer on behalf of the defence. This cross-examination would draw out character traits of the woman's personality which had not been evident in the court to that point.

Dr Falconer reminded Agnes MacDonnell of the testimony she had given immediately after the Valley House assault and arson. 'Did you say on the 6th and 11th October to the magistrate, "I gave him the keys and he went into the stables. I then went over to the burning premises. I was so startled to find him in the yard and so convinced it was he did it, I said something to him and he said is that your gratitude to the man who came to save your horses! And he then put his arm round my waist and then I was in the midst of the flames and he tried to force me into them."'

'I have no recollection of that,' Agnes MacDonnell replied. 'I must have said what is there. The wonder is that I was able to make a statement at all after what happened to me.'

'You say that on 6 October, you did not see any other man except Lynchehaun?'

'No, I did not.'

'Except Lynchehaun?'

'I did not.'

'Did you not say that you looked up and down to see if there was any other man?'

'There was no other man at all.'

'And then when you were struck you assumed that he was the only man could strike you?'

'I know it was Lynchehaun because I saw him strike me.'

'Did you say this person that struck you was not coming towards you?'

'Yes.'

'Did you ever say that he was not coming directly towards you?'

'I decline to answer your impertinent question.'

Dr Falconer repeated his query before Justice Gibson interceded once more in favour of the witness: 'I think what the lady says is quite right, that you are impertinent to her.'

'But did you not say, Mrs MacDonnell, that he was not coming towards you?' Dr Falconer persevered. 'Did you not say that?'

'I will tell you what I said. That he was dodging in and out of the whin bushes on the way down to the haystack and that he was walking like a person who did not wish to be seen. He was almost abreast of me but was about a foot behind. I cannot tell you more plainly than that.' Agnes MacDonnell spat out the words at Dr Falconer.

'When you went into the house after being in the flames, why did you not put on some articles of dress?'

'I don't think, after rushing from the shocking burning, that I was in a condition to go coolly into my bedroom and dress with my leg burning from the knee to the ankle.'

Dr Falconer then turned to the sensitive issue of landlord-tenant relations. 'Have you had notices served on a great number of your tenants, Mrs MacDonnell?'

It was a question that she would have been prepared for. 'I have not,' she replied without hesitation. 'I have fifty-two tenants altogether. I summoned some tenants for possession of the Sandybanks and when they were told they had no right to it, I had no further trouble with them. When my housekeeper,

Bridget Padden, got married to Johnny Gallagher, I objected to their living in the Valley House because they did not ask my permission. That was all.'

'In an early deposition you said you had this money, £88 in gold, £3 in notes, and silver in the house.'

'That statement was perfectly accurate, whenever made. I was sufficiently recovered in my faculties to know what money I had.'

'Did you ever tell Miss FitzGerald, your nurse, that whoever struck you was not Lynchehaun?'

'No. I never said anything of the kind to her or to any other person. I could not say such a thing, for it would not be true. The moment he struck me, I knew it was Lynchehaun.'

'Can you say, Mrs MacDonnell, whether, when you had the misfortune to be in the condition you were in, police constables were talking to you about this case?'

Agnes MacDonnell appeared to detect an unpleasant nuance in this question, for her answer was defensive: 'Not one of them came near me. How dare they come into my bedroom to do any such thing!'

Dr Falconer concluded his examination. 'That will be all.'

A constable helped Mrs MacDonnell from the stand. She turned to walk from the court without a further glance at the accused. Heads turned to follow her progress through the door until she was gone. The tension in the room slackened perceptibly.

The prosecution case relied heavily on Mary Gallagher's testimony that James Lynchehaun attempted to force Agnes MacDonnell into the flames at the Valley House, and secondly, on Agnes MacDonnell's identification of Lynchehaun as the person who afterwards attacked her. It was, therefore, not surprising that Mary Gallagher was subjected to an arduous cross-examination by J. J. Louden for the defence.

'The fire was in the yard?' Mr Louden asked her.

'It was in the stables in the yard,' Mary Gallagher replied.

'When you entered the wicket, where were all these people?'

'I don't know. It was not at them I was looking.'

'What were you looking at?'

'I was looking at the fire.'

You told us of Lynchehaun having his arms round Mrs MacDonnell's waist. What clothes did she have on her at the time?

'Her nightdress.'

'Upon that occasion Lynchehaun did not commit any violence upon Mrs MacDonnell except to hold her round the waist?'

'Well, he had hold of her and brought her very close to the fire.'

'After she came out of that stable with you was her chemise scorched in any way?'

'I don't know, sir.'

'You saw no marks of burning on the lady's chemise?'

'Well, no sir, I did not look.'

'Mrs MacDonnell walked quietly with you from the stable to her own house?'

'She did not.'

'Didn't you say you took her out of the stable?'

'I did but I didn't go to the house door with her.'

'From the time she left the stable with you up to the time she reached her own house did Lynchehaun attempt to molest her?'

'No, sir.'

'Why did you tell Mrs MacDonnell to come out of the house? What did you want her out for and she in her nightdress?'

'Well, because I thought she was frightened when she seen the way the stables was being burned, and I seen the way she was talking to James Lynchehaun.'

'Would she not have been safer inside than outside her house? Was she not coming out to almost certain death?'

The MacDermott objected to this line of questioning.

His Lordship sustained the objection. Mr Louden's insinuation was, he said, one of the most shocking he had heard.

'Having asked her to come out of her house why did you not speak to her when she came out?' Mr Louden then asked Mary Gallagher.

'Well, sir, she was at the people then and I thought she was all right.'

'Where did you go to from the crowd at the gate?'

'I went home, sir.'

'And I take it you did not see James Lynchehaun, the defendant, until you saw him in your own house that night?'

'No, sir.'

Mary Gallagher left the stand. Her clear testimony to the court would prove decisive. When Dr Falconer rose to summarise the case for the defence he used, to clever effect, the arguments put earlier by the Crown counsel. 'The MacDermott,' he started with feigned deference, 'that great criminal lawyer, skilled in prosecuting and trained in all the arts and forensic ability to wind the web of evidence to prove guilt around the prisoner – that lawyer has recommended to the jury that if they have any reasonable doubt about the man's guilt, then they should give him the benefit of it. This was a dreadful crime. The indignation of the civilised world has been aroused at it. But you should not allow your indignation to convict the prisoner in the dock without the clearest proof.'

With regard to the fire, Dr Falconer said, the defence case was that the witness was not in the flames at all because the poor lady would have got greater burns if she was. The prisoner's case was that he tried to take Mrs MacDonnell out of the flames instead of trying to put her into them. If Lynchehaun was the guilty ruffian the Crown represented him to be, why did he go and rap at Mrs MacDonnell's door and call her attention to the fire?

'Agnes MacDonnell was undoubtedly in the middle of the burning,' Dr Falconer argued, 'when she went out to see where the horses were and what James Lynchehaun was doing. Mary Gallagher told them he was struggling with her for twenty minutes. Did they believe that? Did they believe that powerful man would not have succeeded in his purpose sooner if he so desired it? Agnes MacDonnell was quite incapable of giving one scintilla of evidence or of making a statement they could rely on.

His argument was that when Mrs MacDonnell went from the wagon door to the haystack it was quite dark. She was absolutely dazed and did not know what she was doing. He suggested that the reason she said that she saw Lynchehaun was that she was after having an interview with him, a struggle if they liked with regard to the fire, and she thought that everything was Lynchehaun in her fright. Dr Falconer put it to the jury that a woman in her condition, and in the darkness of the night, could not tell them with any confidence who it was that struck her. 'Somebody struck the woman, but there was not a single witness but the lady herself to say that Lynchehaun was in the lawn when Mrs MacDonnell was there. I put it to you that it is not an obligation of the prisoner to prove who committed this crime; it is the duty of the Crown to prove that no person but the prisoner could have committed it.' He added that, in his view, it would have been far better had Mrs MacDonnell remained in her house when she got back in and locked the door.

As for the fire at the big house later that night, said Dr Falconer, there was clear evidence that from the time Mrs MacDonnell was brought to Gallagher's house, Lynchehaun remained there under police supervision and could not, therefore, have set the Valley House on fire. If the police were guilty of negligence or breach of duty in this case, was James Lynchehaun to suffer as a result? He reminded the jury that there were others who had infinitely greater motives for the crime committed that night than the prisoner. 'Everybody in this court has nothing but pity for Agnes MacDonnell. It is most desirable that the outrage committed should not go unpunished. But, it will be a sorry affair indeed if a person is convicted without sufficient evidence.'

Dr Falconer concluded his case for the defence with a powerful plea to the jury: 'The prisoner does not ask for mercy, for if the man is guilty, he does not deserve mercy at the hands of justice. Foul as was the outrage committed, a far worse outrage will be committed on society if, for the sake of clearing the country of a stain, you make yourselves a party to committing a man without sufficient evidence. The law does not act as an avenger.' He struck his papers down on the bench and resumed his seat.

At a quarter to six on Wednesday evening Mr Justice Gibson proceeded to sum up the case he had heard, turning first to address sombre words at the jury: 'I have no doubt that you will base your verdict on the evidence you have heard sworn in this court and upon nothing else.' The Justice's summing-up address would take two hours during which time he spoke in a strong, forceful voice, only occasionally pausing to sip some water. He was, he said, in no doubt as to the significance of the indictment presented to the court: 'This is the most unpleasant and revolting case that it has ever been my duty to hear and I do not exaggerate when I say that some of the details which I heard have made me sick. Many witnesses have been examined and it requires a good deal of attention and effort of memory to recall all the testimony that has been given.'

The Justice dealt first with the issue of motive for the Valley House crime. Mrs MacDonnell was, he said, a lady of somewhat peculiar or independent character but her dealings with her tenants had not been unhappy. 'Sometimes crimes are motiveless and nobody could recognise in this case any motive that could justify the abominable savagery with which Mrs Agnes MacDonnell was treated. It was nothing short of a miracle of the Almighty that this brave lady's life was saved to give testimony in this court.'

Justice Gibson next turned to some matters raised by the evidence heard by the court. 'The question arises as to how Lynchehaun, who was quarrelling with this woman, and who lived half a mile away from her, went up to move the horses of this woman he did not like. How had he got into the yard when the whole place was locked up?' This was a question the jury needed to consider. He wished, he said, to draw the jury's attention to another pertinent piece of evidence, which was Agnes MacDonnell's statement of the night of 6 October. 'In none of these statements, nor up to the 11th October, did Mrs MacDonnell refer to the injuries done outside the yard. It is for you, the jury, to say whether at that time her mind was still recovering from the physical shock and revulsion at what had happened to her.'

In the course of his address his Lordship made reference several times to District Inspector Rainsford, perhaps conscious of the criticism which the police officer had attracted during the Dugort Inquiry. In his view, Justice Gibson said, the Inspector had, in the conduct of the case, exhibited high qualities which entitled him to promotion in his profession. 'I believe him to be a most capable and excellent officer.'

His Lordship turned to the jury at the conclusion of his address. 'This is a shocking case. It is necessary to preserve all one's coolness and manhood in trying a case like the present one. You are asked to do nothing but justice. Are you satisfied upon the evidence that the prisoner is guilty? If you are, no man ever deserved conviction more. On the other hand, if you are not satisfied of the prisoner's guilt, you are bound to acquit him. The responsibility for your verdict is yours and yours alone.'

The issue paper was handed up at half past seven in a tense, hot courtroom. Most of those present remained in their seats. They would not miss the final act in this court drama.

The jury returned after an absence of three-quarters of an hour. When they were settled in their seats, Justice Gibson put the question, 'What is your verdict?'

The spokesman for the jury rose to his feet. The accused looked on and appeared unperturbed. The seconds ticked by in the silent room. The spokesman read out the jury's verdict: 'Guilty – on the first two counts.'

A hum of conversation broke out in the room. His Lordship hammered his gravel smartly, calling the court to order. The prisoner heard the verdict without any apparent change of expression. However, those closest to him observed a tremor in his hands.

Justice Gibson turned to James Lynchehaun and asked, 'Have you anything to say as to why sentence should not be passed upon you?'

Lynchehaun replied, 'No, my Lord. But there was some difference in the evidence as to when the McGintys and Gallagher came into the yard. There was a discrepancy there my Lord.'

His Lordship made no reply to this comment. He proceeded to pass sentence. 'James Lynchehaun, you have been convicted after a spirited and able defence by counsel – a gallant defence, I may say, in a hopeless case. No one who has heard the evidence in this court could have a shadow of doubt of your guilt. It is by a miracle of the Almighty that you are not now in the dock convicted of murder and that I am not now imposing a sentence that would send you a month hence to a felon's grave. The jury could find no other verdict without being false to their oaths. An able man, you might have attained brilliant success for yourself.'

It was at this point that the prisoner lost his composure. He interrupted Justice Gibson in a cracked voice, 'I am in the prime of my life, my Lord. I am only in the prime of my life. Have mercy on me. Have mercy on me.'

His Lordship shook his head. 'I pity you from the bottom of my heart but I can pass but one sentence. Your crime is murder, except for the accident that by a merciful intervention of providence this woman was endowed with splendid courage and vitality, though, poor wreck, she will live for a few and miserable years. The sentence of the court is penal servitude for life. God be merciful to you James Lynchehaun and soften your heart.'

The court rose. Lynchehaun's wife and child rushed towards the convicted man and clung to him, wailing loudly. James Lynchehaun was then escorted from the room. The crowd pressed through the doors into the evening sunshine. The Achill islanders returned to their homes.

Part 2

12

Convict Escape

September 1902

Agnes MacDonnell tilted her head and looked skywards through her veil at the towering Church of Our Lady of the Holy Rosary in Castlebar. It must have seemed to her as if the construction work on the ecclesiastical building over the previous seven years had mirrored her own project in rebuilding the Valley House. Each time she had travelled over and back to Castlebar the clang of the stonemasons' chisels on limestone and the hammering of nails on timber and slate rang out across the town. When she passed by she could see the horses and carts pull their loads of stone up steep ramps as pulleys hoisted building materials through the tall scaffolding.

She had heard the talk back in Achill about the Bunnacurry monk with the crimson cheeks who had travelled across America raising funds for the Castlebar Church with his guile and free-flowing words. It was the same monk who had associated with James Lynchehaun and she was more than pleased when she heard from the Rector that the friar had been transferred out of Achill shortly before Lynchehaun's conviction. She hoped he would not return. The building work on Castlebar Church was now complete. It was a year since Bishop McEvilly presided at the Pontifical High Mass to mark the formal dedication when 200 dignitaries dined in the Town Hall, which had been decorated with flags and colour streamers. She had been surprised to read the newspaper reports of the extravagance of the occasion where the guests had dined on turbot, veal cutlets, roast duck and beef, washed down with the finest wines, port and whiskey.

At last, Agnes MacDonnell was back living in her home, happy to have moved out of the cramped conditions at the gate lodge before the winter set in. She had overseen the rebuilding work on her own, following the death of her husband just a few years after the Valley House destruction. Each day she rose early, instructed her employees in their tasks on the estate, oversaw every detail of the work on her house, and rode her mare on the Sandybanks in the afternoon. Things were almost back to the way they had been at the Valley House, with just the last of the plastering work to be completed. But the two workmen she had employed, Thomas Brown and Thomas Duffy, were giving her a hard time. Their work was shoddy and some of the plaster was already blistering and chipping away. Her agreement with them had been that she would provide the lime and sand for the work but now they were turning this against her, claiming that the materials were of poor quality. She had told them in no uncertain terms that she would not pay until the task was completed to her satisfaction. They could sue her for the money she owed but she would hold fast. If there was one thing she had learned since her arrival in Achill it was that she needed to be resolute and unflinching in defending her rights. She would not give an inch.

Agnes MacDonnell was heading to the monthly assizes in Castlebar. She travelled by horse and car, rather than by train, when she had business to attend to in Newport. The veiled woman of Valley was a constant presence at the Castlebar Assizes where cases involving her property were frequently listed. Even if she herself did not always attend in person, her presence seemed to pervade the room like a lingering shadow during the hearings. On that September day in 1902, Aneas Gallagher was her unfortunate target. She was suing him for six shillings, this being the price she put on the bent which, she alleged, he had cut on the Sandybanks, across from the gate lodge, and carried off for thatch. She was determined to make an example of him and to put a stop to the skulduggery. John Gallagher, her herdsman, had found traces of the bent strewn along the roadway and claimed that Aneas Gallagher had a new room at his house thatched with the bent. There was no other place on the island where similar bent grew.

Aneas Gallagher made his own case in the court and questioned Agnes MacDonnell's herdsman in an impudent manner: 'Did you see me cut the bent?'

'No.'

'Did you see me carry it away?'

'No.'

'Did you see me put it on the house?'

'No.'

'Did you bring bent that road yourself?'

'Not this year.'

'Do you know that bent grows on the Achill Mission property?'

'It is not the kind of bent that was on your house.'

'Do you swear that it was bent that grew on Mrs MacDonnell's land?'

'I do.'

The magistrate had the difficult job of arbitrating between two contrary pieces of evidence. Conscious of the strained relations between landlords and tenants in north Achill, he needed to be careful not to inflame hostilities even further. He had, he said, no doubt but that the bent was cut on Mrs MacDonnell's property. However, this could not be proved, and he had no choice but to dismiss the suit. If such a case came before the court again with clear proof, he added, he would impose a penalty that would deter people from interfering with Agnes MacDonnell's property once and for all.

The magistrate would have suspected this was not the last he would see of Agnes MacDonnell in his court for the antagonism towards her had grown, rather than abated, since the attack, and her animals appeared to be on the receiving end of this enmity. Some time earlier she had made a claim to the Malicious Injuries Court for £15 compensation for the loss of her horse which, she alleged, had been driven over a cliff in the townland of Valley. Her employee, J. J. Lowry, had given evidence of having gone to the farm and not finding the horses that should have been grazing there. He reported the matter to Mrs MacDonnell and to the police. In response to a question about Agnes MacDonnell's popularity in the area, Lowry had replied in court, 'She is very badly treated. There is a grazing farm she wants to let and nobody will take it.'

Sergeant Thomas Homes of Dugort RIC had provided an insight into the escalating bitterness in relations between Agnes MacDonnell, her neighbours and tenants in the years since James Lynchehaun's conviction. The sergeant testified that there was such ill will towards her that the RIC had established a protection hut in Valley because of fears for the woman's safety, a practice not uncommon in other parts of the country where agrarian agitation was rife. The sergeant said that the incident of the horse was reported to the RIC at the Valley protection hut, and he had attended the scene at a place where the road ran close to the sea. There, about a half mile from Valley, he saw an object within some fifty yards of the strand. 'I waded in and found it was the carcase of a horse which answered to the description of the missing animal from the Valley estate. I examined the ground and found tracks of horses' hooves. I also saw a man's footprints and I took a cast of these.' Sergeant Homes told the court that he had no doubt in his mind but that the death of the horse was a malicious act.

Agnes MacDonnell had given evidence in court on that occasion. She said that the colt in question was a handsome animal and that her herdsman, Lowry, had estimated its worth at £30.

The magistrate asked why she was claiming only £15.

'Well, I am not a horse-dealer, my Lord, and I put what I thought was right on it,' she replied, to some amusement and disbelief in the courtroom.

Compensation of £15 was granted, with £3 expenses for J. J. Lowry, £3 10s for the police, and 10s for Agnes MacDonnell.

Those in attendance when Agnes MacDonnell made her frequent appearances in Castlebar Court may have wondered if the horror of her defacement had numbed her sensibility and instilled in her an even steelier resolve and ruthlessness than previously. Perhaps she derived confidence in her actions from the fact that her most bitter adversary was safely incarcerated in prison many miles from Achill.

Back in north Achill the new roof of the Valley House peeped through the surrounding trees on a mild September afternoon when Agnes MacDonnell rode her mare across the Sandybanks towards Ridge Point, with her back to Slievemore. Pressing her knees against the mare's body, she urged the animal ahead, her veil blowing against her face. It was a decade and a half since she had first ridden a horse in those parts, eight years since her life had been changed forever. The twinge of her injuries flared up in extreme heat, or cold, or when an unexpected memory brought fear into her heart. With the passage of years her body had grown thicker, her hair had grey flecks at the temple, and fine lines radiated out from her good eye. When she reined in the animal at Ridge Point she could look out across the bay towards Doohoma and the Erris peninsula, feeling some satisfaction that her life had returned to some equilibrium. They had not driven her out.

On returning to her rebuilt home Agnes MacDonnell was surrounded by the new furniture and fittings acquired with the insurance proceeds: leather-upholstered armchairs; a Chesterfield suite with patterned loose covers; a Walderman piano transported from London; the fine mahogany dining room table and sideboard, and Austrian bentwood chairs. She sat, resting, when there was a loud knock on the front door. She stood, smoothed down her clothes, rearranged her veil in front of her face, and walked to the front hall where she saw two constables standing outside. They had news for her: James Lynchehaun had escaped from Maryborough Prison.

Public notices were erected across Achill:

£100 Reward
Escape of convict James Lynchehaun from
Maryborough Prison

James Lynchehaun, convicted of attempted Murder
and Arson

James Lynchehaun, convicted of Murder and Arson,
having escaped from Maryborough Prison on night of 6
September 1902, I hereby offer a Reward of £100 to any
person who will give information to the Police leading to
the re-capture of this convict.

His description is as follows: Brown hair, hazel eyes,
light-brown eyebrows, coarse mouth, fresh complexion,
stout make, very short neck, height 5 feet 9½ inches,
cut mark on back of left hand above little finger on the
outside, cut on first finger of left hand. He escaped from
Maryborough Gaol without boots or coat, but wore
Prison trousers, shirt and socks. He may assume a disguise.
He was clean shaven when he escaped.

The above reward will be paid to the person entitled
to it, by any Officer of the Royal Irish Constabulary, or
through an Officer of any other Police Force.

11 September 1902
NEVILLE CHAMBERLAIN, Col,
Inspector-General, R.I.C.

It was as if history was being repeated as the people of Achill
rushed to read *The Mayo News* report of James Lynchehaun's
second escape. Here was a story to thrill their imaginations and
lighten their dreary lives. Another episode in the Lynchehaun
saga was unfolding.

Escape of James Lynchehaun

On Saturday night last, about 10 o'clock, James Lynchehaun
made his escape from Maryborough Convict Prison. He
was domiciled in one of the cells in the new wing, from
which he managed to break loose in some extraordinary
fashion. Thence it would appear, he made his way up
the great staircase (the upper portion of the wing being

unoccupied), broke out on the garden roof and descended into the yard below by a downpipe. With the aid of two planks and a rope he succeeded in getting over the outer wall (some 27 feet high), at a point situated at a considerable distance from the new wing. James Lynchehaun is, perhaps, the most famous convict in Ireland, and has had altogether a remarkable career. He is a native of Achill and about 43 years of age, of light complexion, rather low-set, and of powerful build. He was originally a school-teacher, and then became a member of the Manchester Police Force. Subsequently he became agent or land-steward to Mrs MacDonnell, the Valley House, Achill. Some five years ago he was sentenced to penal servitude for arson and for an atrocious attempt to murder Mrs MacDonnell. The circumstances excited tremendous sensation at the time, owing to the fact that Lynchehaun, during the magisterial enquiry, while being removed from Dugort to Castlebar, jumped off the side-car, and escaped from his escort. He remained at large for six months, during which a force of 250 police were continuously beating the immediate neighbourhood for him.

The £100 reward offered by the authorities for information leading to the rearrest of James Lynchehaun was speedily increased to £200. Four prison officers were relieved of their duties in Maryborough Prison, pending an enquiry into Lynchehaun's escape by the Prison Board. Extra police re-inforcements made their way to Achill. A special guard took up position at the Valley House and constables were seen pedalling at speed through the island.

The news shattered Agnes MacDonnell's equanimity. Despite the strengthened police presence around her home, she must have looked out into the darkness with apprehension as the winter nights closed in. Every noise was ominous, every shadow in the house menacing and sinister. Was James Lynchehaun about to destroy her life once more?

13

Dear Friends

September–November 1902

James Lynchehaun looked up at the September sky. It was like the blue of the ocean around Achill on a clear fine day. From where the sun rested in the west, he knew that it was late evening and that he must have slept for several hours. He loosened the jute bag he had fastened around him and looked about to get his bearings. He had nestled in a ditch at the bottom of an incline in a field that was sharp with the stubble of oats, and from where he could hear the sound of running water beyond the ditch. As the heaviness of sleep lifted, he began to feel the bruises and aches in his body and in the soles of his feet, which were scorched with sores and blisters from walking in stockinged feet. He squinted through his right eye to where the swelling from his lower forehead had spread after his fall from the prison wall. He twisted his head towards the warmth of the sinking sun in the west.

In the period of his prison incarceration James Lynchehaun's body had grown flabby and heavy, missing the pull and stretch of oars on the Atlantic, and the bend and swipe of the scythe in the corn fields of Achill. He had spent all but two months of those seven years of confinement in Mountjoy Prison, north Dublin, where the discipline had been severe and rigorous. For maximum security he had been confined indoors, mainly in an underground workshop where he was engaged in tailoring work. Then, just a few weeks previously, he had been moved to Maryborough in the midlands where a large extension was being added to the prison. James Lynchehaun quickly saw the opportunity presented by the scaffolding, wires and ropes that were strewn around the prison building site.

He pulled from his pocket a piece of turnip that he had picked from a field that morning, smashed it against a wall to shake off the clay and break it into lumps that he could chew. His mouth hurt when he ground the hard vegetable flesh between his teeth, his gums already scratched and sore, but the juices slid sweetly down his throat. Making his way through an opening in the ditch he moved in the direction of the flowing water; when he reached the river he bent down on his hunkers, and cupped his hands to splash his smarting face and spatter the liquid into his parched mouth. He then thought that he heard a faint rattling sound which, as he listened, grew louder and more shrill. It was a train. He would head in its direction and follow the railway line to Dublin where he would surely find a safe house.

After he had made his escape from Maryborough, he kept running until he was close to collapse. When he was sure that he was not being pursued, he had continued walking for most of the first night and, in the morning, found himself in a field of golden corn. During those first few days of freedom it seemed as if he was going around in circles, moving as if mesmerised, hiding and sleeping by day and walking by night. On one occasion – starved, parched and torn with shrubs – he approached a farmer's house in desperation. Lynchehaun's friar friend would later write of the fugitive's desperate plea to the farmer and of his pretence that he was 'a misfortunate, deserted soldier'. The farmer took mercy and assisted Lynchehaun with food, clothes and a jute sack.

The sack became his most helpful companion, shielding him when he crossed barbed wire fences and whitethorn hedges, protecting his flesh from snarling dogs' teeth, and providing warmth by night. His food comprised mainly turnips and oats that he rubbed between his hands and shelled with his teeth. Blackberries were a luxury when he came upon them.

The corn fields gave him the cover to hide and to sleep during the day and he counted himself lucky that the weather was mild and balmy. He kept moving in the direction of the colonnade of locomotive smoke as the train's hollering grew louder; he would reach the railway line before dark.

If he had managed to read the newspaper reports about his prison escape, James Lynchehaun may have been amused at certain accounts that spoke of the escapee's good fortune at being abroad in such benign countryside: 'It is safe to say that the fugitive could not find in any part of Ireland a better cover than is to be found within a radius of five miles of Maryborough. Hedges and woodland, furze and blackthorn scrub, corn fields – in the most of which the grain is standing – all combine to make an excellent cover.' Fortunate or not, James Lynchehaun had to keep walking, step by painful step.

Across the width and breadth of Ireland people asked how James Lynchehaun had managed to escape from the most secure prison in the land. Had he bribed somebody within the prison? Who were his accomplices? A buzz of excitement and a thrill of adventure swept through the country as the forces of the Crown gave chase. Would James Lynchehaun outwit them once again?

The new Maryborough Prison extension comprised four storeys with a handsome, cut-limestone facade. Inside, the building ran in four galleries reached by a wide stairway with the highest gallery opening out on to a roof garden surrounded by a parapet wall. The top floor was unoccupied and the exit to the roof not yet fully secured. On the day of his escape Lynchehaun was employed in fitting a gate that opened out onto the roof but which had not yet been fitted with a padlock. Each prison cell was fitted with a spring lock that closed automatically when the door was pushed shut. On the outside of each cell door a black mark indicated when the bolt was open and a white mark when the lock was closed. Before retiring, each prisoner closed his own door by slamming it shut.

Felix Meehan was serving as Governor in Maryborough Prison at the time of Lynchehaun's getaway. Many years later, after he had retired, he gave an intriguing version of Lynchehaun's escape. 'For the first time,' he told a newspaper reporter, 'I am able to record how Lynchehaun managed to get out of what was regarded as the safest prison in the British Isles. It was a piece of paper torn from a book of Euclid that gave Lynchehaun his "key" to freedom.' Meehan told how, on the night of 6 September 1902, Lynchehaun was safe in his cell reading his books of Euclid and working out problems, as was his custom. Lynchehaun tore a page from his book and used this to change the black portion of the lock indicator to white. He then plugged the socket of the lock so that it did not bolt, and wedged the door with a piece of wood so that it could not be pushed in. The inspecting warder judged Lynchehaun's cell door to be secured from the evidence of the white indicator.

Lynchehaun had made up his bed to give the impression that he was asleep under the covers, and had left his shoes at the foot of the bed. When the prisoners had settled for the night, he made his escape up the stairs and out through the unsecured gate on to the roof where he grasped an air-shaft, which projected above the building parapet, and slid against it to the ground. Using a plank from the yard he scaled the perimeter wall at the northwest corner where the ground sloped upwards. He carried with him a rope that he looped on to coping stones at the top of the wall and jumped to freedom. The *Western People* reported that 'Walter Laing, who was on duty at ten o'clock, walked the corridor and was satisfied that every door was closed. About twenty minutes later, he checked the cells and missed the most important individual in the institution.'

Four prison officers were suspended from duty following Lynchehaun's escape. A general enquiry was set in train by the Prison Board into the management of the prison. The perceived foolhardiness of the prison authorities evoked ire in *The Mayo News*: 'The removal of 200 of the worst criminals from Mountjoy to Maryborough Prison before the latter was finished is regarded as such a stupid proceeding that the only wonder is that there was not a general exit of prisoners from the unfinished cage.' Of the four suspended prison officers, one received a further suspension, one was dismissed from the prison service, a third was requested to retire on a pension reduced by a third, and the fourth was transferred to another prison with a reduction of salary.

On 10 October, a month after Lynchehaun's prison breakout, Michael Davitt set sail for the United States of America to attend the United Irish League Convention in Boston, and to fund-raise in a number of American cities.

Where was Lynchehaun? Was he still in Ireland or had he fled the country? The whole countryside hummed with rumour and gossip, tale and anecdote, concerning the fugitive's whereabouts. Children hurried indoors at dusk in dread of the convict. There were rumours that several crossroad dances were cancelled out of fear of the roaming renegade. Reports of sightings came thick and furious: from the south, in Limerick, Clonmel and Kilkenny; from Dublin; from the north, in Carrick-on-Shannon; even from the cities of Manchester and London. It seemed as if, since his escape, Lynchehaun had criss-crossed Ireland and England, eluding the police in every location. The newspapers could barely keep track of the avalanche of stories about sightings of him:

Clare: Lynchehaun, it was said, was hiding in Meelick, Co. Clare, four miles from Limerick City. All the available constabulary proceeded there on foot and on bicycle. They searched all day with no result.

Tipperary: There were several arrests by the police in Tipperary South Riding, of parties supposed to be Lynchehaun. However, the suspicions of the constabulary were proved to be groundless. Some amusement was caused in a street in Clonmel by the arrest of a burly fellow, who turned out to be a liberty patient from the asylum. J. Rahilly, the driver of the mail train from Limerick to Waterford, was arrested late at night on the train's arrival in Clonmel on suspicion of being the fugitive Lynchehaun. He was only released when a night man identified him as the engine-driver of the train, which was allowed to continue its journey after a considerable delay.

Kilkenny: There was high excitement in the city when it was rumoured that Lynchehaun had been arrested, and was confined in John Street barrack where a large crowd gathered. The rumour, however, turned out to be untrue as the 'arrest' was only the detention of an inoffensive tramp named Brady, who bore a resemblance to the apparently invincible Lynchehaun.

London: A Reading clergyman, the Reverend G. L. Werle, was twice approached by police during a visit to London on suspicion that he was the escaped convict. The mistake arose through the anxiety of a guard on the City and South London Railway to claim the award offered by the Irish authorities for Lynchehaun's capture. The guard had been a member of the Royal Irish Constabulary and imagined a close resemblance between Reverend Werle and the escapee.

Leitrim: Mr Frederick J. Ball, RIC County Inspector, Carrick-on-Shannon, was taking his usual exercise on horseback on the road between Carrick and Boyle when he encountered a man whom he took to be the fugitive. He returned with all haste to Carrick-on-Shannon barrack where he announced his 'find'. Acting-Sergeant Kennedy, together with Constables Thornton, Finn and Dineen, all mounted bicycles and proceeded to the area indicated. On their arrival, the object of the exciting chase was found to be a well-known bandmaster who was returning home from Carrick-on-Shannon where he had been engaged the previous night instructing members of the brass band.

Dublin: In the early hours of an October morning, a posse of RIC and Dublin Metropolitan Police officers besieged the inhabitants of a house in York Street. Information had reached the authorities that Lynchehaun had been secreted away in the vicinity. After thoroughly inspecting the premises, the Superintendent and District Inspector were required to withdraw their men.

Mayo: A month after Lynchehaun's daring escape there was increased constabulary activity in the Newport and Achill areas. Two houses in Mulranny were searched and the house of Patrick

Keane, Glenhest, was visited at two o'clock in the morning by a large party of police. After a thorough search of the vicinity the officers retired. Lynchehaun was still at large.

Manchester: On the evidence of a warder from Maryborough Prison, a man giving the name of Frederick Meakin was arrested by the Manchester police and charged with being the escaped convict James Lynchehaun. Meakin was picked from among 3,000 workmen as he was leaving the Westinghouse Works in Manchester. He told the magistrate that he has been employed in the Works for some weeks and had previously been in the army in South Africa for two and a half years. He was remanded in custody for further investigation.

Sligo: There were suspicions that Lynchehaun was in Tubbercurry, County Sligo. District Inspector T. O'Brien was reported to have issued strong instructions to his officers: 'You will please have two rising patrols at each of your stations between the hours of 12 midnight and 6 am. These patrols should leave barrack and be armed with revolvers. The patrols should lie in ambush and at likely places where this criminal would possibly pass.'

However, despite the best effort of the law enforcement authorities across Ireland and Britain, James Lynchehaun was undetected as the winter drew in.

The brown-robed monk needed to be careful, for it was a criminal offence to aid or to abet a fugitive from the law, and he did not wish to draw unfavourable attention to himself. He stood at the door of the school house in Achill Sound. Constables were visible everywhere he went on the island, and he knew he would have to keep his visit short. The teacher he met was a lodger in the Lynchehaun household in Polranny, and the friar spoke to him urgently: he had received a letter from Belgium where his friend was in pressing need of assistance to get to America. Would the teacher pass this information on to James Lynchehaun's family?

On the day that Lynchehaun skipped Maryborough Prison, Brother Paul Carney had been out of Ireland on a four-month questing mission, travelling in England and Scotland to raise money to liquidate debts at Kiltullagh Monastery, Granlahan, just a few miles from the townland where he grew up. Within weeks of his escape Lynchehaun was in touch with the friar. While the police were scouring the countryside in his pursuit, the escaped prisoner was making his way to Belfast, en route to Glasgow, where the friar cajoled and pleaded for church donations. Brother Paul Carney was already compiling his verbose narrative about James Lynchehaun's exploits, and he later wrote of the fugitive's experiences in the Scottish city:

> Although he [Lynchehaun] worked by day he fretted all night and suffered from insomnia so that he lived a dying life between hope and fear. He procured the daily papers, especially *The Freeman's Journal*, which he scanned closely to see were there any reports about him. In them he read of several arrests in different parts of the country on suspicion of being the far-famed Achill troglodyte and escaped jail-bird. The reports increased his fears. While Jim was conducting his dray in the streets of Glasgow he felt as timorous as a frightened hare. He suspected that every man who looked sharply at him was a detective sent to arrest him.

Arrangements were made for a clandestine meeting between friar and fugitive and, from this time onwards, Brother Paul Carney was closely involved in Lynchehaun's flight from the authorities. 'Then and there,' wrote the monk, 'they had a long, private conversation about Jim's escape from the convict prison, and how he came to Scotland, and now how to get out of it and arrive on the continent either of Europe or America. The want of money seemed to be the greatest obstacle.' Between the pair a decision was made that Lynchehaun would proceed, in the first instance, to Antwerp until sufficient funds were available for his passage to America.

On his return from Scotland the friar made his way to Achill and, soon afterwards, £40 in cash found its way to Lynchehaun in Europe. The fugitive sent a letter of thanks:

> My dear friend,
> The long desired relief has come to me which I will soon utilize to cross the Atlantic and try to reach the land of freedom where there is work and food for all. If once there I have a number of friends to assist me ... However, I hope the British authorities will not go to the trouble of extraditing me either here or in America. They may let the matter die out and I will help them in doing so.
>
> Both they and I have lost much valuable time, I running from them and they running from me. Yet you never saw a fox that got so clear from so many hounds as I did from my pursuers. I have baffled all their ingenuity.
>
> If I get safe to America I am resolved to lead a new life according to your advice to me. As drink has caused my ruin I'm resolved to refrain from it in future ...

By November, James Lynchehaun had achieved his goal of reaching America where Michael Davitt was then engaged on his fund-raising tour. The pair came face to face in Chicago, a meeting which was reported in *The New York Times* some time afterwards:

> In the latter part of November 1902 Mr. Michael Davitt lectured in Chicago, and, as he was an ex-convict, Lynchehaun thought he [Davitt] would sympathise with him and let him know if the English government could extradite him. If Davitt was an ex-convict it was for an honourable cause, that of trying to free his country from foreign yoke, while Lynchehaun's was a dishonourable one, that of arson and attempted murder. So when Jim went to interview Davitt the latter despised him and refused to converse at any length with him; he even went and reported him to the Mayor of Chicago who ordered police and detectives after him.

Lynchehaun disappeared from public view once more. However, as the year drew to a close, it seemed as if his ghost continued to roam through Ireland. In mid-December *The Mayo News* reported that the Coroner for north Dublin had held an inquest into the case of a body found on St Joseph's Strand, when evidence of discovery was given by James Eves, a labourer employed on the Hampton Estate between Balbriggan and Skerries. Dr F. B. Nolan concluded from his post mortem examination that it was the body of a man aged about fifty-five years and, in his opinion, the remains had been in the water for about a month. From the clothing on the deceased he had formed a view that it might be the body of an escaped prisoner, to which the Coroner replied, to considerable mirth in the court, 'The escaped Lynchehaun, perhaps?'

In the dying days of 1902 Michael Davitt arrived back at Queenstown on board the steamer *Umbria* after his successful American trip. The ship was due off the coast early in the morning but the wild Atlantic weather meant that it was eight o'clock before she reached the mouth of the harbour. Large crowds greeted Davitt with cheers of welcome when he alighted from the tender at the deep-water quay. The hero was home.

14

Edward VII v James Lynchehaun
September–October 1903

'I am James Lynchehaun.' The words tumbled out as he blinked rapidly. For the first time since entering the Federal Court of Indianapolis, James Lynchehaun was admitting his true identity. The crowd packed into the courtroom and all the surrounding corridors. An atmosphere of pent-up emotion pervaded the room; there was a feeling that mayhem could erupt if Judge Francis Baker did not keep a tight check on the proceedings.

Attorney Charles Fox, counsel for the British Government, was cross-examining the accused. 'You signed the name Thomas Walsh in a paper in this case, did you not?'

'I did, sir,' replied Lynchehaun.

'When did you begin to use the name Walsh?'

'About two years ago, sir.'

'Where did you come from to this country?'

'From France, sir.'

'What name did you have on the passenger list on the steam boat?'

'John Brown, sir.'

'Were you not asked whether you had committed a crime when you went through the immigration office in New York?'

'No, sir.'

Unlike the court proceedings in Castlebar seven years

earlier, James Lynchehaun was testifying personally in the United States as the case of Edward VII v James Lynchehaun got under way. The British Government was seeking the extradition of Thomas Walsh, alias James Lynchehaun, to serve out his prison sentence for the Achill felony. The prisoner's counsel, the eminent Mr Henry Spaan, kept his eyes focused on his client in the witness-box. Lynchehaun's wife sat in the courtroom throughout the nine-day trial, looking nervous and sad, her young son at her side.

Two witnesses from Ireland gave evidence of the prisoner's identity. William Tyndall, a prison trade instructor, said that the accused had been under his charge in Mountjoy Prison, Dublin, for six years, and afterwards in Maryborough for a short time. 'I have no doubt,' he testified, 'but that the accused man is James Lynchehaun.' Sergeant Richard Hicks of the RIC, Castlebar, said that he had seen the prisoner twice, once at the Castlebar Court hearing and once again since that time. 'The man under arrest here I identify as James Lynchehaun.'

The stakes were high and there was no doubt in the minds of those present as to the legal significance of the proceedings they were witnessing. A local newspaper, *The Indianapolis Sentinel*, summed up for its readers the legal issues involved. 'The Lynchehaun case which opens today has resolved itself into a very simple question: Is assault an extraditable offence? The lawyers say that it is not mentioned in any treaty. If this is found to be the case, there is no reason why Lynchehaun should not be a free man to-morrow.' For James Lynchehaun's supporters the legal action was a battle to establish the sacred right of asylum for political offenders. They would refer to it afterwards as an 'an epoch-making case' and probably the most important extradition suit that was ever tried in the United States of America. The case of Edward VII v James Lynchehaun was presented to the public as the pitting of Irish-America against the power and supremacy of Great Britain.

Just a few weeks earlier, in a peculiar coincidence, the British monarch King Edward VII, whose name was set against that of James Lynchehaun in the Indianapolis court, had peered through an Irish mist in the direction of Achill. While on a royal tour of Ireland, the king had acceded to a late request that the royal yacht *Victoria and Albert* would steam between Clare Island and Achill as it sailed south from Donegal to Killary Harbour. At about eight o'clock on that morning, large numbers had gathered on Achillbeg at the southern tip of Achill Island. They had come by boat and by cart from across Achill and from the mainland and waited with mounting anticipation as bonfires blazed and bunting flapped in the Atlantic breeze. However, over the next few hours a thick mist settled on the coastline, the waves grew higher out on the ocean and, by noon, it was clear that the royal yacht could not approach the island. And so, King Edward VII did not get to gaze on the island of Achill.

It had been late August when James Lynchehaun's entanglement with the law in the United States started at 530 Vinton Street on the west side of Indianapolis. The fugitive had fled Chicago the previous November after his ill-fated meeting with Michael Davitt. He wrote afterwards to his wife in Ireland, asking her to collect whatever money she could and to join him in America. On 18 April she and her son travelled to New York on the *Campania*, unaware that the RIC had received intelligence about their journey and that two detectives, Sergeants Young and Arthur, were also on board. On reaching New York the detectives followed Mrs Lynchehaun and her child to Pittsburgh and from there to Cleveland where she met up with her husband. The family disappeared from public view for a time until the detectives traced them to Philadelphia and finally to Indianapolis, where they resided under the name of Walsh.

In the early hours of 25 August, Catherine Lynchehaun was awakened by sharp knocking and, on opening the door, she was confronted by United States Marshals Rankin and Martin, Sergeant Young of the RIC, and E. J. Weize of the Pinkerton Detective Agency. The police officers arrested James Lynchehaun under a warrant sworn out against Thomas Walsh and took him into custody. Five days later, two Scotland Yard detectives left Liverpool for the United States carrying British warrants seeking the extradition of James Lynchehaun.

News of the arrest spread through Indianapolis in a matter of hours and, in no time, the Irish-American community in the city had rallied to Lynchehaun's assistance, while the prisoner was becoming something of a celebrity. 'The Irish rebel was the most popular prisoner in the jail,' Sheriff Metzger told reporters. "More people come to see him than all the rest of the prisoners in the jail. At one point seventy-four sympathisers talked to him through the prison gates, and the telephone jangled constantly with people sending their best wishes.'

The case was attracting exceptional attention. A Defence Committee comprising of powerful friends of Thomas Walsh, alias James Lynchehaun of Indianapolis, was organising support on his behalf and had soon raised $5,000 in donations. The Committee retained the legal service of Henry Spaan and issued a series of resolutions which would appear strange to many who were close to the events of October 1894 in Achill:

> Whereas on the 25th of August 1903, a poor Irish exile, who had found an asylum in our city, and who was peacefully supporting his little family at honest toil, was arrested as an escaped convict at the instigation of an alleged British representative of the British Government, assisted by the Pinkerton detectives, who dogged his footsteps even in the sacred precincts of the Church.
>
> Whereas, even if the identity of Walsh as Lynchehaun should be established, we believe that by being served to penal servitude for life, and having served eight terrible years of penal servitude in a British prison, torn from the arms of his grief-stricken family, he has served more than time sufficient to expiate the offence of assault and battery, with which he was charged.
>
> The Committee resolved that the imprisonment of any human being at penal servitude for life, for committing a simple assault and battery, is an inhuman and un-Christian act, and a travesty upon justice. They also resolved that the British Government, which deals out entirely different and unreasonable punishment to the Irish from what she

does to the English or any other citizens of the Empire, is guilty of gross injustice in the case of this man.

Through the intervention of the Defence Committee, James Lynchehaun was discarding the mantle of fugitive criminal in favour of that of political hero. The Committee was determined to push the case that the prisoner's previous actions had been driven by a political intent. If Lynchehaun was the man sought, the Committee resolved, 'We candidly believe that, as a recognised leader among the people, he became the special object of the bitter hatred of the landlords and that his offence is really a political rather than criminal one, and that it is our duty to see that he gets fair place.'

Lynchehaun's defence team called a number of witnesses, mainly from Cleveland, who had lived in Ireland prior to 1894, and who described for the court the rancour which existed between landlords and tenants on the island of Achill. The first such witness called by Mr Spaan in the Indianapolis court was Daniel Conway, whose voice was so muffled, and his accent so unintelligible, that the questions to him had to be repeated several times.

'I was a district officer of the Irish Revolutionary Brother-hood,' Conway stated under oath. 'I helped to initiate James Lynchehaun into the order.'

'What were the objectives of the order?' the attorney asked.

'We wanted to overthrow the English landlords at the first opportunity and to set up a republican government of our own.'

Asked who the members of the Brotherhood were, Daniel Conway replied, 'The order was composed of tenants who were physically able. They were all sworn to secrecy.'

Patrick Veasey, Michael McNamara and James Corrigan were next examined and each gave evidence of the state of wretched-ness of the Achill islanders who, they testified, lived in huts and hovels, surviving on a daily diet of Indian meal, potatoes and shellfish, their lives beaten down by unscrupulous landlords. The defence team deliberately unfolded an argument that the evil treatment inflicted on the tenants of Achill had inevitably led to the growth of violent resistance. The testimony of the defence witness, Thomas

Lynch, 'a reputable citizen of Indianapolis' was to prove decisive. A native of Achill and, on his own admission, a member of the Irish Republican Brotherhood (referred to in the court as the Irish Revolutionary Brotherhood), he described the character of that movement and of the supposed part played in it by the prisoner. In reply to Henry Spaan's question regarding the rights which the Achill tenants asserted over the land, Thomas Lynch replied, 'This land came down to them from time without record, from their great, great, ancestors, and they naturally felt that it belonged to them. By right of title it belonged to them, and their ideas were to banish by any means whatever, to banish the landlords from the place so that the lands would belong to the people.'

'Were those matters spoken of in public meetings?'

'Certainly, that was the drift of those meetings and the object of them.'

'Now then, the tenants, was it their theory that the land occupied by them and their ancestors from time immemorial, belonged to them by right. Is that correct?'

'Yes, sir, they called those landlords usurpers, who took away what rightfully belonged to them.'

'What was the general feeling of the people towards the landlords?'

'Why, the general feeling towards the landlords was harsh, and they considered the landlords the English representative in Ireland, and their feeling towards them was just the same as towards the English Government, and their ultimate objective was to banish them out of the country and form a government for the people and by the people.'

Thomas Lynch swore to the court that he had known the prisoner in Achill and had attended IRB meetings addressed by James Lynchehaun.

'What ideas did the prisoner express at those meetings?'

'To, if possible, procure the land for the people.'

'And anything else?'

'His talk was just to procure the land for the people and to break the power of the landlord, and in that way the power of the English government in the place.'

'Now, you may state if you know whether or not he was considered a leading character among your people over there in Ireland on those subjects?'

'He certainly was.'

At this point in the cross-examination a man shouted out from the back of the court, 'Free him, Judge. Free him.' Judge Baker looked towards the wild-eyed interrupter and ordered the marshal to remove him from the courtroom.

James Lynchehaun mounted the stand after the defence witnesses had concluded their testimony. The strain was beginning to show and he appeared nervous and jittery, his features drawn and his eyes rolling. When *The Mayo News* later published the proceedings of the extradition case, that newspaper took a jaundiced view of the evidence that Lynchehaun was about to present, claiming that it was of a kind that would 'startle all who are acquainted with the actual facts as set out at Castlebar on 15 July 1895'.

Mr Henry Spaan first questioned James Lynchehaun about the selection of jurors at his Castlebar trial: 'Were the jurors asked by attorneys for the Crown if they were members of the Land League?'

'Yes,' said Lynchehaun. 'When the jurors said they belonged to the Land League, they were told to step aside.'

Attorney Fox, for the prosecution, interrogated the accused about his earlier life in Achill and his relationship with Agnes MacDonnell of the Valley House estate. 'Have you ever spoken of ill feeling against Mrs MacDonnell on the part of her tenants?'

'I have, sir. Mrs MacDonnell evicted tenants from her houses and scores from her estate.'

'You have testified to the burning of the house and barn of Mrs MacDonnell, have you not?'

'I have, sir. One of her tenants was selected by lot, at a meeting of the Irish Revolutionary Brotherhood at which I was present, to set fire to her barn. And there was a plan perfected to kidnap Mrs MacDonnell and give her a good beating.'

'Kidnapping? What do you mean by that?'

'Why, to take her away from the crowd while her barn was

burning and give her a beating.'

Lynchehaun said that on the night the stables and the Valley House were burned he had gone to the home of Mrs MacDonnell when the barn was set alight and asked her for the keys to the stables, which she gave him. He testified that when he saw the woman in danger, he approached her and she drew a revolver and shouted at him, 'This is your work.' He said that he knocked the revolver from her hand in self-protection. She then struck him in the face and, at that point, he struck her with his fist. She staggered towards the crowd that had gathered where the barn was ablaze. The crowd then turned on Agnes MacDonnell and attacked her, causing the injuries she suffered. Lynchehaun asserted that he had struck Agnes MacDonnell in accordance with the orders of the Irish Revolutionary Brotherhood meeting that she be punished and driven out of Achill forever.

'Now, I will ask you if in your conduct that night you were actuated by any motive of personal feeling directed against Mrs MacDonnell?' Attorney Fox said.

'Not the slightest personal motive.'

'And what was done there, you may state what that was a result of?'

'That was the result of the combination of the tenants and of the Irish Revolutionary Brotherhood men. We wanted to send her back to England, sir, to send her out of the country, back to England.'

'And what you did there that night, you may state whether or not that was done in furtherance of carrying out the plan that you had advocated from the public platform, that is to regain the lands of Ireland for the Irish, to drive out the landlords, and establish a republican form of government in Ireland?'

'That was the sole and only reason.'

'Did you show any personal motives at all against the woman as an individual, apart from this general motive?'

'Not the slightest.'

'So far as you know, did any of the parties have any personal grudge against the woman?'

'Not personally.'

'Did you talk with them on the subject?'

'I knew the feeling of every man, woman and child on the estate. I knew their feelings so far as the tenants were concerned.'

During Lynchehaun's evidence, emotions ran high in the court and there were several bitter clashes between the opposing legal teams.

At nine o'clock on the morning of 12 October, prosecution attorney Charles Fox summed up the arguments on behalf of the British Government. *The Mayo News* reported that his 'was an able effort, having to do with an unsentimental and a more or less unpopular side of the argument'. Attorney Fox maintained that James Lynchehaun's crime was not a political one and that the real issue had been befogged in the court. He asserted that a political crime was one that grew out of a political disturbance, had designs on the ruling government, or fermented an insurrection. He held that the burning of houses, the clipping of cows' tails, and similar depredations, were not overt acts of revolution but crimes prompted by personal animosity and evil. The Achill crime, he argued, could not in any sense be considered a political one since there was no armed conflict between the prisoner and the Government authorities.

Mr Jessie La Follette made further closing arguments for the Crown. His principal contention was that Commissioner Moores did not have the authority to surrender the prisoner or to make a final decision in the case. 'The Commissioner's jurisdiction is simply to review the evidence and present his findings to the executive arm of the government. The Secretary of State is the official in whose hands lies the final decision.'

At eleven o'clock Mr Henry Spaan stood to summarise the legal arguments on behalf of the prisoner. At the outset, he said, he wished to dispel the suggestions that the defence case was based on sympathy. 'We do not desire this man to be acquitted on that ground,' he told the court, 'we desire him to be judged on the fundamental principle which underlies the treaty under consideration, and that is that no man shall be extradited for a political crime.' That right, he contended, was a fundamental principle of government and the accused had a right to be judged in accordance with American ideals of liberty. Nothing less was being asked of the court.

A central tenet of Henry Spaan's defence was that James Lynchehaun had taken upon himself the burden of the oppressed. 'He had seen the bowed shoulders, the seamed and scarred forehead, the frames bowed with labour and insufficient food. He had seen the wailing of starving infants, of evicted wives and mothers. He had seen injustice done from one end of the island to the other, and those acts of injustice had burned and seared into his heart, and he took up the burden of the people. He became a leader among them and made political speeches. He was at once a marked man by the English Government.'

The defence attorney then turned to the general condition of Ireland: the prevailing poverty in the country, the hopeless and downtrodden state of its people, the hideous and distressing cruelty of the Government and the landlord class. In no place in Ireland, he said, was there more anguish than on the windswept, remote western island of Achill where James Lynchehaun's so-called crime against the landlord, Agnes MacDonnell, was perpetrated. This was the place where the Irish Revolutionary Brotherhood was most active and where Lynchehaun, a leader in that organisation, was a marked man.

Henry Spaan continued: 'Agnes MacDonnell represented the harshness and tyranny of the Government and the landlords. She seemed animated by a desire to do her tenants all the harm possible. She even fenced up a lake of fresh water, denying her ill-fated tenants God's greatest gift to man with the exception of air. In other words, Mrs MacDonnell showed a cruel disposition towards the peasantry. Her acts were rightly resented by the political organisation of which James Lynchehaun was a member. His crime was not personal, else why did so many take part in it? Lynchehaun's crime was only the outcome of the conditions of the Isle of Achill – conditions the same as elsewhere in Ireland.'

Henry Spaan built his arguments to a powerful climax: 'To conclude, the prisoner should be judged by you in the light of all history, in the light of every struggle for freedom under the sun, in the light of every heart-burning of the Irish man, that came to him from his birth, in every wrong of his race, in the light of all the sadness and tragedy of existence as he lived it on the forlorn sea-bound coast of the Isle of Achill. When you do this, if the court please, you will do justice to this heartbroken and defenceless man. I have done. I thank you for your kindly attention.'

Mr Spaan's address was listened to with great attention in the courtroom, which was crowded mostly with Irish people and many women. The justice rigidly checked any attempts at applause or clapping but those who listened to the defence attorney's sentiments showed their delight with smiles, sideways glances and an air of repressed excitement.

The court rose. It would be two weeks before Commissioner Moores delivered his decision in a case that had grabbed international attention.

15

He is no Robert Emmet

October 1903

It was the last day of October. Heads leaned forward in the Indianapolis courtroom, necks tensed in anticipation. Hands grasped the wooden benches as dozens of pairs of narrowed eyes followed every movement of the court officials. Foreheads tightened in furrows with the strain of waiting for the court judgement. After almost two weeks of consideration, the decision in the James Lynchehaun case was about to be handed down.

It was one of the most significant days in the career of Federal Commissioner Charles W. Moores, a man with a high forehead, dark neat hair, and a studious air. He understood that this was the most important judgement that he was likely to deliver in his judicial career. He had worked long hours in crafting the words that would be reported far beyond the Indianapolis courtroom and, in writing up his arguments, he had called on all his skills of legal acumen, political savvy, and shrewdness. In reaching the judgement he had had to balance several sensitive issues: the many legal case precedents which he had scrutinised in great depth; the raucous and powerful lobby from within the Irish community in Indianapolis, who had vented raw emotions concerning the destitute condition of the inhabitants of Achill; the expectations of the British Government; the wily cunning of the accused in his ability to weave a political web around the brutal Valley House events of October 1894. All this Charles W. Moores had to take into account as he fashioned his judgement, *In the Matter of the Proceedings for the Extradition of James Lynchehaun.*

The prisoner waited, his head jerking like an overexcited animal, his eyes joggling in their sockets as he repeatedly glanced in the direction of his wife and son. The set of his mouth showed a certain air of smugness at the attention he was receiving. He was a man who understood that he was at the centre of a tug-of-war between the might of Great Britain and the United States of America. James Lynchehaun had come a long way.

Commissioner Moores started to read: 'On August 24, 1903, a complaint was filed with this Commissioner on behalf of the British Government. It was a demand for the extradition of the prisoner upon the charge that, having been convicted in Ireland of the crime of assault with intent to murder, and sentenced to penal servitude for life, he had escaped and was still at large. Upon this complaint a warrant issued directing the marshal to bring the prisoner before the Commissioner, to the end that evidence of his criminality, within the terms of the British treaty, be heard and considered.' The evidence, said the Commissioner, had now been heard and it had fallen to him to decide 'whether or not the prisoner shall be committed to the executive department of the United States to be surrendered'. However, before such a route could be taken, he had the awesome task of determining a most important matter, whether the offence for which the prisoner was to be punished, if extradited, was 'of a political character'. 'These questions,' he said, 'must be determined upon the evidence before the court; the stories told in the press and elsewhere for the purpose of influencing public sentiment for and against the prisoner are no part of this case.'

Commissioner Moores was clear that, from the evidence he had heard, a number of facts had been proven: that, on 6 October 1894, James Lynchehaun assaulted his landlord, Agnes MacDonnell, with intent to kill her; that he was convicted of this crime on 15 July 1895, and sentenced to penal servitude for life;

that he was in prison executing this sentence until September 1902 when he escaped and found his way to Indianapolis. The Commissioner then observed, somewhat surprisingly, that 'we have no evidence of the extent of Mrs MacDonnell's injury save in the record of the Irish court that "the prisoner wounded her with intent to murder," and, in his own statement, that this blow was followed by a kidnapping in which perhaps fifteen took part, and by "a very bad beating and a bad kicking" by a party of men and women.'

Of all the aspects of the Lynchehaun trial in Indianapolis, it appeared to Commissioner Moores that it was the coverage of the social and political conditions in Achill that aroused the most intense passions. 'Evidence was received,' said the Commissioner, 'to show the social and political conditions in the county where the crime was committed, and throughout Ireland from 1881 to 1894, and the court was asked to take judicial notice as a historic fact that these conditions have prevailed in Ireland for a hundred years.' It was obvious, he said, that landlordism was at the core of this political and social tension: 'Upon Achill Island, and throughout a large part of Ireland, the feeling between tenants, forming one class or party, and the landlord, forming another, was very bitter.' The Commissioner said that he had no doubt but that 'agitation was to be continuous so as to keep the idea of revolution always before the people'. There was a sense, he said, in which 'the revolt of tenant against landlord was an assault upon the political and social order of the state'.

Turning to James Lynchehaun, Commissioner Moores said that he was in no doubt as to the troublesome nature of the prisoner before him who had been 'both an agitator and an organiser. He had been a member of the Land League and of the Irish Revolutionary Brotherhood for thirteen years, serving in official positions in each. His hostility towards the landlords and the authorities was known. He was watched by the police. No doubt, to the authorities he was a very troublesome character whom they deemed deserving of severe punishment should his advocacy of lawlessness ever lead him to crime.'

The Commissioner said that he had learned, in the course of the court evidence, that Achill Island, in the west of Ireland, was a particular locus of extreme landlord and tenant tensions. 'Expressions of hatred towards the landlords were heard everywhere among the Achill Island tenants who had been aroused by what they considered cruel wrongs at the hands of the owners of the soil. Evictions had been frequent and had been accompanied with destruction of the property both of landlords and tenants.' He understood that land was central to this political tension. 'The land question was the only political question before the Irish people. Legislation intended to relieve the strain seems to have increased it, and the more the rebellious spirit of the tenantry was curbed, the more lawless it became.' Nowhere, said the Commissioner, was the tension of landlord and tenant more acute than in the townland of Valley in north Achill. 'On the MacDonnell estate the tenants were rebellious because of prosecutions and punishment for trespass, evictions, and demands for higher rents, charges for seaweed, grazing and turf, the rights to which the tenants had always claimed. Vile names were given to Mrs MacDonnell. She became, in the view of the islanders, the representative of a class whom they must drive out.'

With a tedious, verbose delivery, the Commissioner was progressing relentlessly towards the substance of his judgement: the decision as to whether the crime of the accused could be deemed to be of a political character. It was apparent that he had wrestled in his mind with all of the issues involved. 'It is not a question,' he said, 'of how detestable the acts were, nor of whether or not they have been punished adequately, nor of whether the trial of 1895 was a fair one. The question is one of law to be determined according to those principles of justice which we find in the decisions of the courts and, according to the definitions that jurists have presented for our consideration.'

The Commissioner turned his attention to the arguments made by the British authorities in seeking Lynchehaun's extradition. 'The demandant has argued that a murderous assault cannot possess a political character if committed against a private citizen, unless committed in time of war. The argument is unsound. If a criminal assault were ever political it would seem that the very fact that it was committed against an official would make it so.' It must have been difficult for Commissioner Moores to hold the attention of his restless audience but he was determined to deal with the legal issues with precision and thoroughness. He also had to balance his judgement by pointing out the unpalatable features in the record of the accused: 'The prisoner's first oath to the court that was to hear his plea for liberty was a denial of his identity. This must have been deliberate perjury. One is apt to think that a political refugee should be a hero and a patriot. And much has been said in this trial about Robert Emmet. It is a far cry from that immortal dreamer to the agitator who, after his cowardly assault upon a defenceless woman, seeks to charge against his unhappy associates the odium of a detestable crime.'

These words provoked a boisterous stamping of feet in the court and an outbreak of loud whispering. When order was restored the Commissioner came to his concluding remarks. 'It is evident to me that the assault on Mrs Agnes MacDonnell was incidental to, and a part of, a popular disturbance; that the popular disturbance, including the prisoner's part in it, had its origin and cause in a popular movement to overthrow landlordism and was done to further that movement, and that this movement, futile though it was, did disturb the political and social order of Ireland; that these people would have been in a state of open insurrection had not the right to bear arms been denied to them; and, that the riot of October 6 was for political purposes and that its participants were engaged in a partisan conflict whose object was a change of laws and an upsetting of existing political conditions. The real question is this, would the crime have been done had there been no political motive and no concert of actions to affect that motive? I am convinced there were moving causes that led to the climax of October 6, and that their relation to the riot and the assault was so intimate that they lent their character to the assault itself.'

The Commissioner paused for breath before delivering his concluding statement to the hushed room: 'Disgraceful though an assault on a woman must always be, I am convinced that under the terms of the extradition treaty with Great Britain this was an offence of a political character for which the prisoner cannot be surrendered.'

The applause broke out before Commissioner Moores had finished speaking. Shoes pounded the wooden floor and fists thumped the air as the crowd cheered and applauded in a noisy tumult. Commissioner Moores had to shout out his words over the commotion to pronounce to the court, 'Let him be discharged.'

On the day Commissioner Moores issued his judgement, the Defence Committee penned an *Explanatory Statement* as a foreword to its publication of the *Complete Proceedings in the Great Extradition Case of Edward VII vs. James Lynchehaun, as tried in the United States Court of Indianapolis.* It was a rather defensive document by the Committee, perhaps conscious that not everyone within the Irish community in Indianapolis and America was jubilant at the Lynchehaun decision, and that many were sceptical about some of the evidence put forward by the defence. 'In view of criticisms and comments made on the Lynchehaun case,' the statement went, 'the Defence Committee desires to state briefly the motives of its action and the circumstances of this remarkable defence.' The Committee was at pains to claim that the battle fought on Lynchehaun's behalf was done on a point of principle i.e. to establish the right of asylum for political offenders. 'At no time,' the statement went, 'did the personality of the defendant enter into the case.'

Reaction to the Indianapolis court decision was swift and sharp. *The Globe* newspaper expressed the outrage of many: 'The next assassin of a President will plead Commissioner Moore's judgement with irresistible force if he escapes across the Canadian line. The Americans will have no cause for complaint if the result throws out of gear the whole machinery of extradition between the United States and Great Britain.' In a similar vein, *The Pall Mall Gazette* observed, 'By the same reason used by Commissioner Moores it would always be possible to refuse the extradition of anarchists guilty of the most dastardly crimes.'

The Duluth News of 3 November described in its headline the reaction to the judgement in Britain:

LONDON PAPERS ARE DISPLEASED
They Think Politics Influenced Decision in Case of
J Lynchehaun

It was soon reported that the Assistant United States Attorney, La Follette, who had supported the counsel for the British Government in the extradition proceedings, had indicated that a warrant could be sworn against James Lynchehaun before a court outside of Indiana in a further effort to have the accused sent back to Ireland to finish out his sentence. Mr La Follette continued to contend that the United States Secretary of State was the only person who should decide on an interpretation of the extradition treaty.

Within days of Lynchehaun's release from custody in Indianapolis, *The Morning Herald* commented that the Irish man had taken out his first US naturalisation papers. By the end of November the British were examining further measures under the expulsion laws of the United States and decided to appeal the Indianapolis decision to the United States Supreme Court. And so it was that the following year the Lynchehaun case ended up in Washington in *Henry C Pettit, United States Marshal for the District of Indiana v. Thomas Walsh*, and Mr Justice Harlan set out the legal parameters on which the Supreme Court would make its findings:

> This is a case of extradition. It presents the question whether a commissioner specially appointed by a court of the United States under and in execution of statutes enacted to give effect to treaty stipulations for the apprehension and delivery of offenders, can issue a warrant for the arrest of an alleged criminal, which may be executed by a marshal of the United States, within his district, in a state other than the one in which the commissioner has his office. It

also presents the question whether a person arrested under such a warrant can be lawfully taken beyond the state in which he was found, and delivered in another state before the officer who issued the warrant of arrest, without any preliminary examination in the former state as to the criminality of the charge against him.

The United States Supreme Court affirmed the decision of the Indianapolis Circuit Court:

As applied to the present case, that stipulation means that the accused, Walsh, could not be extradited under the treaties in question, except upon such evidence of criminality as, under the laws of the state of Indiana,— the place in which he was found,—would justify his apprehension and commitment for trial if the crime alleged had been there committed ... But as there are no common-law crimes of the United States, and as the crime of murder, as such, is not known to the national government, except in places over which it may exercise exclusive jurisdiction, the better construction of the treaty is, that the required evidence as to the criminality of the charge against the accused must be such as would authorize his apprehension and commitment for trial in that state of the Union in which he is arrested.

A full decade after flames had burst into the night sky in north Achill, James Lynchehaun had taken on and defeated the legal forces of Great Britain and the United States of America. His reputation had soared to new heights. The reaction to the judgement in Lynchehaun's home place was, however, tempered with disbelief at the political cloak put on Lynchehaun's activities in the United States courts. This skepticism was expressed by *The Mayo News* some time afterwards when it described certain aspects of the Indianapolis evidence as 'flagrant perjury'.

As news of the Indianapolis court decision was spreading far and wide, the outcome had the effect of drawing renewed attention to Achill. *The Times* of London published a lengthy account of a visit to the island by its correspondent who concluded that Achill was 'a very desirable holiday resort for tired brain workers, anaemic persons and those wearied with city life'. Curiously, he came upon a strange story about the popularity of fox-hunting on the island. It appeared that, before the construction of the new bridge at Achill Sound, it was a rare occurrence to see a fox in Achill, but that situation had since changed. 'The foxes,' he wrote, 'have evidently rushed across the bridge, finding a magnificent country on the island side, with innumerable caves and inaccessible precipices for their unmolested increase. So bold have they become that on almost any night they may be seen visiting the villages and the sea shore on the prowl for stray fowl or fish offal on the strand.' It appeared that the prowling fox had almost wiped out the hare, the grouse and other game on the island.

The Times reporter was favourably impressed on his visit to The Colony at Dugort with its 'three unpretentious hotels' and where the energetic agent, Mr Grierson, had planted thousands of trees. The writer had some sympathy for 'the justly popular, hard-working Dr Croly, who has all of Achill for his sphere of duty.' Also, the visitor found the island vegetation to be most entrancing. 'The whole surface of the island is bog-covered, clad with beautiful purple heather, and totally devoid of trees except for a few at Dugort and the Sound, where a plantation around a house is an agreeable variation, and where gigantic fuchsia trees, osmunda ferns, honeysuckle and bramble bushes luxuriate.' For the journalist, the landscape presented an exotic picture with the villages of Achill recalling 'a high up Himalaya hamlet, a nestling encirclement of tillage in square patches, chiefly of rye, with deep drains between, around a cluster of primitive huts'.

The landscape was not the reporter's only concern, however, for the visitor had some stern words for the Congested Districts Board, established over a decade earlier and around which there had been such high expectations. He heard complaints from the islanders of the refusal of the officials to listen to any local advice. 'One of the head officials of the Board,' he wrote, 'decided that oats should be grown at Dooagh. The local people assured him that oats would not ripen there. He insisted that the crop be grown. A plot was chosen, dug up and manured according to instructions and under the special observation of the officials, with the result predicted by the natives. The oats refused to rise a fraction beyond three inches of the ground.' It was common talk throughout Achill that the Board officials were incurring needless costs driving about in cars where local people could give the information required at considerably less expense.

The correspondent wrote that the MacDonnell estate at that time had '47 tenants and 1,530 acres grazed by the landlord'. He made no mention of the attack on the Valley House almost a decade earlier or of the more recent escape of Agnes MacDonnell's attacker from secure detention. Neither did he pick up on what many in Achill were asking: Could Agnes MacDonnell continue to live alone in the place where, each night, she retired to bed with fears of who might be prowling around her estate in the darkness? Could Agnes MacDonnell hold her ground? Would James Lynchehaun return to Achill?

Part 3

16
Sure They'd Never Touch Lynchehaun
Summer 1905

The writer, John Millington Synge, looked through the window of his room in Deehan's Hotel, Belmullet, north Mayo, at the early morning scene. Below him, small groups of men and women moved along the street leading from the square down to the jetty where they would catch the steamer. Most walked in their bare feet, carrying their boots under their arms. Through the open window he could smell the heavy kelp-smoke spiralling from the town's chimneys into the dawn sky. Synge was a tall, well-built man with a heavy moustache that seemed to drag his face downwards into a long, melancholy appearance – an El Greco face. Beneath the hazel eyes his cheeks appeared sunken from recurring bouts of illness. In the middle of the room his Blickensderfer typewriter sat on a table among strewn papers. These were a busy few weeks for the writer as he had to get regular articles out to *The Manchester Guardian* newspaper detailing his travels.

Synge knew that Achill was a major source of harvester migrants and had heard that, a few days previously, 'a special steamer went from Achill Island to Glasgow with five hundred of these labourers, most of them girls and young boys. From Glasgow they spread through the country in small bands and worked together under a ganger, picking potatoes and weeding turnips, and sleeping for the most part in barns and outhouses.'

He was told that the migrants' wages varied from a shilling to two shillings a day, depending on the demand for their labour. The men, it seemed, went more often to work in the north of England and earned better wages. 'Three or four of them,' he wrote, 'generally bank together with one of them as a chosen spokesman and then they contract the farmers for various jobs of turnip-weeding and such for prices that work out three or four shillings a day.' While some of the migrants returned after a month or two, he had heard that many stayed on until October or November, if they could find enough work.

It was Synge's second visit to north Mayo in less than a year. He had come the previous September when James Lynchehaun's victory in the United States Supreme Court a few months earlier was on everybody's lips. He had travelled with his bike by steamer from Sligo as far as Belmullet. He should have been going to the Aran Islands and had earlier written to Lady Gregory about his dilemma: 'I was to have started to Aran to-morrow morning but I hear there is smallpox in Kilronan, so I am a little uncertain what I shall do. My people want me not to go at all and of course, if it should spread, it would not be pleasant to be there in an epidemic.'

The writer's impression on reaching the Mayo coast on his fist visit was of a wet and rather miserable place, debased and demoralised. Belmullet was 'squalid and noisy, lonely and crowded at the same time and without appeal to the imagination'. However, Synge's musical ear had been drawn to the enchanting sounds as he passed up and down the town: a gramophone in one house, a fiddle in the next, a fragment of a traditional lullaby, a baby's cry, and the sounds of girls and young men romping in the dark. Synge's visits to Mayo would later take on an imaginative significance when he decided to locate his new drama in the wild Erris landscape. His notebooks from that first September trip contain early sketches of the play. Originally titled *The Murderer (a farce)*, Synge experimented with other titles like *Murder Will Out*, *The Fool of the Family*, *Christy Mahon*, and, finally, *The Playboy of the Western World*. It was the story of a wild man hero-worshipped by a community for his supposed dastardly deeds.

Synge noted down names, dialogue and phrases that would feed his thoughts as his drama took shape: 'hearing the cows breathing and sighing like Christian sinners in the white light of the moon'; 'looing and mooing like heifers you see looking out through a gate in the wet mud, and they seeking their food in the cold evenings of the year'. Although Synge did not visit Achill, the tall tales surrounding James Lynchehaun from the nearby island became part of the creative backdrop to the work and the play's early drafts included a reference to the notorious Achill fugitive. When the drama's hero, Christy Mahon, revealed to Pegeen and a group of men in a public house that he had murdered his father, one of the men remarked, 'Sure they'd never touch Lynchehaun when they knew the kind he was. It's only a common, week-day kind of murderer them lads would lay their hands on.'

John Synge would have been aware of the Achill context of the Lynchehaun story, and of the proselytising activities of the Achill Mission, from his own family background. Both his grandfathers and his brother were clergymen while his mother was deeply imbued with evangelicalism. His uncle, Reverend Alex Synge, had gone to Aran as part of the nineteenth-century evangelical movement a half-century before his nephew arrived on the island.

John Synge would draw on images of the savage-hero in Irish life from the case of James Lynchehaun, and also from the story of O'Malley of Murvey – the Connacht man who killed his father – which Synge first heard on the Aran Islands. There was, too, the case of Danny, the rate-collector of Erris, north Mayo, who was murdered in 1888. These narratives became entwined in Synge's imagination as he walked, cycled, made notes and listened and talked to locals in north Mayo, within sight of Achill Island.

When Synge returned to Mayo in the summer of 1905 it was with his friend, the painter Jack Yeats. The pair travelled west for a month on an assignment from *The Manchester Guardian* for a set of articles and illustrations on the Congested Districts of the west of Ireland. Synge was pleased with the £24 he would earn for the work but slightly peeved – at least he pretended so – that his painter friend had struck a better bargain for expenses: 'The dirty skunks paid him more than they paid me, and that's a thorn in my dignity!' They had set out by train from Dublin on 3 June with Synge playfully suggesting that the elder of the two should be in charge for the month-long journey. Synge, they found, was two months older than Yeats, 'so he was the boss' and charged with keeping the account of their expenses, which he noted in meticulous detail: train tickets, long-car hire, hotel accommodation, food and tips. Jack Yeats carried a collection of small, ring-bound, cartridge-paper sketch books to record drawings of their expedition: a China man in Belmullet market; the harvesters waiting to catch the steamer at Belmullet jetty; a jackass with an ornamental tail; Synge sporting his friend's hat on Belmullet pier.

The leg of the journey from Connemara to north Mayo was tortuous, Synge complained afterwards in a letter to his mother. 'We started from here [Carna] at 11 a.m. with a two-hour's drive on the Clifden line, then we had to train all the way back to Athlone and wait there 5 hours to get the connection to Ballina, so that in the end we reached Ballina at 3 o'clock this morning, then drove there the 40 miles on the long car in a downpour and got here at 10.30.' Synge was relieved and pleased to find a letter from his mother waiting for him at Deehan's Hotel, as well as a parcel containing his pyjamas, £6s and – to his relief – cigarettes. Even if the journey to Belmullet had been thoroughly exhausting, he was able to reassure his mother about his health. 'I am all right and have had no asthma since I left Gorumna on Monday; it is a mysterious illness.'

While moving through north Mayo Synge missed the stone walls of Connemara and found, at first, an overwhelming wretchedness in the Mayo landscape of miserable cottages and endless bogs. 'All the land about here,' a woman told him, 'is stripped bog and it is no use at all without all kinds of stuff and manure mixed through it ... you'd want great quantities of sand and seaweed and dung to make it soft and kind enough to grow a thing in it.'

It was when the pair joined the festivities in Belmullet town square on St John's Eve that Synge's spirits lifted. The visitors mingled with the crowd amid donkeys and pigs, heather brooms and blacking brushes, tinkers and card-trick men, and the movement of people arriving in from the islands. They stood 'watching the fire-play, flaming sods of turf soaked in paraffin, hurled to the sky and caught and skied again, and burning snakes of hay rope'. This strange incident would appear in Synge's text of *The Playboy* in an encounter between Christy Mahon and his drunken father: 'It's that you'd say surely if you seen him and he drinking for weeks, rising up in the red dawn, or before it maybe, and going out into the yard as naked as an ash-tree in the moon of May, and shying clods against the visage of the stars till he'd put the fear of death into the banbhs and the screeching sows.'

The men travelled south of Belmullet to the places that reached down towards Achill Island. It was the area where Lynchehaun had boasted to have crossed to after his escape from custody in Polranny a decade earlier. They passed a sandy ford where girls gathered cockles on the strand, a sight that would be dramatised in *The Playboy* scene with the village girls, Sara Tansey, Susan Brady and Honor Blake, doing likewise. They travelled to Geesala, a townland nestled between Blacksod and Tullaghan bays, and took lodgings in Gunning's Inn.

At Doolough Strand, close to Geesala, riders whipped their horses into a canter across splaying sand to the shouts of the crowd in the annual summer horse race. In Act III of *The Playboy* Synge transformed this incident into an off-stage mule race at the sea's edge when Mahon, unaware that he is watching his own son Christy, shouts, 'Look at the mule he has, kicking the stars' and, on recognising his son, adds, 'I'd know his way of spitting and he astride the moon.' The enraged father was mesmerised by the spectacle of Christy transformed into a hero figure. Almost a half-century after Synge's visit to Mayo, the horse race which the writer could not represent on stage in *The Playboy* would be magnificently recreated in John Ford's movie *The Quiet Man*, with its obvious allusions to Synge's drama. The film's hero, Sean Thornton, arrives in a Mayo village, having killed a man, and is challenged to prove his mettle, as Synge's Christy Mahon had been.

Had they gone as far as Doohoma, a few miles further south, Synge and Yeats could have looked directly across Blacksod Bay to Achill Island and to Ridge Point, close to Agnes MacDonnell's home at the Valley House. Doohoma was the place where the Achill boat crossed from the island to the north Mayo mainland. This was the ferry referred to by the Widow Quinn in *The Playboy* as she tried to whisk Christy Mahon away: 'I'll take him in the ferry to the Achill boat.' As Christy grappled with his captors he called up the ghost of the 'madman' Lynchehaun: 'Cut this rope, Pegeen, and I'll quit the lot of you, and live from this out, like the madman of Keel, eating muck and green weeds on the faces of the cliffs.'

The weather was stiflingly hot as Synge and Yeats prepared to leave Belmullet, and Synge complained of being worn out from the effort of getting out fresh material every second day for *The Manchester Guardian*. His temper was not improved by the fact that his typewriter was broken, although he managed to patch it up and hoped it would last until he reached home. They were about to leave north Mayo and to head inland 'to the congested portion of the inner edge of the county'. Synge knew that, in the district of the Erris Union, he had witnessed the most distressed conditions in the whole of Ireland.

From his two journeys to the Erris district, John Synge had packed his notebooks with jottings of images, conversations, and phrases that would dance through *The Playboy* text. The places extending from Doohoma and Geesala to Carrowmore Lake and Bangor Erris were recreated in the drama. It was in these places that Christy Mahon was 'abroad in the dark night poaching rabbits on hills', going 'with a dung fork and stabbing a fish', and watching 'the light passing the north or the patches of fog' until he'd hear 'a rabbit starting to screech'. Christy would tell Pegeen that they 'should be pacing Neifin in the dews of the night, the times sweet smells do be rising and you'd see a little, shiny new moon, maybe sinking in the hills'. He longed for them both to be 'astray in Erris', where they could make 'mighty kisses' with their 'wetted mouths'.

These were the places where savagery and fine words were linked together for the writer and where 'a daring fellow is a jewel of the world' when a community makes a hero out of his savage deeds. They were the places 'facing southwards on the heaths of Keel' in nearby Achill, where the dark deeds of James Lynchehaun had taken hold of a community's imagination.

By late June, Synge was back in Dublin, his assignment for *The Manchester Guardian* complete. During the trip Synge had combined his journalistic and artistic tasks by pounding out newspaper articles on his typewriter while also imaginatively shaping *The Playboy* drama. Synge could not have realised that, in just over eighteen months, this artistic work would unleash waves of controversy and acrimony. The sarcastic words of Christy Mahon's father would later appear prophetic: they will 'have a great time from this time out telling stories of the villainy of Mayo and the fools is here'.

By the end of the year Synge had met the head-turning and flirtatious actress Molly Allgood who became the inspiration for the character of *The Playboy*'s Pegeen. She was eighteen, he was sixteen years her senior, and hovering constantly between sickness and health. For his remaining years, Molly would be at the centre of John Synge's life as the controversy surrounding his savage drama hero swirled about him.

17

A Murderous Race of Savages
January 1907

Dublin's Abbey Theatre was crammed full, with many in the audience having standing room only. John Synge had seen the crush on the street when he arrived at the theatre but was unprepared for what he met when he entered the auditorium. 'Take off your hat. Have some manners,' they mocked him, with an eruption of boos and jeers. The pit and gallery were taken up by an audience that was largely hostile to his play. 'Tramp, tramp, the boys are marching,' a group above him sang out as they stamped their feet in unison. When the curtain went up on *Riders to the Sea*, the first performance of the night's programme, it was to a respectful reaction and Synge hoped that the trouble might be contained that night. But no sooner had Act I of *The Playboy* got under way than the rumpus broke out once more.

'Rotten. Go back to England,' he heard through the mayhem.

'That's not Ireland. Maybe it's Lancashire,' a voice shouted.

The writer's rasping cough went unnoticed in the bedlam. The rattle in his chest hurt his ribcage and it felt like his head would burst with the noise that swelled through the theatre. He could sense the fever coursing through his body as the jeers and hisses crackled and fizzled in the auditorium. A bugle screeched in the gallery, feet pounded in the stalls and screeches whistled through cupped fingers. Then Synge heard the words clearly and distinctly: 'Hurrah for Lynchehaun'. He knew that, for this interjection at least, he had nobody but himself to blame, since he had dragged the Achill felon, the English landowner Agnes MacDonnell, and the patricide case of Murvey into the controversy surrounding his latest play.

The noise from the audience did not smother the voices of the actors as fully as it had done on the previous two nights, as the presence of the constabulary helped to keep the lid on the worst excesses of the protestors. Synge was glad when the curtain fell on the last act, for he was exhausted, and he knew that his cough would keep him awake for most of the night. It had been a gruelling five days, and he had felt poorly with influenza for the entire week. He had woken at his mother's home in Glenageary the previous Sunday with a splitting headache, worn out from the lack of sleep. The outbreak of fury from a section of the audience at the Abbey the previous night had reverberated in every bone of his body as he sat in Glendalough House writing a letter to Molly Allgood. The pair were secretly engaged and planned to marry, but his ill health was proving an obstacle.

He was lonesome, he told her, unable to settle at anything, and troubled by what had happened at the inaugural performance of *The Playboy*. As he wrote, Synge appeared to grow calmer and more philosophical, suggesting to Molly that, perhaps, the excitement around the play might bring some positive outcomes. 'It is better any day to have the row we had last night, than to have your play fizzling out in half-hearted applause. Now we'll be talked about. We're an event in the history of the Irish stage.' He did not exaggerate, for the disturbances that greeted *The Playboy* would make theatrical history. Molly had, Synge assured her in his letter, played the part of Pegeen Mike in the play wonderfully; he had even overheard a man in the audience remark, 'What a beautiful girl!' How he wished that she was beside him to talk over the whole show and possible improvements.

The quarter to eleven bell rang out in his mother's house, usually a signal for Synge to put on his shoes and set out on his walk with Molly. Perhaps, if he wired her next day, she could come down on the quarter to two train to Bray and they could take a walk together? Even though he felt poorly that morning Synge had to go into the city to meet up with Lady Gregory, who had sent a wire to W. B. Yeats in Scotland telling him: 'Audience broke up in disorder at the word shift.'

Synge had been nervous on Monday morning as he waited for the newspapers' verdict on *The Playboy*. *The Freeman's Journal* could barely contain itself in expressing its protest at the unmitigated libel in the play against Irish peasant men and women: 'The blood boils with indignation as one recalls the incidents, expressions, ideas of this squalid, offensive production, incongruously styled a comedy in three acts.' That such a piece could have been conceived and written was strange enough to *The Freeman's* correspondent, but that it should have been accepted, rehearsed and enacted at a theatre supposed to be dedicated to high dramatic art was incomprehensible. The paper was unequivocal: even if the events presented in the drama were true, it was not necessary to enquire if they should be represented on stage. 'It is quite plain that there is need for a censor at the Abbey Theatre,' the piece concluded.

In the same edition, *The Freeman* published a letter to the editor from 'A Western Girl' who voiced her emphatic protest against the play. 'We are asked to believe that a community of Connacht peasants receive with open arms a stranger who says that he is fleeing from justice for the murder of his father.' Worse still, the letter went, the play had shown Irish peasant women flinging themselves into the arms of a parricide. 'Is it necessary for me to say that in no part of Ireland are the women so wanting in modesty as to make such advances to a total stranger, much less to a criminal?' The letter writer was especially disappointed that the charming actress, Miss Allgood, was forced 'before the most fashionable audience in Dublin to use a word indicating an essential item of female attire, which the lady would probably never utter in ordinary circumstances'.

On Tuesday, after two nights of *Playboy* disturbances at the Abbey, Synge managed to walk himself into even deeper trouble. W. B. Yeats had returned from Aberdeen and he and Synge had lunched together in the Metropole Hotel where they gave their views on the ongoing controversy to reporters. Yeats was supportive. *The Playboy*, he said, was Mr Synge's masterpiece and he was adamant that it would continue. 'We will go on until the play has been heard, and heard sufficiently to be judged on its merits.' Any member of the audience, he said, who wrote to complain that they had been unable to hear the play, would be sent a free ticket, and the play would continue for as long as there was one person who wanted to hear it and was prevented from doing so.

When the reporters asked Synge if he had anything to say about the word that had caused such uproar in the Abbey, the writer replied that it was an everyday word in the west of Ireland, which would not cause offence there, but might be taken differently by people in Dublin.

And what was the main point of the play? he was asked.

Synge replied that the idea of the play was suggested to him 'by the fact that a few years ago a man who committed a murder was kept hidden by the people on one of the Aran Islands until he could get off to America, and also by the case of Lynchehaun, who was a most brutal murderer of a woman and yet, by the aid of Irish peasant women, managed to conceal himself from the police for months, and to get away also.'

The following day Synge modified these comments somewhat in a letter to *The Irish Times*: '*The Playboy of the Western World* is not a play with a "purpose" in the modern sense of the world, but although parts of it are, or are meant to be, extravagant comedy, still a great deal that is in it, and a great deal more that is behind it, is perfectly serious, when looked at in a certain light.' However, Synge could not have had any cause for complaint when *The Freeman's Journal* quickly added fuel to the fire with its provocative headline, 'Play Founded on Lynchehaun Case'.

Some weeks later, as Synge was recovering from a prolonged bout of illness, he wrote to his friend Stephen McKenna complaining that the interviewer had 'hashed up' what he had said in the Metropole, and explaining his reference to the parricide and Lynchehaun cases: 'That's the whole myth. It isn't quite accurate to say, I think, that the thing is a generalization from a single case. *If* the idea had occurred to me I could and would just as readily [have] written the thing, as it stands, without the Lynchehaun case or the Aran case. The story – in its ESSENCE – is probable, given the psychic state of the locality. I used the cases afterwards to controvert critics who said it was *impossible.*'

On the Wednesday of the eventful first week of *The Playboy* performances, Yeats had to attend the courts where Patrick Columb, clerk, was charged with being guilty of offensive behaviour in the Abbey between ten and eleven o'clock the previous night. Yeats, in answer to questions from Mr Tobias, appearing for the police, had testified:

> I am managing director of the Abbey Theatre. I was there last night when a play called The Playboy of the Western World was performed. From the first rising of the curtain there was obviously an organised attempt to prevent the play being heard. That was from a section of the pit. The stalls and balcony were anxious to hear the play. The noise consisted of shouting and booing and stamping of feet. I did not hear six consecutive lines of the play last night owing to the noise. The section that caused the disturbance was not part of the regular audience. The conduct of the section was riotous and offensive and annoyed and disturbed the audience.

Mr Lidwell, for the defendant, asked, 'Did you read the play?'

'Yes,' replied Yeats, 'and passed it.'

'Is it a caricature of the Irish people?'

'It is no more a caricature of the people of Ireland than Macbeth is a caricature of the people of Scotland or Falstaff a caricature of the gentlemen of England. The play is an example of the exaggeration of art.'

'Is this play typical of the Irish people?'

'No, it is an exaggeration.'

Patrick Columb was found guilty of disorderly behaviour

and ordered to pay a fine of 40 shillings, with the alternative of one month's imprisonment.

By the end of the week Synge was exhausted. His cough was getting worse and continued to keep him awake at night. The doctor was called and diagnosed severe bronchitis and ordered the patient to bed, while all the time Synge was longing to be out on the hills with Molly, his 'changeling'.

There was more positive news on Saturday when a thoughtful and generally supportive letter in the papers from Stephen Gwynn, Member of Parliament for Galway, drew attention to the marvel of the 'sheltered murderer': 'By a very old tradition, based on the general injustice of the mode of government, Irish peasants are bonded together against the criminal law.' There was, he argued, every disposition among the Irish peasantry to shelter a man wanted by the police: 'Hence, for instance, the escape of Lynchehaun.' It was easy to see, he said, 'how grim imagination can shape out a lonely inert community where nothing happens, in which a man who has done a deed is a man of note ... the more notable in proportion to the horror of his deed.' Stephen Gwynn added, however, that he could see that if *The Playboy* succeeded, it could be held as justifying the view of Ireland 'as peopled by a murderous race of savages'.

Synge was too ill the following Monday to attend the public debate on *The Playboy* organised by Yeats at the Abbey. The discussion was chaired by P. D. Kenny, known as 'Pat' – a Mayo man, born in Aughamore, just a few miles from the birthplace of Brother Paul Carney and some two decades the friar's junior. Pat and the young Carney may well have passed one another on the road to Ballyhaunis or to Knock, one a young lad, the other serving his trade as a baker in Ballyhaunis.

Pat had given his own views of *The Playboy* in *The Irish Times* where he wrote provocatively: 'I cannot but admire the moral courage of the man who has shone his dreadful searchlight into our cherished accumulation of social skeletons. He has led our vision through the Abbey stage into the heart of Connacht, and revealed to us there terrible truths, of our own making, which we dare not face for the present. The merciless accuracy of his revelation is more than we can bear.' As for the issue of the feminine underclothing mentioned in the play, he said, 'I have often heard discussions more familiar among the peasantry themselves without the remotest suggestion of immorality, and if Dublin is shocked in this connection, it is because its mind is less clean than that of the Connacht peasant woman.'

It had been a tumultuous week. Synge wrote to Frank Fay asking him to get copies of each newspaper that covered *The Playboy* storm: he wanted six copies of *The Irish Times* for Wednesday and Thursday, six copies of *The Herald* and six of Saturday's *Telegraph*. He also asked for a copy of *An Claidheamh Soluis* where Patrick Pearse had accused the playwright of using the stage 'for the propagation of a monstrous gospel of animalism', and for producing 'a brutal glorification of violence, and grossness, and the flesh'. For Pearse, Synge's play was indefensible and its production had serious implications for Anglo-Irish drama: 'Mr Yeats triumphs for the moment; but he has lost far more than he has gained. As for Anglo-Irish drama – it is the beginning of the end.'

The Mayo News edition of Saturday 2 February took up *The Playboy* debate with the headline:

Calumny on Mayo Life

---o---

Play Alleged to be founded on the Lynchehaun Case

Dubliners Protest against its Production

The piece described the astonishing occurrences at the Abbey Theatre when the management of 'the so-called Irish and National Institution' attempted to produce a drama written by a Mr Synge. Following a summary of *The Playboy* plot, the writer added that it was no surprise that the Abbey audience strongly protested against the performance 'as a vile calumny on Irish peasant life'. Concerning Mr Synge's citing of James

Lynchehaun during the controversy, *The Mayo News* expressed its strong views.

> Mr. Synge, the author, was drawing very much on his imagination when he described Lynchehaun as 'a brutal murderer of a woman', for the lady whom he attacked, Mrs Agnes MacDonnell, is enjoying, we are glad to say, excellent health at the present time in her home at the Valley, Achill. Knowing Mayo life, we assume as intimately as Mr. Synge, we can say that his efforts to represent Mayo women as the willing harbourers of parricides are founded on calumny, or, as the 'Freeman' says, calumny gone raving mad. He has cited the case of Lynchehaun, but perhaps he does not know that when the audacious scoundrel was being sentenced at Castlebar Assizes, Judge Gibson paid a special compliment to the 'peasant woman' who was the principal means of bringing the criminal to justice. He told this simple, truthful Achill girl that she was a credit to the religion she belonged to and to the island from whence she came.

Agnes MacDonnell, the woman who continued to enjoy 'excellent health', was, it seemed, as determined and single-minded as ever, on the evidence of proceedings at the Achill Assizes. In a court sitting overseen by Mr R. Carr, there was an exceptionally large number of cases to be heard. However, through the intervention of local peacemakers, a large number of these were settled out of court, but not that of Agnes MacDonnell. She had summoned Anthony Lavelle, for the trespass of four cows on her lands, and her employee, John Gallagher, gave evidence on her behalf.

The defendant, Lavelle, spoke in his own defence and argued that his cattle were grazing on a common area where the fences were broken, allowing the beasts to enter Mrs MacDonnell's property. The presiding magistrate responded to this plea by asserting that a landowner was not bound to erect fences to keep out the animals of others. 'You are bound to keep your cattle off her land. Do you believe that Mrs MacDonnell is bound to force other people's cattle off her land?' Anthony Lavelle was dogged and sullen, claiming that it would not take two hours to build a fence where his cattle entered.

A decree of two shillings for trespass and two shillings in costs was given against the defendant. The magistrate repeated his view that people ought to know that nobody was under an obligation to fence out other people's cattle unless an agreement was made to do so. Before the case concluded Anthony Lavelle told the court rather ominously, 'Her cattle were in my share of land often, but the next time I'll catch them and I'll make her pay for them.'

Agnes MacDonnell continued to wrap the protective cloak of the law around herself and her assets in Achill. Meanwhile, her bitter enemy James Lynchehaun had made legal history across the Atlantic and now, closer to home, his name was enmeshed with an historic literary controversy.

18

A Distinguished Visitor
Summer 1907

Everybody in Achill wanted to read the newspaper story. The islanders whispered about its contents in the shops and on the pavements in Achill Sound, while those who could not read listened, wide-eyed, as snatches of the story were read out to them. The newspaper passed from monk to monk in Bunnacurry Monastery where some eyed their fellow friar, Brother Paul Carney, with some suspicion; he was back in Achill after an absence of a decade and spent hour after hour in his room writing in his journals. The members of the Royal Commission on Congestion talked of the story among themselves when they visited the schoolhouse in Achill Sound to take submissions from the public. Dr Croly read the piece in his home in The Colony and spoke of its contents with a shake of the head to fellow worshippers after Sunday's church service. Agnes MacDonnell's employees asked one another if Lynchehaun had been in the vicinity of the Valley House, prowling among the tress and whin bushes. Would they keep the paper to show to Mrs MacDonnell when she returned from London? Had she heard the news?

The Mayo News edition of 10 August 1907 was a sensation. It arrived in the middle of a wretched summer long remembered for the incessant rain and lack of sunshine. After favourable conditions in February and March, the unseasonable weather set in during April, becoming almost winter-like. Temperatures during May had been abnormally low with a persistent sleety rain and sharp easterly winds. The weather had delayed the planting of the potato crop as the ridges lay ready and waiting, covered with a thick layer of sea wrack. When growth came, it was estimated to be anything from ten days to a month behind that of previous seasons, and the severity of the weather had especially hampered the progress of the oats crop. There had also been a falling off of visitors to the island and the car owners and hotel keepers complained at the lack of business. The prospect of rain hung over the island and the inhabitants of Achill needed some diversion from their misery.

When the islanders stared at the newspaper pages, it was as if they were looking straight into his face again. Lynchehaun's razor-bright eyes gazed out from *The Mayo News* where four large pictures were blazoned across the page: a haughty bearded inmate from Castlebar Prison in 1894; a side profile of the prisoner with a heavier, rounded face in Maryborough Jail in 1902; a prosperous-looking, moustached man with a thick jowl in Indianapolis in 1903; and, sensationally, a sketch titled 'Mr Cooney of New York, alias James Lynchehaun, Esq., of Cleveland, Ohio (Tourist in Achill 1907)'. The pictures and story were accompanied by a headline which sent a thrill of excitement through its readers:

LYNCHEHAUN
His Recent Visit to Achill
THE RESULT OF A WAGER

Those who read and re-read the report may have picked up a hint of defensiveness on the part of the newspaper, which acknowledged some scepticism surrounding Lynchehaun's supposed secret visit to Achill the previous month: 'The news was at first received with considerable doubt, even in Achill, but it is now very well known that Mr James Lynchehaun, alias Mr Cooney of New York, has been amongst us and has paid what was probably his last visit to his aged parents and friends.'

It seemed that the secret visit was kept under wraps until Lynchehaun had departed Achill and Ireland and was safely out of British jurisdiction.

The Mayo News was repeatedly forced, over the following weeks, to substantiate its story. By the end of August the paper was on the defensive, claiming that 'before making the sensational announcement that the champion jail-breaker had quietly revisited his native hills last month, we took every possible precaution against being "hoaxed" or mistaken on the subject'. In particular, the paper stressed the accuracy of their report that a Westport resident, who knew Lynchehaun from infancy, spent an hour or so with the notorious fugitive at the Railway Hotel. Lynchehaun had, according to the newspaper, spent just one night with his parents in Polranny during his stopover, and also dropped in on an old neighbour, who failed to recognise him until he made himself known, and had 'yielded, rather reluctantly to their solicitations to take himself out of harm's way as speedily as possible'.

The news scoop provided an opportunity for *The Mayo News* to fill pages of news columns with previously published material about Lynchehaun's exploits over the dozen years since the Valley House outrage. At the same time, the paper retained a certain reserve and reticence about the 1894 events, maintaining that it was 'unnecessary in these columns to refer to the shocking details of the assault' for which Lynchehaun had received a life sentence.

There were those who believed that *The Mayo News* accounts of the fugitive's return to Achill were penned by James Lynchehaun himself, so different was the narrative style to the paper's regular reportage. If this suspicion were true, it may have accounted for the tentative and rather diffident tone in aspects of the paper's presentation: 'It is stated with every semblance of truth that during the past few weeks James Lynchehaun visited his native Achill and spent a pleasant time with his friends. It is also stated, quite unnecessarily we think, that the distinguished visitor travelled incognito, and thus escaped attentions which, to one of his modest temperament might have been unpleasant.'

The story went that a mild-looking American gentleman of middle-age had arrived by train in Mulranny one sunny afternoon and asked a car owner if he could be taken to friends named Cooney in a certain part of Achill. What were Lynchchaun's feelings on returning to his native place? 'Not being weavers of fiction,' *The Mayo News* reported, 'we are unable to describe what the feelings of the passenger were as he drove though the scenes of his first marvellous escape midway between Mulranny and the island.' For weeks the newspaper continued to robustly defend its coverage of Lynchehaun's stopover and the paper persisted by producing new evidence in support of its account. One such piece of evidence was a facsimile of a letter-card, published in the paper and reportedly sent by James Lynchehaun to an acquaintance in Mulranny with the message, 'You were the only man in Ireland who could tell who I was.'

As the month of August drew to a close, a crowd gathered outside the schoolhouse in Achill Sound to watch the arrival of important visitors. The members of the Royal Commission into Congestion in Mayo were holding one of its meetings in Achill, with Sir Francis Mowatt presiding. A delegation from Corraun handed in a written statement to the meeting and their message was clear: 'Buy out the landlords, enlarge the holdings, and teach the people to set up new and reproductive works.' The compulsory purchase of the land from the landlords was on everybody's lips, alongside the sensational accounts concerning Lynchehaun's homecoming.

By September the story of Lynchehaun was still making news and *The Mayo News* ran its most breathtaking headline to date in a compilation of accounts of Lynchehaun's escapades and adventures after he left Ireland following his Achill visit:

Lynchehaun !

---o---

Now in Buffalo USA

---0---

HE SENDS US TWO LETTERS

Describing His recent Tour

Arrested on Board HMS The Talbot

His Visit to Achill – Recognised by his Brother's Dog

Delivers a Speech and Raises a Row in Belfast

Exploits in Germany

At midday, on Saturday 1 September, the paper received two letters addressed to its editor, Mr Doris, with Buffalo, USA postmarks for 28 August. The letters were written in pencil and bore the signature of James Lynchehaun. 'Both are, beyond all doubt,' the correspondent wrote, 'in the handwriting of the outlaw.' The letters, if true, filled in some of the missing details of the escapee's Achill sojourn. 'I went especially to see my dear old father and mother. The scene cannot be described either in fiction or history.' Lynchehaun also claimed in the letters to have had a peculiar experience with his brother's dog: 'I want to tell you a strange but true episode. My brother, Tom's dog sniffed and smelled me all over. He embraced me with all kinds of affection. I could not get him away. He put his forepaws around my neck. He followed me for miles. I fired three revolver shots to scare him. No use. I took him up by the paw, shook it and kissed him and he returned home. I spoke to him only in Irish and he went straight home. That dog is a genuine Irish hound – see him, red coat of hair.'

During this time the ageing Brother Paul Carney resided at Bunnacurry Monastery, having been transferred back to his beloved island two years earlier. Each day he sat hunched in his room, his pen moving over and back across the pages of his leather-bound journals. He had grown even heavier with the passage of time, his feet turned outward for balance when he took a break and strolled in the monastery walled garden. Occasionally, if the day was fine, he followed the path down to the slipway from where he could look out on Inishbiggle and inhale the ocean scents from Blacksod Bay. But the walk tired him, causing spots of perspiration to glisten on his face like a ripe apple after a shower of rain. The friar had received a letter from his friend: 'I have been home to see my dear father and mother,' Lynchehaun wrote, 'neither fiction nor history has recorded, or ever will, such a scene. See the old people and they will tell you all, much better than I can describe or write, while on my flying tour.' It appears that the friar and the felon did not meet up during the latter's clandestine visit.

Brother Paul Carney was then in his sixties and had spent almost a decade honing his skills as a questor of funds for church causes across America, in England and Scotland, and throughout Ireland. He was content now to enjoy the peace and quiet of Achill, to reflect, and to write. He thought often about his friend and asked himself if, perhaps, he had stoked Lynchehaun's savagery. Had his words or actions inflamed his friend to his brutish acts? The friar had much to ponder but was unwavering in his determination to write down the exploits of his friend. He would leave behind a record in his *Lynchehaun Narrative*, and was, at the time, engaged in gathering anecdotes and stories about the years since his friend's victory in the Indianapolis court. He wrote of an intriguing encounter between Lynchehaun and the Vice-President of the United States: '12 January 1906. An Indianapolis paper on this date states that Vice-President Charles Fairbanks called on James Lynchehaun, the Irish escaped convict ... and found his condition much improved at his home. Lynchehaun had been in a serious condition for several weeks from rheumatics.'

The friar also wrote of a meeting between Lynchehaun and another important visitor to Indianapolis, Douglas Hyde – founder, and later president of the Gaelic League. Hyde was speaking at the Athenaeum Club in the city, and described the encounter with James Lynchehaun in his own book *My Journey to America*:

> Lynchehaun is in Indianapolis. England tried her best to get hold of him, but the Irish got together and they defeated England's attempts. They did that through spite and hatred of England, and it appears that they did not know that he was a blackguardly ruffian. The scoundrel himself said, 'When I die Indianapolis will be written on my heart', and, indeed, he has good reason to be thankful to the people of that city. He was on the platform when I spoke, and he came to shake my hand, half ashamed to come near me. At first I did not realise who he was, but (then) I said to him in Irish, 'I heard of you before', and I turned away from him.

Brother Paul Carney's friend had come a long way since his humble beginnings in Achill. The friar doggedly continued with his narrative. He would not go to his grave until he had completed his task and set down the saga of James Lynchehaun for posterity.

Agnes MacDonnell must have been waiting for this to happen. She would have known in her bones that Lynchehaun would return at some point and that he would not leave her in peace. Every day that she spent on the island she must have expected him. She had carried her wounds for more than a dozen years. She could not escape the memories and was reminded of the revolting events of 1894 each time she touched her disfigured face. Sometimes, it seemed as if the despoilment had made her heart smaller and numbed her emotions. But she had held her ground in the face of every threat, menace and pressure. The land, the law, and the Church – these had been her buttress and her bulwark. She had endured.

She was unyielding with her tenants, pursuing her rights in the courts with determined tenacity, most often in the Castlebar courtroom where she had last faced James Lynchehaun; sometimes in the Achill Assizes; occasionally in the Mulranny Land Court. It was in Mulranny that Mr Justice Fitzgerald had held a special session to consider her claim when she appealed the rents set by the Land Court for the Valley estate tenants. She had briefed John Garvey to speak on her behalf. 'These tenants,' he said in court, 'have a right of seaweed, excellent turf, and the grazing of 1,500 acres of mountain for part of which Mrs MacDonnell is liable for a rent of £10 a year to the Irish Church Missions.'

J. C. Roberton, representing the tenants, described the abject condition of the tenants on Agnes MacDonnell's estate: they had built their own houses and reclaimed any of the land that was of use; they had to travel thirty miles to their nearest market town in Newport; they were forced to migrate as harvesters to England and Scotland to earn their rents for the landlord; the land which they occupied would scarcely yield a miserable crop of oats, potatoes, and meadow.

The Justice was not impressed by Agnes MacDonnell's appeal when the rent had changed by the paltry sum of two shillings. 'It's scarcely for the dignity of the court,' he said, 'that it should have to consider such an appeal. Who on earth can tell if a holding is worth twelve shillings or ten shillings?' Agnes MacDonnell cared little for the dignity of the court. It was easy for the judge to talk; he did not have to put up with what she had endured for twenty years while she sought to manage her property. She knew from experience that if she gave her tenants an inch that they would take a mile. Recourse to the law was her only protection.

She had heard the far-fetched yarns about Lynchehaun's visit to Achill and knew that the man had extraordinary notions since he beat the Empire in the Indianapolis court. She had even heard that he had also visited the Industrial Exhibition in Dublin and stayed in no less a place than the Shelbourne Hotel.

Perhaps, in quiet moments or in the blurred space between sleep and wakefulness, Agnes MacDonnell imagined that she came upon James Lynchehaun – as in times past – on the road between Valley and Dugort. She may have pictured him as a figure dwarfed between mountain and sea at some distance from her; a man moving towards her and closing the space between them in the shadow of the mountain; a face that grinned and bared its teeth before merging with the grey-black mountain of Slievemore.

Part 4

19

The Curse of God on You All!

1912–1913

Dr Thomas Croly watched the crowd through the curtained window. There must have been a few hundred people in the gathering outside the office of Grierson, agent for the Achill Mission estate. Some of those who waited blew warm breath into their palms, rubbing their hands together for warmth against the January wind that rolled down from Slievemore on to The Colony. The doctor had heard the footsteps pass his door for what seemed like hours, had listened to the angry mutterings and to the dry coughs that irritated his medic's ear. Each time he looked out, he saw a face he recognised, even if he could not recall the name, from his years of criss-crossing the island day and night on his house calls. There, in the middle of the assembly, he could see the troublesome cleric, Father Martin Colleran, who was driving a wedge between landlord and tenant in a way that his predecessor, Connolly, had never done. Father Colleran was leading his flock on a dangerous course and the doctor was fearful about where it would end.

The doctor's retirement as Medical Officer in Achill after more than three decades of service should have been the start of a peaceful time when he could ease into a life of relaxation in Dugort, enjoying the goodwill of St Thomas' community and of his former patients. Frequently, he crossed the road from his home, walked the short distance downhill facing the Atlantic, and then turned in along the driveway to the church where he had served on the Select Vestry since his arrival in Achill. He attended the weekly church service to sing out the words of 'Redeemer, Now Thy Work is Done', and organised church maintenance and administration tasks.

Everything had been going to plan when, earlier in the year, the Westport Union Board of Guardians considered his application for a full pension on retirement and the newspapers reported their favourable decision: 'Dr Croly has been insufficiently remunerated for his work in Achill and therefore the fullest remuneration should be accorded him.' He did not foresee the nasty direction that events would then take, and was sickened to the core by the vocal public objections to the Union's decision. That one of the prime movers behind the objections was Emily Weddall, a fellow Trustee at the Achill Mission, was all the more upsetting. She took issue with the pension decision in strong letters to the newspapers arguing that Dr Croly's work in Achill was not given free gratis. He was, she said, already well remunerated for his dispensary work and lavishly paid for his private calls. Moreover, she wrote, he received a considerable amount of voluntary labour from the Achill people, who cut and dried his turf, carted manure, and carried out many other services on his behalf. Emily Weddall believed that these 'sad little acts' for the doctor were done out of fear and were not spontaneous outbursts of gratitude as some had claimed. Mrs Weddall proposed that, when a replacement doctor was appointed to Achill, 'a new scale of charges should be instituted more in keeping with the place'. The public controversy was a bitter humiliation for Dr Croly at the end of his career.

Emily Weddall had antagonised the doctor ever since her arrival in Achill six years earlier. She had made a point of associating publicly with the tenants, and attending the Assizes when they were brought before the court for disturbances of the peace. Things had come to a head when her husband, Captain Weddall, died and she sought permission to erect a Celtic cross at his grave in St Thomas' cemetery. The Special Vestry had considered her request at a special meeting attended by eleven members and Dr Croly afterwards recorded their decision: 'The Vestry, with one dissenter, were against such cross being erected in the graveyard.' The doctor knew that Emily Weddall blamed him and had got her revenge with his public mortification over pension rights. What he disliked most was the way she projected herself as a custodian of Irish culture, attracting summer crowds to Scoil Acla at Dooagh, and gaining favourable attention all over the country. He had even heard that she had stood at the graveside of John Millington Synge following the writer's untimely death three years previously.

The doctor bent his ear towards the open window when the drone of the outside assembly grew quiet, and he could see that Father Colleran was preparing to speak. In recent times Dr Croly had begun to think that relationships on the island were as rancorous and as discordant as they had been twenty years earlier when the nasty business at the Valley House flared up. Now, the vociferous demands of the tenants were more belligerent and strident than he could ever recall. Colleran and his likes had a lot to answer for.

The national newspapers were again turning their attention towards Achill, showing them all up in a bad light. In a recent report he had read: 'All over Ireland tenants are buying out their land, yet the landlords of Achill do not allow their tenants to get the benefit of the Act like the people outside. The matter is made doubly urgent because of the conditions under which the poor people of the Valley and the Achill Mission estates are compelled to live.' The land agitation activities of Michael Davitt and others had started a chain of events that had led to the introduction of the various Land Acts by the British Government. The most recent of these had been the Birrell Act of 1909, which extended the 1903 Wyndham Act by allowing the compulsory purchase of tenanted farmland by the authorities. The pressure in Achill was mounting. The island tenants were demanding that their landlords sell to the Congested Districts Board. They would settle for nothing less.

Father Colleran had started to speak to Grierson but he was really addressing the crowd. Those standing at the back of the gathering twisted their heads to turn an ear in the speaker's direction. 'This demonstration is a peaceful one,' the priest started. 'There is no threat of violence, of boycotting, or of any illegal methods. I want you to understand this. We have come here this morning with one purpose. The people want a plain answer to a plain question.' The land agent appeared to cringe back against the wall as the people pressed in close. The priest raised his arm and pointed at the land agent. 'This is the question we have. Are the Trustees of the Achill Mission willing to sell to the tenants through the Congested Districts Board or are they not? What is the answer?'

The pack of people took up the refrain in a chorus of shouts, 'What is the answer? What is the answer?'

The cleric lifted his hands for silence before resuming. 'The visits of the Trustees to this island are few and far between. Who knows what their true intentions are? Sometimes they say that they will sell; next time they refuse. The Congested Districts Board has the same problem, it seems, in getting a reply from the Trustees. You, Mr Grierson — you are the representative of the Trustees. I demand an answer for these long-suffering tenants. Are you prepared to sell through the Congested Districts Board? If these tenants receive an assurance from you, then they have their rents ready to pay and will hand them over. All you need to do is lodge the land maps with the Congested Districts Board and these tenants will pay.'

Why was Achill different to the rest of the country? Father Colleran asked. 'All over Ireland people are buying out their land. In places where the people are very comfortable, the Congested Districts Board is spending thousands of pounds in making them yet more prosperous. This island is known to be one of the poorest parts of the country. But nothing is happening here.' At this stage Father Colleran tried to lighten matters with a shot of humour. 'In strict justice,' he observed, 'considering the nature of the land in Achill, people should be paid to live on it instead of being asked to pay you rent.'

Laughter burst out among the crowd. Dr Croly could see how some of those close to his window turned, smiling, to the person beside them, nodding in agreement at the priest's sentiments. The agent, Grierson, was agitated and appeared hoarse when he started to speak. He himself, he said, had always been for the interests of the people and had even suggested, as far back at 1902, the sale of the Achill Mission estate. 'Withholding payment of rents,' Grierson told them, 'won't influence the Trustees. They don't touch a penny of the money.'

This comment gave rise to guffaws among those standing closest to the agent and the mirth spread through the throng. A man yelled, 'Where does the money go then?' and the shout went up through the crowd, 'Where does the money go? Where does the money go?'

Father Colleran asked for quiet. 'Whatever was done with the rent money,' he declared, 'I can vouch for the fact that not one penny of it goes into improving the lot of the tenants. The Land Purchase Act has brought no benefit whatsoever to the people of Achill.'

'Yes,' somebody shouted, 'not one penny.'

The priest, knowing that he needed to bring proceedings to a close in an orderly way, turned and spoke directly to the crowd. 'We came here this morning to demand a definite answer from the Achill Trustees. Mr Grierson has now promised to bring your demands directly to the Trustees. I would ask you now to wait patiently until you hear that the Trustees have lodged the land maps with the Congested Districts Board. Once you have this assurance, you can then hand over your rents. I am asking you all now to disperse peacefully. This must remain a peaceable protest.'

Dr Croly had much to preoccupy him, not least the welfare of his friend, Agnes MacDonnell, who was caught up in the latest land agitation. For almost twenty years, despite his advice, she had insisted on returning to Achill year after year to the place that had almost destroyed her. On the one hand, the doctor found her obstinacy and stubbornness difficult to comprehend; on the other hand, there was something about her persistence and tenacity that he found admirable. Dr Croly knew in his heart that his friend would never give in. He was aware that a deputation of her tenants had already gone to the Valley House to demand that she sell to the Congested Districts Board.

'Did you hear what Agnes MacDonnell said to them?' his wife had asked.

'What?'

'She said she would not sell and that she would not loosen her grip on her land or on her tenants until she had to.'

'It's on account of what happened to her that she's like that.'

'She said she hoped to live to see the day when the curse of God would fall on this place.'

'She'll never give in,' he had replied with resignation. 'She'll hold on to what she has. That's the way she is.'

He could see that the ill feeling towards Agnes MacDonnell was as harsh in Achill as it had ever been in the past. More worrying still, the antagonism was now being vented publicly with one newspaper letter claiming that the conditions of Mrs MacDonnell's tenants 'had no parallel anywhere in Ireland'. The writer complained that even access to water was denied to her tenants who were prevented from using a certain right of way: 'The valuations of the tenants' holdings in the Valley are scandalously low and half of the tenants are huddled together on cut-away bog, unfit for a snipe to live upon, while up to their very doors are between 300 and 400 acres of tillage land of average quality.' Even worse, the letter-writer added, the landlord's fences ran up to the very gables of their poor cottages, with the result that the tenants could only reach their houses around one gable end.

Perhaps the most harrowing episode of all for the doctor was that which occurred a few weeks prior to the protests at Grierson's office when an islander wrote to the papers with an account which touched a raw nerve, dealing as it did with the death of a child. Michael Gallagher told an emotive story of a system of grazing on the Achill estates which was a curse on him and his family. He described how, the previous year, he had taken his two daughters, aged thirteen and fourteen, to Scotland for the potato picking. The early morning rising and the severe work affected his younger daughter who fell ill and, while they struggled on for a while, the girl became so feverish that they had to return home. 'We all came home before the usual time,' he said, 'poorer than when we left.' No sooner were they back than the bailiff arrived for the rent. Every penny owed had to be paid, the collector said, as he could not make any allowance for the sick girl. 'I hadn't a shilling in my pocket,' said Michael Gallagher, 'and so was forced to go round and make a collection from house to house until I scraped up and paid the amount claimed.' The girl grew weaker and soon passed away, while her father blamed the grazing money and the rent for the family's misfortunes. 'All honour then,' he said, 'to Father Colleran and those associated with him for at last taking the bull by the horns.'

Such was the atmosphere in Achill as Dr Croly was facing into his retirement. The calls for the system of tenantry in Achill to be smashed once and for all grew more strident by the day. By the following spring, the demands for the Congested Districts Board to invoke compulsory powers and force the Achill landlords to sell to their tenants were intensifying. Father Colleran articulated the tenants' trenchant demands in a letter to the Board's Henry Doran:

> Achill Sound
> 25th February 1913
>
> Dear Sir,
> Five years ago your Board promised that Achill would be the first estate purchased under the new Act. Since then we have heard not a word from your Board about purchase ... Everybody is helping us except our own legal official saviour; the press of Ireland, England, and the world is ventilating our grievances and helping us and calling on your Board to come to our rescue. When may we expect your aid?

Yours sincerely,
M Colleran, PP

The priest read out the reply he received to his letter at a public meeting in Achill Sound fair green, telling the people that he detected a ray of hope in Henry Doran's letter:

Congested Districts Board
27th February 1913

Dear Father Colleran,
I beg to acknowledge receipt of your letter of 26 inst. complaining of the Board's inaction in respect of Achill. I have not heard before that the Board promised, as you say, that Achill would be the first estate they would purchase under the Act of 1909. No such decision was arrived at by the Board at any time ... The Board cannot purchase the entire area of land under their control in the course of a few years, and there are, I may say, a great many districts quite as poor as Achill, and up to the present, have no attention whatever from the Board. From time to time the Board sent several communications to the owners of Achill Island explaining their willingness to open negotiations for the purchase of it, but until quite recently they got no satisfactory reply. Within the last few weeks communications have been received which indicate that the trustees contemplate offering the island for sale to the Board. The Board are not of the opinion that Achill Island is a property which up to the present time they should seek to acquire by compulsory purchase. They may be wrong in this view. You apparently hold the opposite view very strongly ... If the owners will lodge the maps of the estate with the Board an inspection of it would be made without much delay.

Yours faithfully,
Henry Doran

Within days there was a nasty turn of events at Valley when Dr Croly's worst fears were realised. The only positive aspect of the episode was that, as a retired doctor, he was not called upon on this occasion to minister to the injured and wounded.

In early March 1913, a convoy of carts, laden with hay, approached Valley crossroads from the southern direction, escorted by a number of constables. An agent had purchased a consignment of hay on Agnes MacDonnell's behalf from the estate of the recently deceased parish priest, Father Connolly, and, given the landlord-tenant tensions on the island, a request had been made for police protection. The procession of carts moved slowly in the direction of Valley crossroads, near where a large group of people, mainly women, had gathered. At first it seemed as if the carts would pass without any disturbance. However, as the procession drew level with the crowd, a barrage of turf and stones rained down upon carts, animals and drivers. More people joined the assault and the missiles hailed down with growing ferocity. The police drew their batons in self-defence and charged the attackers.

A scream was heard and the shout went up, 'Her arm is broken.' Sergeant Donnellan was knocked to the ground and taken away unconscious. Several constables sustained facial injuries and had their batons smashed. A considerable time elapsed before the police managed to disperse the attacking crowd and let the carts proceed to the Valley House. Dr Moran later motored from Westport to attend the injured and Sergeant Donnellan was said to be suffering from concussion. It was not known if Agnes MacDonnell was in residence at the Valley House at the time of the disturbance.

Achill was making national news headlines once more as *The Irish Times* reported on 15 March that police reinforcements had been sent to the island and that ten officers had been based at the Valley which was in 'a state of siege'. Nobody knew how it would end. The object of the dispute between the islanders and the landlords, the report said, was not a question of rent but of the selling of the land on the landlord estates to the Congested Districts Board for distribution among the tenants. 'The owners, however, refuse to be coerced into selling their property,' the report added. 'Meetings have been held in different districts and there has been a good deal of drumming and parading such as might be seen long ago on the mainland.'

Twelve women were brought before the Achill petty sessions court on charges of assaulting Agnes MacDonnell's workmen and a number of constables. The small courtroom was crowded when the case was heard, with hundreds gathered outside and a large force of police in attendance, drawn from Castlebar, Westport, Newport and other centres. The defendants were not professionally represented and, before the cross-examination could commence, Father Colleran rose to ask if he could make a statement to the court. Consent was given.

'I would respectfully suggest to the bench,' the priest said, 'that you should adjourn all these cases today. I believe that if you do adjourn them, the guarantee or promise given by the people to the police, and by the police to the people – of not bringing any more police to Achill – will be upheld. Then I believe we will have peace. We do not want to have quarrelling on the island or in the parish. I do not wish it to go abroad on the wings of the press that there is any ill feeling between the police and the people here.'

Father Colleran said that the agitation about the land purchase issue had been going on for six months. During all that time, he claimed, 'and the police will bear out what I have to say, there has not been a single outrage from the beginning up to the present time'. All that had happened, in his view, was 'a skirmish between the police and the people in the Valley' but this was hardly something that deserved heavy censure.

The priest was prepared to give a commitment to the court that any future agitation would be carried out peacefully. He then made a remarkable announcement in relation to Agnes MacDonnell: 'I am glad to say that Mrs MacDonnell of the Valley has offered to sell. She has notified the tenants that, of her own free will, she is offering her estate to the Congested Districts Board in a reasonable time, and that she will get the estate measured and mapped. Until we get the other landlords in Achill to act similarly we will continue the agitation and we will pay no rent.'

The Chairman agreed to adjourn all cases for four weeks. The police departed Achill by mail train.

What of Agnes MacDonnell? Was it true? Was she about to sell her lands to the Congested Districts Board? Was the battle now over? Had she finally given in?

At its meeting on 8 April 1913, the secretary to the Congested Districts Board read into the records a letter from Agnes MacDonnell of the Valley House confirming that she was giving instructions to have maps prepared with a view to offering her estate to the Board. At the same meeting the Board decided to request Mr Grierson of the Achill Mission estate to lodge outstanding maps and documents with a view to having an inspection made of the entire Dugort estate to enable the Board to come to a decision as to whether they should exclude certain lands of the Achill Mission from the sale.

Soon afterwards, the Board directed that the valuation of Mrs MacDonnell's properties at the Valley House should proceed. To all appearances, it looked as though Agnes MacDonnell would soon divest herself of the Valley House lands.

The sale transaction between Mrs MacDonnell and the Congested Districts Board did not, however, take place. It may have been that the valuation price was unacceptable to Agnes MacDonnell and that she was holding out for a better offer or she may have been unwilling to sell additional untenanted land as sought by the Board. Perhaps the wily landowner had used the tactic of offering her lands for sale to deflect the animosity of her tenants.

For the remainder of her life, the lands of the Valley House estate would remain in Agnes MacDonnell's ownership. She had held out.

20
A Blazing Trail
May 1923

Agnes MacDonnell stretched out her hand to take the glass, sipped, and welcomed the trickle of wine in her throat. Darkness was closing in on the Valley House and she could see the criss-crossing branches of the trees through the window. When standing, her body was shorter and her frame shrunken from what it had been. Her hair was still thick but with no hint of the auburn radiance of earlier years. An eye patch covered her destroyed eye but her facial scars were less prominent and appeared to have fused with the lines of age over three decades.

For months now she had followed the stories of rampage and devastation as the Irish turned their ferocity on one another. They had maimed animals in the fields, pushed train carriages into the sea, planted bombs under bridges, smashed telegraph equipment in post offices and turned guns on former comrades. She had waited, expecting at any moment to hear loud footsteps on her driveway and shouts to open up. Could the Valley House once again explode into flames? She knew that there had been IRA threats in Achill, even to St Thomas' Church.

Like many others, she had thought at the start of the year that the hostilities would soon come to an end. She had read in the newspapers that the capacity of the Anti-Treaty forces was weakened and that Mr Cosgrave's Free State Government would soon be back in full control. There was talk of an amnesty and pleas to Mr de Valera to agree to a truce. She had hoped that the worst of the attacks were in the past but the fighting was, if anything, getting worse. For weeks on end, a blazing trail of destruction had swept across Ireland devouring a swathe of big houses. Agnes MacDonnell was apprehensive – was this the moment when she could lose everything? Could her life's work again be brought to ruin?

She had prided herself on being one step ahead of her enemies. Two years previously, in September 1921, just weeks before the Irish delegation led by Arthur Griffith travelled to London for the talks that ended with the signing of the Anglo-Irish Treaty, she had arranged a meeting with her solicitors. In the presence of two witnesses – F. Harrison, engineer, and Lucy Harrison, of 63 Bryanston Street, London – she had formally signed her last will and testament. She left all that she possessed to her son, Leslie Elliot, pleased with his marriage to Irene Orpen two years earlier. It may have been a moment of closure for Agnes MacDonnell. Against all the odds, she had kept her Achill estate intact and secured its future for her family.

If, after two years of Civil War, it appeared that the strife in Ireland might be petering out, this would not happen without a final burst of violent mayhem. On the first day of February 1923, the carnage came precariously close to Achill, to the County Mayo village of Ballyglass, outside Claremorris. Agnes MacDonnell read the accounts of what happened at Moore Hall, the property of the writer, George Moore, whose brother – Colonel Maurice Moore – was a member of the Irish Free State Senate. In the darkness of the February night, a local IRA unit had made its stealthy way towards the big house and ordered the steward to hand over the keys. The armed men hauled furniture and household items from the lower rooms out on to the lawn, pelting more from the first-floor windows. They would later carry off nine cartloads of loot. The men then dragged bales of hay from the stables to the house, doused the residence with paraffin and petrol, and set the building alight. Six hours later the roof fell in and Moore House was a scorched, ash-strewn shell.

The Irish Times speculated on the immediate cause of the Moore House arson attack. 'It is understood that after the arrest of Mr Kilroy, leader of the Anti-Treaty forces in Mayo, a message was sent asking Colonel Moore to intervene in order to save Mr Kilroy's life, and promising that if this was done no more attacks would be made in County Mayo.'

In London, George Moore wrote an irritated letter to *The Times* where he appeared to blame his brother for the catastrophe. 'With reference to the burning of Moore Hall, you speak in *The Times* today of the Hall as being the residence of Colonel Moore, despite the fact that the house is described as mine in all books of reference. In the hope of saving a very beautiful example of Georgian architecture, I tried to dissociate my house from politics, and for that reason Colonel Moore has not visited Moore Hall for the last twenty years. His acquiescence in his election to the Senate and the speeches he has delivered in the Senate, are no doubt the cause of the burning.'

Stories about James Lynchehaun continued to reach Agnes MacDonnell and she could even smile now at the yarns about him: he was a great political figure like Davitt; he was the playboy hero of John Millington Synge; he had outwitted the authorities at every turn; he was one of the revolutionaries causing mayhem throughout Ireland. She had long since taken the view that it was impossible to separate fact from fiction when it came to her assailant.

James Lynchehaun had, it seemed, been back in Achill several times. She heard that he had visited his home a few years earlier, at the end of the war, arriving on the island 'dressed in a Canadian soldier's uniform'. The story went that he left his kit at the police barrack in Achill Sound, went into Sweeney's where he started to drink and 'spoke in Irish to people he recognised, but who did not recognise him'.

'Don't you know who I am?' he had asked them.

'No,' they replied.

'Don't you know who was the first man to drive a horse and cart across Achill Sound bridge?'

'Lynchehaun,' they said.

'The very man,' he had replied.

She had heard another story about the time he was seen walking near Dugort and spotted two policemen in the distance. 'Knowing that they were on the look-out for him, and that he wouldn't have time to make an escape, he hunched himself up like an old man, picked up a shovel, that by chance happened to be lying nearby, and started to clean away the grass from the side of the road.'

According to this tale, the police approached and asked the fugitive, 'You didn't see Lynchehaun passing this way?'

'I wouldn't be sure,' he said, 'but I think it was like him I saw going by there a while ago.'

'This direction?' the policeman asked, pointing the way they were travelling.

'Yes,' he said, so they continued on their wild goose chase.

Agnes had heard that Sergeant Donovan had arrested Lynchehaun in Mulranny, placed him in Castlebar Jail, and afterwards transferred him to Maryborough Prison from where he had once escaped. They even said that representations on Lynchehaun's behalf had been made to Lord French and that he was released some months later on condition that he did not return to County Mayo.

If Agnes MacDonnell could, occasionally, smile at the extraordinary stories, at other times she would wake at night in the Valley House to the sound of the ocean wind beating against the window panes. For a moment she would think that the sound was the rap of a man's knuckles on the outside door and she imagined that she saw, through the glass, a face with steel-bright eyes. Then, the moment of illusion would pass.

She raised a weak hand to her face. The pain had abated over the years and was now like a fierce toothache that had settled into a bearable throb. She reached for the glass and took another sip of wine in the fading light of the May evening. Then, her arm became immobile; it would not move. The wine glass clattered to the ground and an ooze of red liquid trickled across the floor like a dribble of blood seeping from a flesh wound.

She drew long breaths with an irregular, scratching sound. Everything began to blur at the edges; it was as if she were drifting in and out of a heaving ocean. By the time the evening sucked the light from the room, everything within it was quiet. It was the stillness of a space where there was no longer any life. The only sounds were non-human: the clicking of the clock; the creaking of a floor board; the rattle of window panes; the caws of crows on the chimneys of the Valley House. Afterwards, when they pushed the door open, they found her motionless. Her one eye was open; her tongue had slipped between her lips; one arm hung at her side, the other lay across her body.

Agnes MacDonnell's remains were removed from Achill by train on the first leg of her final journey to London. The wind whistled through the carriage wheels and along the wrought-iron filigree of the station's metal canopy. Beyond the station the sea was purple-blue and, further out into the island, the mountain was buried from sight in a grey mist. The locomotive puffed off, the connecting rods of the wheels pushing and pulling as the engine built up speed. The train rounded the bend and Achill receded from view as seagulls hopped from sleeper to sleeper along the railway line. Agnes MacDonnell's past piled up behind her as she departed Achill for the last time.

Afterwards, life in Achill went on as before. The whin bushes flowered in extravagant yellow in front of the Valley House, dusting the ground gold with falling petals; blackbirds hopped on the gravel of the curved avenue; horses tossed their heads in the fields near Ridge Point and raised their nostrils to the sea breeze. Dr Thomas Croly rested in the cemetery at St Thomas' Church, Dugort, under the watch of Slievemore. Friars walked by blossoming apple trees in the walled garden of Bunnacurry Monastery where the elderly Brother Paul Carney visited occasionally from his then home in Roundstone, County Galway. Men and women knelt in the cemetery at Kildownet and prayed for the safe return of their girls and boys who would soon set out for the harvest fields of Scotland.

Within days, *The Mayo News* carried a one-line announcement: 'Mrs MacDonnell, the Valley House, died on Saturday.'

A week later a congregation of twenty-two people gathered at St Thomas' Church for the main Trinity Sunday service at half past eleven. When the donation envelopes for the day were opened, total subscriptions amounted to £25 8s. There is no record of Mrs MacDonnell's death having being noted or of prayers having been offered by the congregation in her memory. Some weeks later the Preacher's Book recorded an offering of ten shillings having been received from Leslie Elliot – perhaps a contribution towards prayers for the repose of the soul of his mother, Agnes MacDonnell of Achill and London.

Epilogue
1937

A public advertisement offered the Valley House for sale by public auction in the summer of 1937:

> Valley House Hotel Licensed
> By Public Auction
> Wednesday 14 July at 12 o'clock
> Ideal, healthy situation.
> Recently renovated; all modern conveniences.
> Exceptional opportunity for ambitious business person.
> Also the entire household furniture and effects, comprising
> over 1,000 lots.
> Inspection invited.
> Joyce Auctioneer. Westport

The Great Southern Railway had discontinued rail passenger services to Achill and tourist numbers to the island had dwindled. A deputation from the island had visited Seán Lemass, Minister for Industry and Commerce, at Government Buildings in January to protest at the decision in October to close the railway line entirely. In early June hundreds of migrant harvesters left Achill by bus and caught the train from Westport to Dublin's North Wall. There, they boarded the steamers for the twelve-hour journey to Glasgow, rolling out their coats beneath them in the ship's steerage. They were met in Scotland by their foreman or 'gaffer' and taken by horse and cart or open-topped lorry to their first farm.

James Lynchehaun was then an elderly man in his late seventies who had resided for some time at the County Home in Castlebar. However, when a number of patients were being transferred from the County Home to the Mental Hospital, he objected strenuously and, at the start of the summer, he joined a harvest squad that was heading to Glasgow. Fortunately for him, he was not part of another ill-fated squad that also set out that summer for the harvest fields of Scotland.

On Wednesday 15 September 1937, a squad of Achill potato harvesters arrived in the town of Kirkintilloch, southwest Scotland, about ten miles from Glasgow. Their employer was W. & A. Graham, Glasgow potato merchants, who bought the potato crop by the acre from local farmers. The company owned a house at 67 Eastside, East High Street, where the Achill squad would stay overnight and travel each day to the surrounding potato fields. There were twenty-four in the squad, fourteen females and twelve males, the youngest aged thirteen. For three months they had worked on farms across Scotland from Ayrshire to the Lothians. The journey to Kirkintilloch early that morning was to be their last move before returning home to Achill in October. They organised their sleeping arrangements and, by eleven o'clock, most of the squad of workers had retired for the night.

Fifteen-year-old Thomas Duggan, son of the Achill squad foreman, woke at about one o'clock that night to the sound of crackling timber and saw that the place was ablaze. The female members of the squad, who were sleeping separately from the men in the three bedrooms, were able to make their escape, some of them having to jump from an upstairs dormer window. They tried desperately to release their brothers, cousins and neighbours, only to find the doors secured by locks. In a short time the flames had engulfed the shed area where the men slept, causing the roof to collapse. By two o'clock the local fire brigade had extinguished the flames, and a salvage van with portable searchlights was brought in to sift through the smouldering debris to locate the remains of the ten victims. Only one body was identified from among the dead.

On Saturday 18 September, the steamer SS *Lairdsburn* transported ten coffins, together with the fire survivors, back to Dublin. At half past ten the following morning the Death Train carrying the remains of the dead pulled out of Dublin's North Wall for the journey back to Achill. On reaching Achill Sound the coffins were carried by relays of forty men across Michael Davitt Bridge to the parish church where they were placed before the high altar for an all-night vigil. The dead were buried next day in Kildownet Cemetery in a large open grave lined with rushes and flowers.

Two weeks later, on Thursday 30 September, the 'Achill Bogie' locomotive with No. 530 emblazoned on her side, got ready to haul the last train out of Achill Sound. The locomotive moved off with a full head of steam, soon rounding the bend and disappearing from the view of Mr Considine, station master, and a small group of staff who waited on the platform until the sound of the train had faded into the distance.

Throughout the month of October buses ferried the returning migrants back to Achill. James Lynchehaun, however, would not return again to the island. In the first week of December, newspapers announced his death in a Glasgow hospital. 'When he died,' reported the *Irish Independent*, 'a letter was found in his pocket from Father Curley, Achill. A clergyman then wrote to Father Curley, who had by then gone from Achill. When Father Curley finally received the letter, he communicated the news to James Lynchehaun's relations.'

A *Connaught Telegraph* reporter wrote: 'After years of trouble with the authorities Lynchehaun came home to Mayo to reside. He spent his days between Achill and Castlebar, and in the latter town he was well known. He informed some of his closest friends that he was writing an account of his life but whether he completed his task is not known. He leaves a wife and son both of whom are in America.'

Another newspaper account of James Lynchehaun's death reported how, the previous year, the Electors Revision Court in Castlebar had considered his application to be placed on the voter register. It appeared that there had been no public notice of the hearing, and that the Gardaí and rate collector had objected to the application by Lynchehaun on the grounds that he was not a property owner. The Registrar refused the applicaton. When informed of the decision to refuse him a vote on account of his residency at the County Home, James Lynchehaun was said to have replied, 'I have no other home.'

Notes

This book draws on archival material that includes, among other sources, the notebooks of Brother Paul Carney covering the life of James Lynchehaun and the friar's fund-raising trips abroad; the Trinity College manuscripts of John Millington Synge dealing with his visits to north Mayo in 1904–1905; folklore material on James Lynchehaun which was gathered in Achill in 1947 and is held at the National Folklore Collection, University College Dublin; contemporary minutes of proceedings for Westport Union Board of Guardians, Congested Districts Board and St Thomas' Select Vestry. The archival material is supplemented by newspaper accounts, court case records (1895 Castlebar case and 1902 extradition case in Indianapolis), and a wide range of other sources which are recorded in the bibliography. Specific sources for individual chapters are indicated below.

Chapter 1: The Island Drowned

The accounts of the *Victory* tragedy and of the funeral of the drowned are drawn from contemporary newspaper reports in *The Irish Times*, *The Freeman's Journal*, *The Mayo News*, *The Connaught Telegraph* and *The Times* of London, and in the journal article 'Clew Bay Boating Disaster' by Aiden Clarke in *Cathair na Mart* (1986).

Oral history accounts of the drowning are contained in the local publication, *Achill Drowning*, and in *The Achill Prophesy* – an Esras Films production for TG4 television.

A succinct overview of James Lynchehaun's career is available in an entry in the *Dictionary of Irish Biography*. 1920 census material from Cleveland, USA, give 1894 as the birth date of James Lynchehaun – son of James and Catherine (née Gallagher) Lynchehaun.

The exchanges between Owen Malley and the Westport Board of Guardians official are from *The Mayo News* of 28 June 1894. The Board of Guardians administered the Poor Law in the respective Unions and collected poor rates from land occupiers as well as seed potato loan repayments. Context from *A New History of Ireland* (Volume VI).

Agnes MacDonnell's contribution to the Achill Relief Fund was acknowledged in *The Mayo News* of 28 June 1894.

The Times' references to the seed potato rent are from that paper's report of the Achill drowning tragedy on 15 June 1894.

The story of the girl walking from Achill to Westport after the drowning is from *The Irish Times*, 16 July 1894.

Chapter 2: The Great and the Good
The account of Michael Davitt's visit to Achill in summer 1894 is taken from *The Mayo News*, 14 July 1894.

General contextual material on Michael Davitt is derived from *Davitt* by Bernard O'Hara, *Michael Davitt* by Darla King and *A New History of Ireland* (Volume VI).

Details of Davitt's visit to open the bridge at Achill Sound are from *The Mayo Examiner* and *The Connaught Telegraph* of 3 September 1887.

The story of James Lynchehaun driving his horse and cart over the new bridge is related in *The Mayo Examiner*, 27 September 1947.

The sources for this section on James Lynchehaun are the RIA *Dictionary of Irish Biography* and Brother Paul Carney's unpublished manuscript, 'A Short Sketch of the Life and Actions of the far-famed James Lynchehaun' (*Lynchehaun Narrative*).

Details of Lady Aberdeen's visit to Achill are from *The Mayo News*, *The Irish Times* and *The Freeman's Journal*. Lady Aberdeen's letter, written prior to her departure for Canada, was published in *The Irish Times* on 24 July 1894. Maureen Keane's biography, *Ishbel: Lady Aberdeen in Ireland*, provided contextual information on Ishbel Gordon.

Reports of Father Fitzgerald's sermon in Dookinealla and of the interview with the Protestant Rector are taken from *The Irish Times* editions of 16 and 17 July 1894.

Chapter 3: Handsome Head of Thick, Reddish Hair
The sources for the general information on Agnes MacDonnell are James Carney's *The Playboy & the Yellow Lady*, Brother Paul Carney's *Lynchehaun Narrative*, newspaper accounts of the Valley House atrocity of 1894, Pat Gallagher and John O'Shea, Achill, and relatives of Agnes and Randal MacDonnell in the UK.

Historical background material on the Valley House estate is included in the Landed Estates database prepared by the Moore Institute, NUI Galway. The estate was bought by Frederick Lambert, 8th Earl of Cavan, from John Goodacre in the early 1870s. Lord Cavan used it as a hunting lodge and holiday residence until his death on 16 December 1887. His widow, Countess Cavan, sold the estate the following year.

The Valley House is currently (as of 2011) open to the public as a hostel.

UK census data provided by Ann MacDonnell show that in 1871 Lydia Agnes MacDonnell resided at 1 Upper York Terrace, London, with her son, Leslie Elliot, and a maid. Her birthplace is stated as Scotland and her birth date as 'about 1846'.

The 1881 census shows Agnes residing at 10 St Anne Hill, London, with son, Leslie (aged 16), and husband, John Randal MacDonnell (aged 53).

The image of Agnes MacDonnell is derived from a portrait in the possession of Ann and Richard MacDonnell, descendants of Randal MacDonnell.

Quote from Mrs Hall is taken from *Ireland, its Scenery, Character and History* by Mr and Mrs S. C. Hall; contextual material from Maureen Keane's *Mrs S. C. Hall: a Literary Biography*. Harriet Martineau quote is taken from her book, *Letters from Ireland*.

The notification of the Valley House auction is from *The Times*, 7 April 1888.

St Thomas' Church, Dugort continues to be used as a place of worship by the Achill community. The Church of Ireland Minute Book of the Select Vestry (1871–1916) records Dr Croly's involvement in St Thomas' activities. The Register of Baptisms, Marriages & Deaths lists the names of those who read recantations, on conversion to the protestant faith, in the period 1844–1846.

Mealla Ní Ghiobúin's *Dugort, Achill Island: The Rise and Fall of a Missionary Community* provides an overview of the Achill Mission activity. Many of The Colony buildings still stand, and Gray's Guest House continues to provide guest accommodation in one of the original settlement buildings.

The account of Agnes MacDonnell's attendance at Achill Petty Sessions is taken from *The Mayo News* of 19 August 1894.

The letters from James Lynchehaun to Agnes MacDonnell,

written between September 1889 and March 1890, were read out at James Lynchehaun's Castlebar trial in 1895.

The summary of the deteriorating relations between Agnes MacDonnell and James Lynchehaun draws on the address by the Crown prosecutor, The MacDermott, at Lynchehaun's trial.

Quotes from Agnes MacDonnell and John Gallagher are from the Lynchehaun trial proceedings as reported in a Supplement to *The Mayo News* on 20 July 1895.

Chapter 4: Hostile Meeting

The meeting of the Achill relief committee, including the exchanges between Michael Davitt and Bindon Scott, was reported in *The Mayo News* of 16 September 1894.

Brother Paul Carney was the author's great granduncle and the material on his family and his birthplace are based on the author's personal family knowledge.

On his death in 1928, Brother Paul Carney left behind two sets of journals: the *Lynchehaun Narrative* and 'Notes of his Life & Travels' (Notes) to which the author gained access. In 1986, James Carney published *The Playboy & the Yellow Lady* based on parts of the *Lynchehaun Narrative*.

The Westport Union Minute Book for the Board of Guardians meeting of 7 June 1894 gives details of the poor-rate amounts owed by Agnes MacDonnell and other Achill landlords.

A report in *The Mayo News* of 28 June 1894 records the rate collector's request for police support in making seizures in Achill for the outstanding seed rates.

The minutes for the Westport Board of Guardians meetings in July, August and November 1894 detail the Union's dealings with the rate collector James Conway. The minutes for 25 October contain the resolution calling for Government assistance in dealing with the fall-out from the poor potato crop.

Details of the police report for September 1894 are from the Belmullet District Report (Public Record Office CO 904/57).

Chapter 5: I Am Cold

The case of the sexton's censure is recorded in St Thomas' Select Vestry minutes of 2 February 1892.

The account of events at the Valley House on 6 October 1894 is compiled from newspaper reports of evidence and depositions at the following: Claim for Malicious Damages by Agnes MacDonnell (November 1894); Enquiry into Escape of James Lynchehaun in Dugort (November 1894); James Lynchehaun before Westport Magistrates (January/February 1895); Castlebar trial of James Lynchehaun (July 1895).

Dr Croly's descriptions of Mrs MacDonnell's injuries are taken from a number of accounts that he gave to the constabulary, to magistrates and at James Lynchehaun's trial.

Chapter 6: An Animal-looking Man
The Irish Times reports are taken from that paper's editions between 8 and 12 October 1894.

The newspaper reports of the Achill outrage are from *The Irish Times*, *The Freeman's Journal*, *The Mayo News*, *Western People* and *The Connaught Telegraph*.

The accounts of the disappearance of Lynchehaun's clothes are from newspaper reports of the Dugort Inquiry in November 1894.

In the 1881 UK census Randal MacDonnell is described as 'Barrister not in practice. Journalist Editor of newspaper.' While some newspaper reports in 1894 describe him as Irish, the census gives his birthplace as Middlesex, England.

Agnes MacDonnell's description of Lynchehaun as 'a fine, strong, dark, animal-looking man' was later taken as a sign of a sexual relationship between the pair. Such a relationship is at the heart of the film *Love & Rage* about the Valley House events. However, scriptwriter Brian Lynch has described the story as fictional in many aspects: 'The script describes their [James Lynchehaun and Agnes MacDonnell] relationship as an affair, but while there is some evidence of a more than business intimacy, the story I tell is purely imaginary.' (www.brianlynch.org)

Chapter 7: He's Off!
The Court Inquiry into the arrest, custody and escape of James Lynchehaun was held at Dugort barrack from 21 to 26 November 1894. The evidence of Commissioner Cameron and of the driver Albert Purvis was reported in *The Mayo News* on 1 December 1894.

Brother Paul Carney's account of Lynchehaun's escape is taken from his *Lynchehaun Narrative*.

There were extensive newspaper reports into apparent sightings of the fugitive Lynchehaun. Several of these accounts were featured in *The Mayo News* of 10 November 1894.

Chapter 8: Frightful Hurricanes

Agnes MacDonnell's claim for malicious damages was reported in *The Mayo News* on 17 November 1894.

The letter of James Lynchehaun to District Inspector Rainsford was read out at the Castlebar trial in July 1895.

Commissioner Cameron's report for the month of November 1894 is taken from the Belmullet District Reports (Public Record Office CO 904/57).

The resolution sent to the Chief Secretary of Ireland was included in the minutes of the Westport Board of Guardians' meeting of 25 October 1894.

Details of the advance money sanctioned for the purchase of seed potatoes were contained in *The Mayo News* on 29 December 1894.

The decisions of the Dugort Court of Inquiry were reported in *The Mayo News* on 22 December 1894.

The storms of December 1894 were reported in *The Freeman's Journal*, *The Irish Times* and *The Times* of London. The account of the storm damage at Eagle Island lighthouse, north Mayo, draws on Rita Nolan's book, *Within the Mullet*.

Chapter 9: Was This Woman Outraged?

The arrival of the prisoner James Lynchehaun at Westport was carried in *The Mayo News* on 12 January 1895; the report included a pencil-sketch of Lynchehaun as he entered the courtroom.

Local newspapers reported several appearances of James Lynchehaun, James Gallagher and Mary Masterson before the magistrates in Westport in January and February 1895.

Evidence of James Lynchehaun's arrest was carried in *The Mayo News* on 16 February 1895.

Dr Croly's detailed evidence in Westport Court was carried in *The Mayo News* on 26 January 1895. J. J. Louden's questioning of Dr Croly suggested a female involvement in the attack on Agnes MacDonnell after the stables were set alight. Local folklore in Achill continues to suggest that Agnes MacDonnell was attacked by local women after the stables were set on fire and not by James Lynchehaun.

Notice of the postponement of the trial of James Lynchehaun to the Summer Assizes in Castlebar was contained in *The Mayo News* of 16 March 1895.

Chapter 10: Queen v Lynchehaun

The map exhibit 'Queen v Lynchehaun' was prepared by the surveyor G. K. Dixon in March 1895 and is currently held at Mayo County Library, Castlebar.

Coverage of the opening of the railway line to Achill is from newspaper reports and from Jonathan Beaumont's *Rails to Achill*. Details of Achill visitor attractions are taken from the Midland Great Western Railway Tourist guides and handbooks.

The court proceedings of July 1895 were covered in all the local and national newspapers in Ireland.

In *The Playboy & the Yellow Lady*, James Carney described the practice of affixing the definite article to surnames (as in 'The MacDermott') as an assertion of respectability by descendants of ancient Irish families.

Chapter 11: That is the Man!

The most comprehensive newspaper coverage of James Lynchehaun's trial was contained in special supplements of the *Western People* and *The Mayo News* on 20 July 1895.

James Carney's book includes an extensive commentary on the Castlebar Court proceedings and on the cross-examination of Mary Gallagher, a key prosecution witness.

Chapter 12: Convict Escape

The drawn-out history of the construction of Castlebar Church is covered in Tom Higgins' *Through Fagan's Gate: the Parish and People of Castlebar Down the Ages*.

The *Western People* of 12 October 1901 carried an extensive report of the Castlebar Church dedication ceremony.

According to information received from family members, Randal MacDonnell died in 1898.

A plaque still exists on the gable of the Valley House giving the completion date for the rebuilding of the house as 1902.

Reports of two malicious damages claims by Agnes MacDonnell for the deaths of horses were reported in the *Western People* on 4 November 1899, and 2 November 1901. The report about the illegal cutting of bent at the Valley House was carried in *The Mayo News* of 29 November 1902.

The account of the dispute between Agnes MacDonnell and her

workmen at Castlebar Quarter Sessions is from the *Western People* of 31 October 1903.

A description of the furniture in the Valley House was included in an auction notice in the *Western People* in July 1937.

The announcement of a £100 reward appeared in *The Mayo News* of 13 September 1902.

Chapter 13: Dear Friends
The scene describing Lynchehaun on the run after his prison escape is a dramatisation of an account in the *Lynchehaun Narrative*. The reference to the benign countryside in the vicinity of the prison is from *The Mayo News* of 20 September 1902.

Details of the prison escape are from the *Lynchehaun Narrative*; from Felix Meehan's account in *The Ballina Herald* of 25 September 1937; from a 1951 *Iris an Gharda* interview with R. J. Bennet which James Carney references in his book.

Sightings of Lynchehaun are taken from *The Mayo News* and *The Irish Times* from September to December 1902.

When the folklore collector Bríd Ní Mhaolmhuaidh visited Achill in 1947, she recalled how Lynchehaun's name had been used to frighten children in her native County Sligo.

Accounts of Lynchehaun's experiences in Glasgow and his letter from Europe are from the *Lynchehaun Narrative*.

The supposed meeting between Michael Davitt and Lynchehaun in the USA was reported in *The New York Times* on 8 September 1903. James Carney covers the meeting in his book, quoting reports from the *Evening Journal* and *Chicago American* newspapers. He also quotes a letter written by Lynchehaun to the *Chicago American* about the Davitt meeting: 'It is true that I applied to Davitt for an interview, which he declined; but why he should become a public informer of me, who never did him an injury, is more than I can understand.'

A report in *The Southern Star* of 5 September 1903 attributed Lynchehaun's earlier arrest directly to Davitt: 'When Lynchehaun extended the hand of greeting, Mr Davitt denounced him and called for the police.'

The case of the body found in north Dublin was reported in *The Mayo News* of 13 December 1902. Michael Davitt's return from the United States was carried in *The Mayo News* of 27 December 1902.

Chapter 14: Edward VII v James Lynchehaun

The coverage of the Indianapolis court case is derived from newspaper reports and from the Defence Committee publication, *An Irish-American Victory over Great Britain: Complete Proceedings of the Great Extradition Case of Edward VII vs. James Lynchehaun, as tried in the United States Court.* The *Mayo News* of 31 October carried a report of the concluding legal arguments.

The account of King Edward VII's journey close to Achill is from *The Irish Times* of 31 July 1903.

The evidence of the defence witnesses in Indianapolis was reported in *The Mayo News* of 3 October 1903, together with the Defence Committee resolutions.

James Carney claimed that the Irish Republican Brotherhood was referred to as the Irish Revolutionary Brotherhood in the Indianapolis Court 'to avoid any unfortunate misunderstanding in the American mind'; he also said that it was unclear whether or not James Lynchehaun had been an IRB member.

James Carney's book includes a critique of the prosecution case in Indianapolis and the 'exaggerated and sometimes perjured' evidence for the defence. He also raises the question as to whether the defence witness, Thomas Lynch, may have been a relative of James Lynchehaun: 'The possibility was hardly adverted to that in this case Lynch was probably an Anglicisation of Lynchehaun and he would thus have been at least a distant relative of the accused.'

James Carney suggests that Brother Paul Carney was present in Indianapolis for Lynchehaun's trial but there is no evidence to support this. The friar's accounts of the trial appear to be drawn from third party – mainly newspaper – reports. The friar was in the United States for two lengthy fund-raising trips, in 1896–1898 and again in 1899–1901. There is no reference in his journals to a third American trip.

Chapter 15: He is no Robert Emmet

Details of Commissioner Moores' judgement are taken from the Defence Committee's publication. The full contents are available in microfilm at New York Public Library (Schwartzman Building). The publication includes photographs of Commissioner Moores and members of the legal teams.

Details of the Supreme Court case, Henry C Pettit v Thomas Walshe, are available at: www.openjurist.org

The report of *The Times* correspondent's visit to Achill is contained in the edition of 28 September 1903.

Chapter 16: Sure They'd Never Touch Lynchehaun
The chapters dealing with J. M. Synge draw on *Fool of the Family* (W. J. McCormack), *John Millington Synge: A Biography* (David M. Kiely); *J M Synge 1871–1909* (Greene & Stephens); *J. M. Synge Travelling Ireland* (ed. Nicholas Grene) and Synge's works.

Some details of Synge's first visit to north Mayo in September 1904 are from the Synge Manuscripts, Trinity College Library, (MS 4395, Notebook 32). The account of his 1905 trip with Jack Yeats draws on the Synge Manuscripts and on *The Manchester Guardian* essays (*J. M. Synge Travelling Ireland 1898–1908*, ed. Nicholas Grene).

Synge's two trips to Mayo are covered in the author's essay, 'Rose and Purple Colours on the Sea: John Millington Synge in Mayo (1904–1905)' in *Cathair Na Mart*, 2010.

The sketch books which Jack Yeats used during the Congested Districts' tour were viewed in New York Library (Berg Room, Schwartzman Building).

Ann Saddlemyer has examined Synge's worksheets and draft manuscripts for *The Playboy* in *J. M. Synge Collected Works* (Volume IV), including the notes Synge made through 1904–1905.

In *Fool of the Family*, W. J. McCormack discusses the influence of the Lynchehaun and O'Malley parricide cases on Synge in constructing *The Playboy*.

All quotes from Synge's letters are taken from *The Collected Letters of John Millington Synge*, ed. Ann Saddlemyer.

In 2004, members of Druid Theatre spent some time in Erris rehearsing a production of *The Playboy* and experiencing the places which provide the drama's location. Members spoke with Bridie Quinn who had traced the references to north Mayo places in the play. Lorna Siggins wrote of the Druid visit in *The Irish Times* on 7 July 2004.

Adrian Frazier's book, *Hollywood Irish*, traces the connections between *The Playboy* and *The Quiet Man*, and between the characters of Christy Mahon and Sean Thornton.

Chapter 17: A Murderous Race of Savages
The Playboy riots and subsequent events were covered extensively in *The Freeman's Journal*, *The Irish Times* and the *Irish Independent*.

The account of the Wednesday night Abbey disturbances is adapted from reports in *The Freeman's Journal* and *The Irish Times* of Thursday 31 January 1907.

An account of the interview with Synge during the week of *The Playboy* disturbances was published in the *Dublin Evening Mail* of 29 January and in *The Freeman's Journal* of 30 January 1907.

Quotations from *An Claidheamh Soluis* editorial are from the edition of 9 February 1907.

The Mayo News coverage of *The Playboy* disturbances is from the edition of 2 February 1907.

The account of the summons against Anthony Lavelle by Agnes MacDonnell is from *The Mayo News* of April 1906.

Chapter 18: A Distinguished Visitor
Information about the poor weather conditions of 1907 is from Alexander William's diary accounts in Gordon T. Ledbetter's *Privilege & Poverty*. Local newspapers carried reports from the Department of Agriculture and Technical Industries on the poor state of the crops in Achill that summer.

The Mayo News carried accounts of James Lynchehaun's supposed visit to Achill in summer 1907 in its editions of 3 August, 10 August, 31 August, 7 September and 5 October that year. James Carney suggested that some of the newspaper accounts were written in a unusual style and he concluded that the material was provided by Lynchehaun himself, and had been subjected to 'slight editorial treatment'.

In the essay, 'Talk, Gossip, Yarns and Anecdotes: Folklore Surrounding James Lynchehaun of Achill', the author examines the issue of *The Mayo News* coverage of Lynchehaun's 1907 visit to Achill.

The facsimile of Lynchehaun's letter-card was published in *The Mayo News* on 31 August 1907; details of Lynchehaun's letters to Mr Doris were published on 7 September 1907.

James Carney's book described Lynchehaun's meeting with Douglas Hyde and carried a translation of Hyde's account.

From Brother Paul Carney's 'Notes' we know that the friar was transferred back to Achill in January 1905, after a ten-year absence, and remained on the island until November 1907. The *Lynchehaun Narrative* includes a reference to Lynchehaun visiting the Industrial Exhibition in Dublin and staying at the Shelbourne Hotel.

Details of the Land Court case taken by Agnes MacDonnell are from *The Freeman's Journal* of 6 November 1908.

Chapter 19: The Curse of God on You All!
The clash over Dr Croly's retirement pension was reported in *The Mayo News* during May and June 1912.

The controversy over the cross for Captain Weddall's grave is described in *Emily M. Weddall, Bunaitheoir Scoil Acla* by Isold Ní Dheirg. The decision of St Thomas' Select Vestry regarding the cross was taken at its meeting on 6 July 1909. An account of the beginnings of Scoil Acla is found in *Scoil Acla 1910–2010* and at: www.scoilacla.com

On 27 March 1909, *The Irish Times* reported that the attendance at John Millington Synge's graveside included Emily Weddall.

The land agitation in Achill in 1912–1913 was part of the final phase of the process of land transfer from landlord to tenant which brought about long term change in social and political structures in Ireland. This process is analysed by Joseph Lee in *The Modernisation of Irish Society 1848–1918*.

The account of the tenant deputation to Dugort and of the tenants' meeting with Agnes MacDonnell are from *The Mayo News* of 5 November 1912. A few days earlier, Father Colleran had written to the land agent informing him of the deputation (letter included in MS 91, 'Correspondence with Achill Mission', at Representative Church Body Library, Dublin).

Michael Gallagher's letter to *The Mayo News* was published on 23 November 1912. The letter complaining about conditions on the Valley estate appeared on 22 March 1913.

The letters of Father Colleran and Henry Doran, Congested Districts Board, were published in *The Mayo News* on 8 March 1913.

An account of the attack on the hay-carts at Valley was carried in *The Irish Times* on 15 March 1913.

The statement of Father Martin Colleran to the Achill Assizes and the claim that Agnes MacDonnell was prepared to sell her lands to the Congested Districts Board were reported in *The Mayo News* of 5 April 1913.

Details of the Congested District Board's consideration of the purchase of the Valley House and the Achill Mission estates are from the Board Minutes (1913–1915).

It was only after Agnes MacDonnell's death that the Land Commission acquired the Valley House lands from her son. In his book *Achill*, Kenneth McNally states: 'In 1927 and 1931 the Land Commission purchased the untenanted and tenanted estates of Leslie Elliot for a price of £2,776 and in so doing removed the last of the island estates from landlord ownership. Of the 1,869 acres comprising the untenanted estate, 575 acres were set aside for the enlargement of 21 adjoining holdings and much of the remainder turned over to common grazing and the extension of turbary rights. Lands on the tenanted estate were rearranged in the same manner to enlarge individual holdings.'

Chapter 20: A Blazing Trail
The Irish Times of 10 February 1923 carried the headline: 'The Blazing Trail in Ireland – Many Houses Mined and Burned.' The paper reported the attack on Moore Hall as well as the letter of 3 February from George Moore to *The Times*.

The *Dugort Preachers' Book* for St Thomas' Church includes an ominous note dated 22 October 1922: 'IRA Threat?'

According to Jim Rankin, Irene Elliot's grandson Leslie Elliot married Irene Orpen in 1919. Irene had three children from a previous relationship with Samuel Berridge; she and Leslie Elliot had no children together.

The stories about Lynchehaun gathered by the folklore collector Bríd Ní Mhaolmhuaidh in Achill in 1947 are contained in the National Folklore Collection manuscripts at the Delargy Centre for Irish Folklore, University College Dublin.

Felix Meehan's recollections of the 1918 Lynchehaun incident were reported in *The Ballina Herald* on 25 September 1937.

Brother Paul Carney suggested that James Lynchehaun left his wife in 1907. According to the 1920 US Census (material courtesy of the Irish American Archives Society, Cleveland), Katherine Lynch – believed to be Catherine Lynchehaun, once wife to James Lynchehaun – and her son, James, were living on Detroit Avenue, Cleveland, where she ran a confectionary business. She died on 1 May 1927 of a ruptured appendix.

The report of Lynchehaun's appeal to Lord French was contained in *The Freeman's Journal* of 4 February 1922; the same edition reported that a man answering to the name of James Lynchehaun had been arrested in Athlone and later released.

Pat Gallagher, the Valley House, heard from his grandmother that Agnes MacDonnell died in a downstairs room of the house and that her body was taken to London for burial. This information was confirmed to him by Vi McDowell (1910–2009) of Gray's Guesthouse, Dugort. The detail of the wine glass beside Mrs MacDonnell's body is from James Carney's *The Playboy & the Yellow Lady*.

The Mayo News of 2 June 1923 carried an announcement of Agnes MacDonnell's death.

The *Dugort Preachers' Book* provides details of the Sunday service at St Thomas' Church the week after Agnes MacDonnell's death.

Epilogue
The notice of the public auction of the Valley House was published in the *Irish Independent* on 8 July 1937. Leslie Elliot had owned the house since his mother's death and had lived there with his wife, Irene. According to Jim Rankin, grandson of Irene Elliot, Irene died in 1942 in Castlebar Hospital. Jim Rankin has been unable to establish the burial places of either Irene or Leslie Elliot.

Even though the Valley House was advertised for sale in 1937, it was only in 1942, following Irene Elliot's death, that the house was sold to the Gallagher family, according to Pat Gallagher, current owner of the Valley House.

In its report of Lynchehaun's death, the *Western People* of 11 December 1937 described an earlier meeting when Lynchehaun told its correspondent of his decision to join the Scottish labour squad.

Reports of James Lynchehaun's application for a vote in Castlebar were published in *The Connaught Telegraph* and the *Western People* on 11 April 1936.

Details of the Kirkintilloch fire tragedy are taken from Brian Coughlan's *Achill Island Tattie-hokers in Scotland and the Kirkintilloch Tragedy, 1937*, and from contemporary newspaper accounts.

Further material on the Achill tattie-hokers (migrant harvesters) was derived from Deirdre Ní Loingsigh's 'We'll have a half day in the bothy making boxty for the boys' (MA thesis).

An account of the final days of the Achill railway line is carried in Jonathan Beaumont's *Rails to Achill*.

Reports of James Lynchehaun's death appeared in the *Irish Independent*, *The Mayo News*, the *Western People* and *The Connaught Telegraph* in early December 1937.

Bibliography

See notes to individual chapters for newspaper references and additional unpublished sources.

Beaumont, Jonathan, *Rails to Achill – A West of Ireland Branch Line* (2005)

Byrne, Patricia, 'Rose and Purple Colours on the Sea: John Millington Synge in Mayo (1904–1905)', *Cathair Na Mart*, 28 (2010)

Byrne, Patricia, 'Talk, Gossip, Yarns and Anecdotes: Folklore Surrounding James Lynchehaun of Achill', *Cathair Na Mart*, 29 (2011)

Byrne, Patricia, 'Teller of Tales: An Insight into the Life and Times of Brother Paul Carney (1844–1928), Travelling Questor and Chronicler of the Life of James Lynchehaun, Nineteenth Century Achill Criminal', *Journal of the Galway Archaeological and Historical Society*, 61 (2009)

Carney, James, *The Playboy & the Yellow Lady* (Dublin, 1986)

Carney, Paul, 'A Short Sketch of the Life and Actions of the far-famed James Lynchehaun' (*c.* 1904 with additional notes added later)

Carney, Paul, 'Notes on his Life and Travels' (n.d.)

Casserley, H.C., *Outline of Irish Railway History* (North Pomfret, 1974)

Church of Ireland (Dugort) Minute Book, Select Vestry, 1871–1916. Representative Church Body Library, Dublin.

Clarke, Kieran, 'Clew Bay Boating Disaster', *Cathair na Mart*, 6 (1986)

Coiste Cuimhneacháin Báthadh Acla, *Achill Drowning* (Westport, 2006)

Comerford, Patrick, 'Edward Nangle (1799–1883): The Achill Missionary in a New Light', *Cathair na Mart* 19 (1999)

Congested Districts Board, Minutes of Proceedings 1910–1912, Volumes 1–3, National Library of Ireland.

Conlon, Patrick, *Franciscan Ireland* (Mullingar, 1988)

Corry, Emmett, *History of the Franciscan Brothers of Brooklyn and America* (Brooklyn, 2003)

Coughlan, Brian, *Achill Island Tattie-hokers in Scotland and the Kirkintilloch Tragedy, 1937* (Dublin, 2006)

Defence Committee for James Lynchehaun, *An Irish-American Victory over Great Britain: Complete Proceedings of the Great Extradition Case of Edward VII vs. James Lynchehaun, as tried in the United States Court,* (New York Public Library)

Delgary Centre for Irish Folklore, University College Dublin, (MS 665 and 1015)

Dictionary of Irish Biography (Cambridge, 2010)

Dixon, G. K., 'Queen v Lynchehaun', map of Valley House crime scene (1895)

Dornan, Brian, *Mayo's Lost Islands – The Inishkeas* (Dublin, 2000)

Dugort Preachers' Book 1921–1935, Representative Church Body Library, Dublin

Frazier, Adrian, *George Moore 1852–1933* (New Haven & London, 2000)

Frazier, Adrian, *Hollywood Irish: John Ford, Abbey Actors and the Irish Revival in Hollywood* (Dublin, 2011)

Gillespie, Raymond and Moran, Gerard, eds., *A Various Country: Essays in Mayo History 1500–1900* (Westport, 1987)

Greene & Stephens, *J. M .Synge 1871–1909* (New York, 1989)

Grene, Nicholas, ed., *J. M. Synge: Travelling Ireland* (Dublin, 2009)

Hall, Mr & Mrs S. C., *Hall's Ireland* (London, 1840)

Henry, Paul, *An Irish Portrait* (London, 1988)

Henry, Paul, *Further Reminiscences* (Belfast, 1973)

Hill, Judith, *Lady Gregory – An Irish Life* (Cork, 2011)

Higgins, Tom, *Through Fagan's Gate: the Parish and People of Castlebar down the ages* (Castlebar, 2001)

Joyce, P. J., *A Forgotten Part of Ireland* (Tuam, 1910)

Keane, Maureen, *Mrs S. C. Hall: A Literary Biography* (Gerrard's Cross, 1997)

Keane, Maureen, *Ishbel – Lady Aberdeen in Ireland* (Newtownards, 1999)

Keenan, Desmond, *The Catholic Church in Nineteenth Century Ireland* (Dublin, 1983)

Kiely, David M., *John Millington Synge – A Biography* (New York, 1994)

King, Carla, *Michael Davitt* (Dublin, 2009)

Ledbetter, Gordon T., *Privilege & Poverty – The Life & Times of Irish Painter & Naturalist Alexander Williams RHA 1846–1930* (Cork, 2010)

Lee, Joseph, *The Modernisation of Irish Society 1848–1918* (Dublin, 2008)

Leerssen, Joep, *Remembrance and Imagination: Patterns in the Historical and Literary Representation of Ireland in the Nineteenth Century* (Cork, 1996)

Love & Rage (film) Lionsgate Home Entertainment, 1998.

McCormack, W. J., *Fool of the Family – A Life of J. M. Synge* (London, 1989)

McDonald, Theresa, *Achill Island: Archaeology, History, Folklore* (Tullamore, 1997)

McNally, Kenneth, *Achill* (Devon, 1973)

Martineau, Harriet, *Letters from Ireland* (Dublin, 2001)

Moffitt, Miriam, *Soupers & Jumpers: The Protestant Missions in Connemara, 1848–1937* (Dublin, 2008)

Ní Dheirg, Isold, *Emily M. Weddall – Bunaitheoir Scoil Acla* (Baile Átha Cliath, 1995)

Ní Ghiobúin, Mealla, *Dugort, Achill Island 1831–1861 – The Rise and fall of a Missionary Community* (Dublin, 2001)

Ní Loingsigh, Deirdre, 'We'll have a half day in the bothy making boxty for the boys', MA Thesis, University of Limerick (2003)

Nolan, Rita, *Within the Mullet* (Naas, 1997)

O'Hara, Bernard, *Davitt* (Westport, 2006)

Pilkington, L., 'The Most Unpopular Man in Ireland: P. D. Kenny, J. M. Synge and Irish Cultural History', *Irish Review* 29 (2002)

Police District Reports for County Mayo (CO 904/57, 1894)

Price, Alan, ed., *J M Synge Collected Works – Volume II: Prose* (London, 1966)

Register of Baptisms, Marriages and Burials (Book 2) for Achill-Dugort. Representative Church Body Library, Dublin.

Robinson, Tim, *Connemara – Listening to the Wind* (Dublin, 1986)

Royal Irish Academy, *A New History of Ireland: Volume VI* (Oxford, 2006)

RTÉ, 'Lest they Perish', film documentary (1985)

Saddlemyer, Ann, ed., *The Collected Letters of John Millington Synge* (Oxford, 1983)

Saddlemyer, Ann, ed., *J. M. Synge Collected Works* (Volume IV) (London, 1983)

Shepherd, Ernie, *The Midland Great Western Railway of Ireland* (Leicester, 1994)

Siggins, Lorna, 'In Playboy Country', *The Irish Times*, 7 July 2004

Synge, J. M., *The Playboy of the Western World* (Dublin, 1974)

Synge Manuscripts (Ms 4000), Library of Trinity College, Dublin

The Achill Prophecy. An Esras Film production for TG4 television, (2008)

Thomas, Conal, 'Early History of Granlahan Monastery' in *Granlahan Magazine* (1996)

Waldron, Kieran, *The Archbishops of Tuam 1700–2000* (Tuam, 2008)

Westport Union Minute Book – Board of Guardians (Ms 12.67–12.696), National Library of Ireland, Dublin

Yeats, Jack, sketch books, 'Ireland with Synge 1905', Berg Collection, New York Public Library

Index